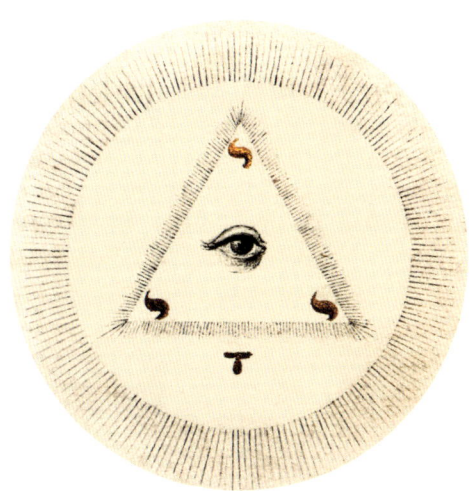

**VINCULVM MAXIMUM
KAI**

Α Ω

ὁ ΜΕΓΙΣΤΟΣ ὁ ΚΥΡΙΟΣ

ὁ ΘΕΟΣ ἈΠΟΤΑΤΟΣ ἘΣΤΗ   τοῦ ΠΑΥΤΟΥ ΠΝΕῚ ὙΠΕΡ ὩΝ

יהוה

*Qui facis Mirabilia magna Solus
Finis coronat opus.*

OCCULT

DECODING THE VISUAL CULTURE OF MYSTICISM, MAGIC & DIVINATION

PETER FORSHAW

CONTENTS

INTRODUCTION AS ABOVE, SO BELOW
8

I. FOUNDATIONS
34

- Astrology — 36
- Alchemy — 60
- Kabbalah — 90

II. OCCULT PHILOSOPHY
114

- Natural Magic — 116
- Astral Magic — 138
- Ritual Magic — 158

III. OCCULT REVIVAL
176

- Occultism — 178
- Tarot — 198
- New Age & Occulture — 222

248–56

GLOSSARY
FURTHER READING
SOURCES OF ILLUSTRATIONS
INDEX & ACKNOWLEDGMENTS

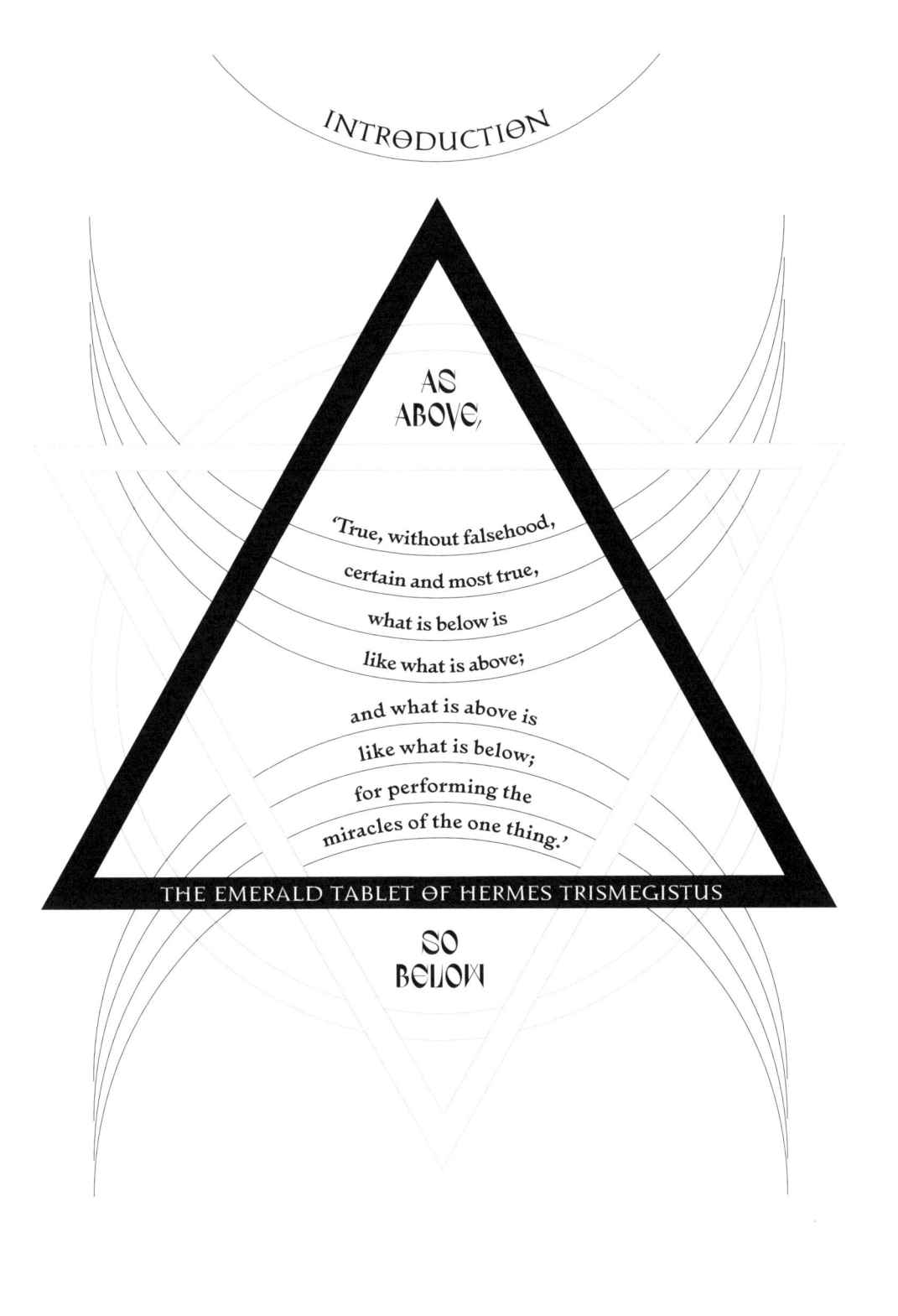

INTRODUCTION

AS ABOVE,

'True, without falsehood, certain and most true, what is below is like what is above; and what is above is like what is below; for performing the miracles of the one thing.'

THE EMERALD TABLET OF HERMES TRISMEGISTUS

SO BELOW

he story of the occult is long, stretching back into antiquity. It is a story of heavens above and earth below, of relations between the gods (or God), mankind and nature, and a belief in the existence of correspondences between all things, of a web of creation, a great chain of being. It tells of the powers of angels and spirits, of beneficent daemons and maleficent demons, the properties of animals, vegetables and minerals, and the potential of human beings. Above all, it is a story of mankind's fascination with wonders and marvels, initiations into secrets and the seeking-out of hidden things.

Over the centuries, this story has been told in many lands and in diverse ways, from the mouths of mages and sages, astrologers and alchemists, Hermetists and Kabbalists, but also through the hands of artists, composers, performers and others drawn to the occult wisdom of the past. This book brings together some of the most intriguing examples of their beliefs and practices, illustrated with original images from books and manuscripts, material survivals (such as talismans, magic mirrors and crystal balls) and works that they have inspired.

The quote at the beginning of this introduction is from the *Emerald Tablet*, a foundational text for many interested in the occult arts of alchemy, astrology and magic, the earliest known version appearing in an Arabic work from the 9th century. It is said to have been written by the ancient Egyptian sage Hermes Trismegistus, a legendary figure whose name means 'thrice-great', as the perfect combination of philosopher, priest and king. Hermes was considered to be the inventor of alchemy, indeed of all the sciences and arts, and was identified by some with the Egyptian god of wisdom, Thoth. He is one of the forefathers of many of the occult practitioners you will meet in these pages. Do not be put off by his obscure or oracular style of expression: the quote has been interpreted in many ways, as speaking of the astrological influence of the planets and stars on all things on earth, as the sublimation and condensation of vapours in the alchemical vessel, or as the relation between the microcosm, the 'little world'

< *page 8*
Éliphas Lévi, *As Above, So Below*, from an English edition of Lévi's *Transcendental Magic* (1896)
This engraving combines kabbalistic terms from the Zohar and alchemical phrases from the Emerald Tablet, encircled by an ouroboros.

> *pages 12–13*
Johann Diricks van Campen (engraver), *The Triumphal Pyramid* (1602), from Heinrich Khunrath's *Amphitheatrum Sapientiae Aeternae* (1609)
This plate shows a fiery pyramid on which is carved the alchemical Emerald Tablet of Hermes Trismegistus, as well as the start of Hermes's revelation by the Divine Mind from the Pymander, the first discourse in the ancient collection of religio-philosophical texts called the Corpus Hermeticum.

Pinturicchio and assistants, *Isis with Moses and Hermes*, 1493

This scene appears in a fresco adorning the Room of the Saints in the Borgia Apartments at the Vatican Palace, Rome. It depicts the Egyptian sage Hermes Trismegistus, considered by some to be a contemporary of Moses, in the presence of the ancient Egyptian goddess Isis, seated on a throne.

INTRODUCTION — *As Above, So Below*

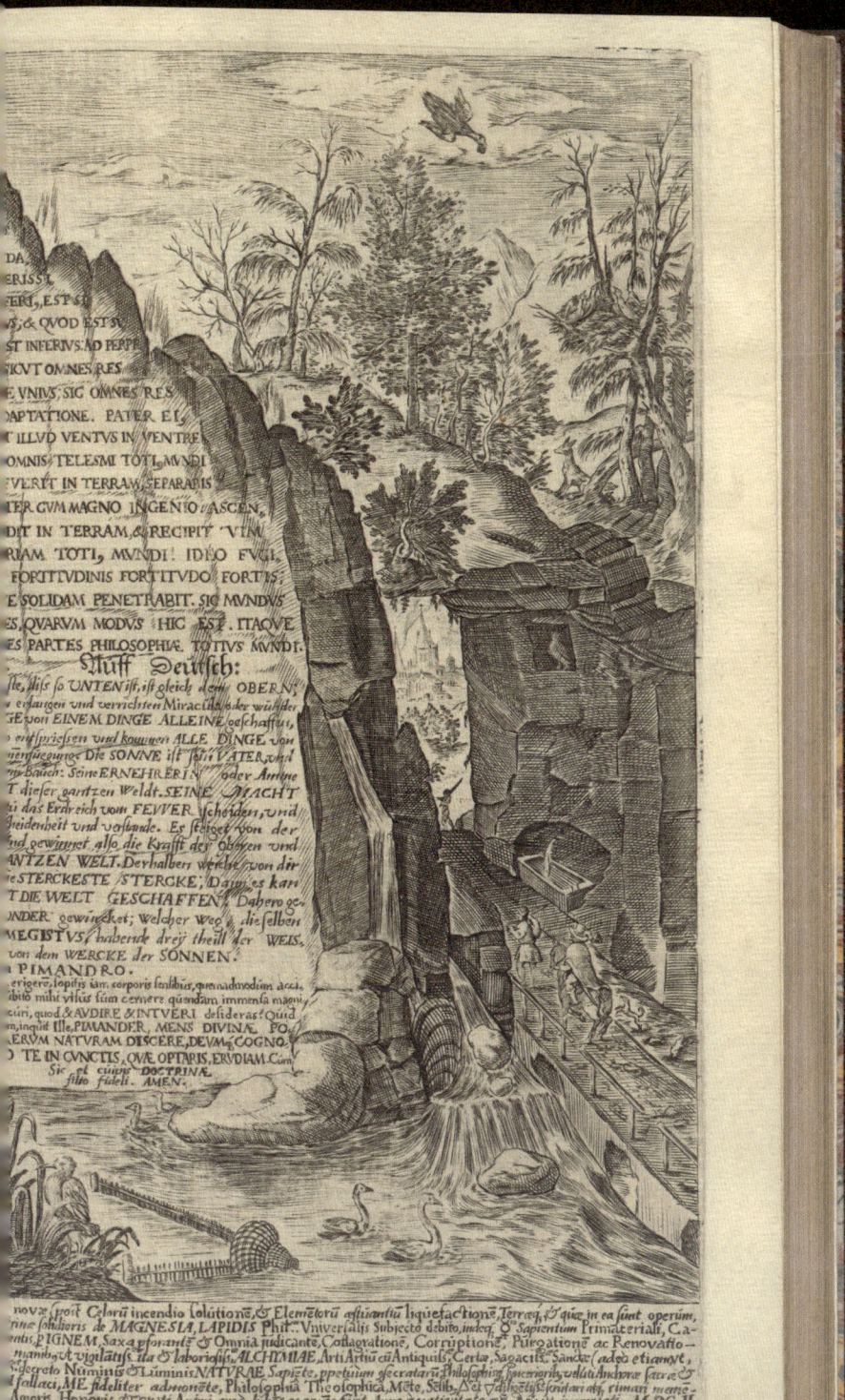

Matthaeus Merian the Elder (engraver), from *Opus Medico-Chymicum* (1618) by Johann Daniel Mylius
The alchemist stands in the centre, in a grove of trees bearing glyphs of alchemical substances. On the left is a solar male figure with an alchemical lion, a phoenix, and spheres of fire and air; on the right, a lunar female figure with a stag, an eagle, and spheres of water and earth. Above are winged creatures, representing stages of the creation of the philosophers' stone, as well as the heavenly orders of angels and the name of God.

of man, and the macrocosm, the universe as a whole. Occult thought can be understood on multiple levels.

An example of the enduring appeal of the *Emerald Tablet* and the syncretic nature of much occult philosophy can be seen in Éliphas Lévi's *Dogme et Rituel de la Haute Magie* (*The Dogma and Ritual of High Magic*, 1854–56). In the frontispiece to the first volume, we find the *Emerald Tablet*'s most famous statement, 'Quod Superius...sicut Quod Inferius': That which is Above is like that which is Below. Lévi, who was extremely interested in the Jewish mystical tradition of Kabbalah, combines this with the terms 'Macroprosopus' ('Great Countenance' or 'Soul of the Macrocosm') and 'Microprosopus' ('Lesser Countenance' or 'Soul of the Microcosm'). In the centre of these phrases is a hexagram or Double Triangle of Solomon, formed by two figures, the God of Light and the God of Reflections. The ultimate unity of all these elements is symbolized by the ouroboric serpent surrounding them, biting its own tail.

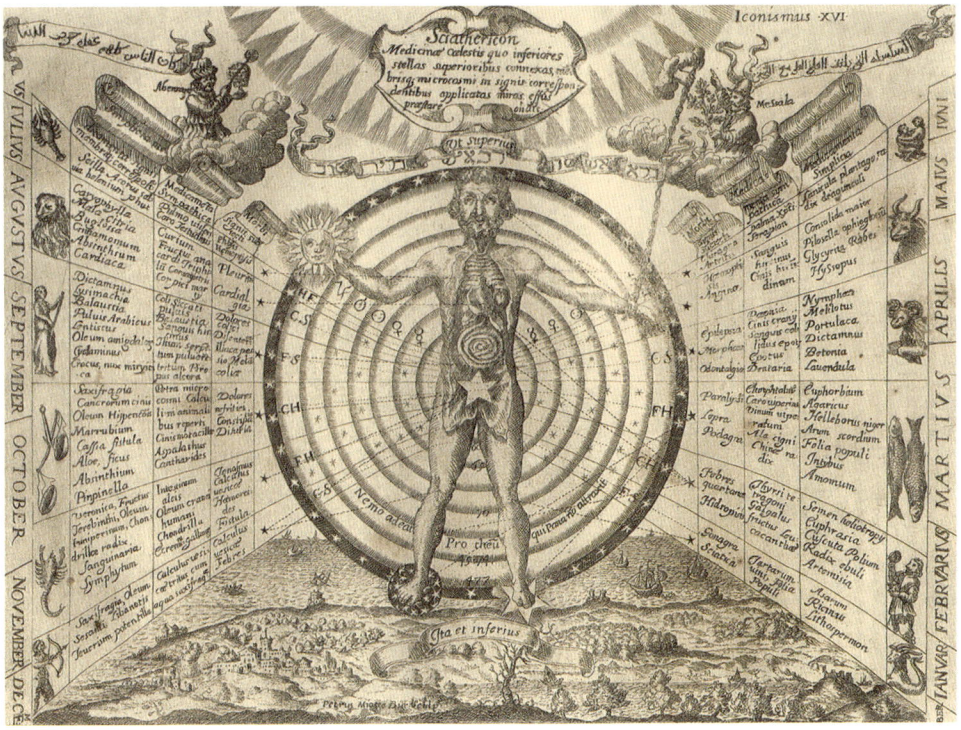

Pierre Miotte (engraver), *Sciathericon Microcosmicum*, from Athanasius Kircher's *Ars magna lucis et umbrae* (1646)
This engraving illustrates the relations between man, the microcosm, and the 'greater world' or macrocosm, including the twelve signs of the zodiac – revealing how the planets affect different parts of a man's body.

Given the complex nature of such symbols, the occult worldview can seem perplexingly opaque at first encounter. After all, the Latin word from which the term 'occult' derives, *occultus*, means 'hidden', 'secret' or 'concealed'. The foundational practices introduced in the first part of this book, however – in particular, astrology – existed long before they were disseminated in Latin and more widely adopted in the West. Stargazing – a practice that encompasses the mapping of the heavens, and the attempt to find significance in the regular movements of the planets against the background of the stars and constellations – dates back over 4,000 years and developed in places as diverse as Mesopotamia, China and India. In terms of astrology in the West, an especially influential confluence of Babylonian and Egyptian astrology took place in 4th-century BCE Egypt after its conquest by Alexander the Great (356–323 BCE), whose tutor was the famous philosopher Aristotle (384–322 BCE).

16   INTRODUCTION —*As Above, So Below*

DECODING SLOANE 181

One of the best examples of literally 'hidden' occult knowledge is found in a painting concealed within the inside front cover of a manuscript in the British Library, Sloane MS. 181, *Tabulae Theosophicae Cabalisticae* ('Theosophical Cabalistic Tables'), connected with the alchemist, mage and Christian Cabalist Heinrich Khunrath (1560–1605). The painting is divided into two halves and shows the diversity of his interests. On the left we see the adept at prayer in his study, surrounded by many aspects of his occult practice.

1.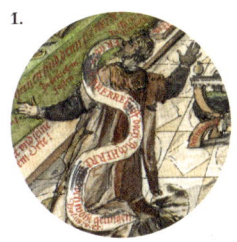

ADEPT IN PRAYER
The adept kneels in prayer. Written on the scroll coming from his mouth are words based on Psalm 118:25: 'O Lord, help: O Lord, give good success.'

5.

DIVINE NAMES
Written on the wall in Greek, Hebrew and Latin is a list of divine names relating to Christian Cabala, including Ehieh, Elohim and Adonai.

2.

ATHANOR
Also known as an alchemical furnace, athanors provided low, constant heat for alchemical digestion, a process that could take several weeks.

6.

PHILOSOPHERS' STONE AND BOOK
A dark philosophers' stone labelled 'wonder-working stone of the wise', above a book with images of Christ and Adam Androgyne.

3.

BLAZE OF LIGHT
The light is full of verses about God and fire, including Exodus 3:2 (Moses and the burning bush) and Ezekiel 1:5 (vision of the cherubim and Yahweh's chariot).

7.

EVIL SPIRIT
To the left of the adept's table, there is a typical alchemical flask containing a trapped evil spirit that looks a bit like an insect.

4.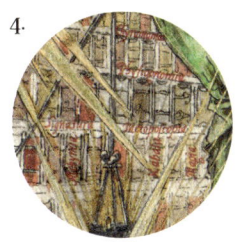

BOOKCASE
A bookcase labelled with subjects such as physiognomy, magic, alchemy, chiromancy, astrology, astronomy, Kabbalah, physics and metaphysics.

8.

GLOBES
These celestial and terrestrial globes symbolize the Above and the Below – central concepts of alchemy, drawn from the text of the *Emerald Tablet*.

The Three Magi, Basilica of Sant'Apollinare Nuovo, Ravenna, Italy, 6th century
The magi are shown bringing gifts of gold, frankincense and myrrh to the infant Christ.

Several centuries later, around the time of the birth of Christ, Egypt also became the birthplace of the art of alchemy, although other alchemical traditions also developed around the same time elsewhere, for example in China and later in medieval India. Often classed as the third of these foundational occult sciences, magic also appears in both Mesopotamia and Egypt. In many early modern Western accounts, however, magic is said to have originated in Persia, with the pre-Christian prophet Zoroaster and the legendary magus Osthanes, passing to ancient Greece as early as the 5th century BCE, then being adopted into Latin; the term *magia* first appeared in the poet Virgil's *Eclogues* around 40 BCE, with the Persian *magoi* becoming familiar in the Christian West due to the biblical account of the three magi who were guided by a star to Bethlehem following the birth of Christ.

In the 9th and 10th centuries, much Greek material relating to these arts and sciences was translated into Arabic, followed by a flood of translation from Arabic into Latin during what has been called the 12th-century Renaissance. The transmission of Arabic and Persian learning to the West – through, for example, the scriptorium of King Alfonso X 'the Wise' of Castile and

Zoroaster with two demons, from a later manuscript (1425) of the 13th-century pseudo-Aristotelian treatise Secretum Secretorum

The Persian Zoroaster was described by the Roman natural philosopher Pliny the Elder as the 'inventor of magic', and here we see him standing in a magic circle, discussing secrets of nature with demons.

León (1221–84) – introduced learned magicians to new conceptions of the occult sciences and an impressive new corpus of works on astrology, alchemy and magic. The impact of *al-ʿulūm al-khafiyya* or *al-ghariba*, the Islamicate occult sciences, on the West is particularly apparent from the 11th to the 13th centuries.

During this period, the notion of 'occult qualities' (*virtutes occultae*) in nature was discussed by distinguished philosophers such as the Dominican Thomas Aquinas (1225–74) and the Franciscan Roger Bacon (*c.* 1220–92), as well as the physician and self-proclaimed prophet Arnald of Villanova (1240–1311). These were qualities of substances that could not be explained by classical Aristotelian philosophy through the manifest, observable physical properties of the four elements (earth, water, air and fire), such as light, heat, motion, taste, colour or odour. A famous example of an occult quality was the power of a lodestone to attract iron. The effect was visible to the eye but its cause was 'occult' because magnetism could not be understood as a specific mixture of the four elements. Other examples include the belief in influences emanating from the planets and constellations, and the idea

PROFILE
FOUR ELEMENTS

The notion of four elements is fundamental to occult philosophy. The astrological zodiac, for example, is divided into four elemental groups of earth, water, air and fire signs, following the four element model proposed by the Greek philosopher Empedocles (*c.* 450 BCE). He considered them to be four indestructible and imperishable simple bodies, the four roots of matter, from the lowest and most gross, earth, to the highest and most subtle, fire. In medicine, the Greek physician Hippocrates (*c.* 460–*c.* 370 BCE) related these macrocosmic elements with the four humours in the human microcosm: yellow bile with fire, blood with air, phlegm with water, and black bile or melancholy with earth. Health was dependent on a proper balance of these humours. The image below of the human immersed in the four elements is from a 15th-century French manuscript, *On the Properties of Things*, by the English Scholastic Bartholomaeus Anglicus (d. 1272).

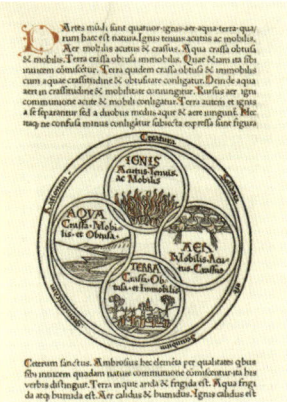

PROCLUS' ELEMENTAL PROPERTIES

This page (1472) from Isidore of Seville's 7th-century *De natura rerum* shows the four elements, each with three properties according to the philosopher Proclus (412–485): from fire (sharp, subtle, mobile) to earth (blunt, dense, immobile).

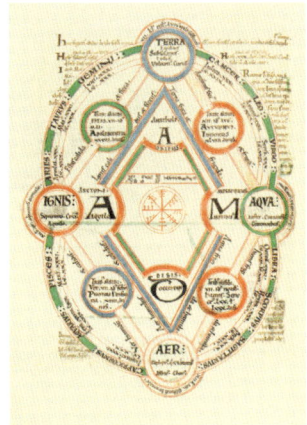

PHYSICAL AND PHYSIOLOGICAL FOURS

This 12th-century copy of Byrhtferth of Ramsey's 'Diagram of the Physical and Physiological Fours', from the English monk's *Enchiridion* (1011), relates the four elements to the seasons, compass directions, winds and stages of life.

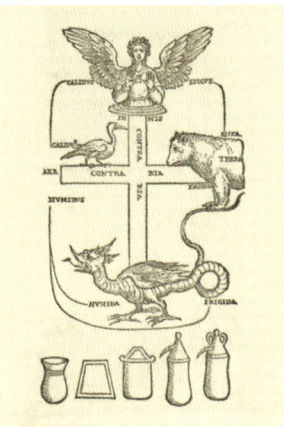

ALCHEMICAL CROSS OF THE ELEMENTS

This alchemical cross of the elements is from the 1546 edition of Petrus Bonus's 14th-century *Pretiosa margarita novella*. The four elements are represented as an angel (fire), bear (earth), wyvern (water) and bird (air).

PERSONIFIED ELEMENTS

In Johann Daniel Mylius's *Philosophia Reformata* (1622) the elements are personified as women standing on the traditional signs for the four elements, and on their heads are vessels containing figures representing the respective element. From left to right: earth, water, air and fire.

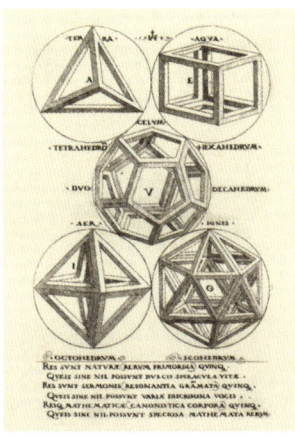

PLATONIC SOLIDS

The (here mislabelled) Platonic solids in Augustin Hirschvogel's *Ein aigentliche und grundtliche anweysung in die Geometria* (1543), showing the elements as a triangular pyramid (fire), cube (earth), octahedron (air) and icosahedron (water), plus a central dodecahedron, representing 'Heaven' or Ether.

INTERCONNECTED ELEMENTS

The 19th emblem in Michael Maier's *Atalanta fugiens* (1617/18) discusses the elements as interconnected. A line above the illustration states, 'If you kill one of the four, suddenly all will be dead.' They are depicted as men wielding fire, air, water and earth, and are opposed by a figure with a club.

‹ Portrait medal of Giovanni
Pico della Mirandola
by Medallist T.R.,
16th century
*Pico is known for introducing
the Jewish mystical tradition
to the Christian West and
has been called the father
of Christian Cabala.*

› Portrait medal of Marsilio
Ficino by Niccolò di
Forzore Spinelli, *c.* 1499
*Pico's contemporary, the
Florentine humanist Marsilio
Ficino is famous for his
translations of the writings of
Hermes, Plato and important
Neoplatonists, as well as for the
natural and astral magic in his
Three Books on Life (1489).*

that stones and metals could attract and hold those influences; the sympathies and antipathies believed to exist between animals, vegetables and minerals, and their related curative powers; the wondrous (electrical) rays of the torpedo fish; and the occult (i.e. 'interior') properties of alchemical substances. Knowledge of such things was born of long experience and observation. Nature was a repository of occult powers, and this often hard-won knowledge was kept secret from the uninitiated and profane.

In the 15th century, one of the leading figures in the Renaissance recovery of ancient wisdom, the Italian priest, astrologer and translator Marsilio Ficino (1433–99), introduced the West to the philosophy of Plato (*c.* 428–424 BCE) and the Neoplatonists Plotinus (*c.* 204–270 CE), Iamblichus (245–325) and Proclus (412–485), as well as the philosophical works attributed to Hermes Trismegistus. Ficino put forward a 'genealogy of wisdom', of wise men who anticipated the coming of Christ, including Zoroaster, Hermes, Orpheus, Pythagoras and Plato. His contemporary, Giovanni Pico della Mirandola (1463–94), acquainted the Christian West with the mysteries of Jewish Kabbalah, said to have originated either with Adam in the Garden of Eden or Moses on Mount Sinai, although the historical tradition is generally traced back to 12th-century Spain and France. In his *Conclusiones nongentae, in omni*

Dedication copy of *Three Books on Life* by Marsilio Ficino, 1489
This beautifully illuminated manuscript on how to prolong life and combat scholarly melancholy, according to astrology and astral magic, was prepared for Ficino's patron, the Florentine banker and statesman Lorenzo de' Medici.

genere scientiarum (*900 Conclusions on All Kinds of Sciences*, 1486), a series of 900 theses on a variety of topics related to philosophy, theology and mysticism, Pico combined material from a wide range of traditions (Latin, Arab, Greek, Chaldean, Egyptian, Jewish). Pico's interest in Jewish Kabbalah is considered a watershed in the history of Hebrew and Aramaic studies in Europe, and he is widely considered to be the father of Christian Cabala (as the term is often written in Latin).

In the early 16th century, the German humanist, polymath, soldier, physician and theologian Heinrich Cornelius Agrippa (1486–1535) was the first person to write explicitly of 'occult philosophy'. These words appear in a manuscript of 1510, left in the safe-keeping of his mentor, the 'magical abbot' Johannes Trithemius (1462–1516), while Agrippa was on a 'most secret mission' to the court of Henry VIII in England. The manuscript was substantially revised and eventually published as the encyclopedic *De occulta philosophia libri III* (*Three Books of Occult Philosophy*) in 1533. It is clear that Agrippa was using this term as a synonym for magic and his three books form the basis for Part II of this book. Agrippa discusses the relations

DECODING ROBERT FLUDD'S HEAD

A well-known engraving from Robert Fludd's *Utriusque Cosmi Historia* ('History of Both Worlds', 1617–21) shows three worlds above Fludd's head and gives some sense of how man gains knowledge of the different realms of existence.

1.
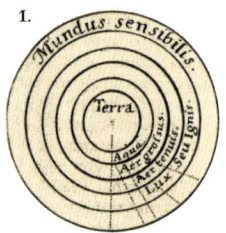

SENSIBLE WORLD
The lowest of the three worlds is the everyday 'Mundus sensibilis', the Sensible World, with its four elements: earth, water, air (gross and subtle), and light or fire.

5.
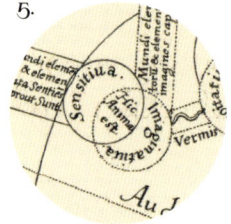

IMAGINATION
We conceive of the Imaginable World through the imagination, identified here as a faculty of the soul in which images occur in thoughts, memories and dreams.

2.
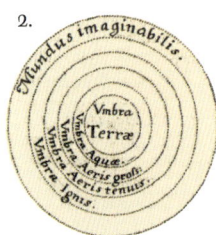

IMAGINABLE WORLD
The world between divine form and worldly matter has the label 'Mundus imaginabilis', the Imaginable World, a world of visions of potential and possibility, where we see the shadows of earth, water, and so forth.

6.
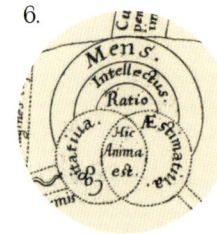

THINKING AND JUDGING
We relate to the Intellectual World through thinking and judging, and the three cognitive faculties of reason (*ratio*), intellect (*intellectus*) and mind (*mens*).

3.
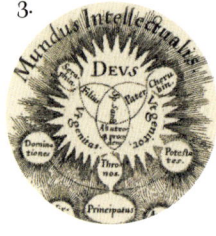

INTELLECTUAL WORLD
The highest world is the 'Mundus intellectualis', the Intellectual World, in which we see God, identified as the Holy Trinity, surrounded by the nine angelic orders.

7.
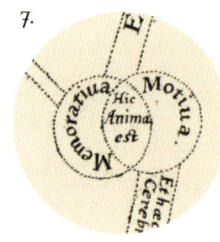

MEMORATIVE AND MOTIVE FACULTIES
At the back of the head are the memorative and motive faculties of the soul, responsible for remembering and recollection, and for setting the body in motion, respectively.

4.
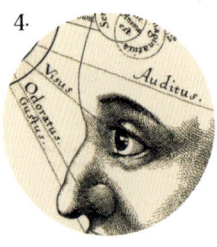

SENSES
We perceive the Sensible World through our five senses (hearing, sight, smell, taste and touch). Fludd connects each sense to its respective sense organ.

8.
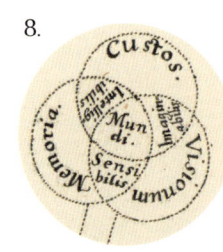

MEMORY
Memory, the guardian of visions, the storehouse of ideas and images gleaned from all three of the worlds: Sensible, Imaginable and Intellectual.

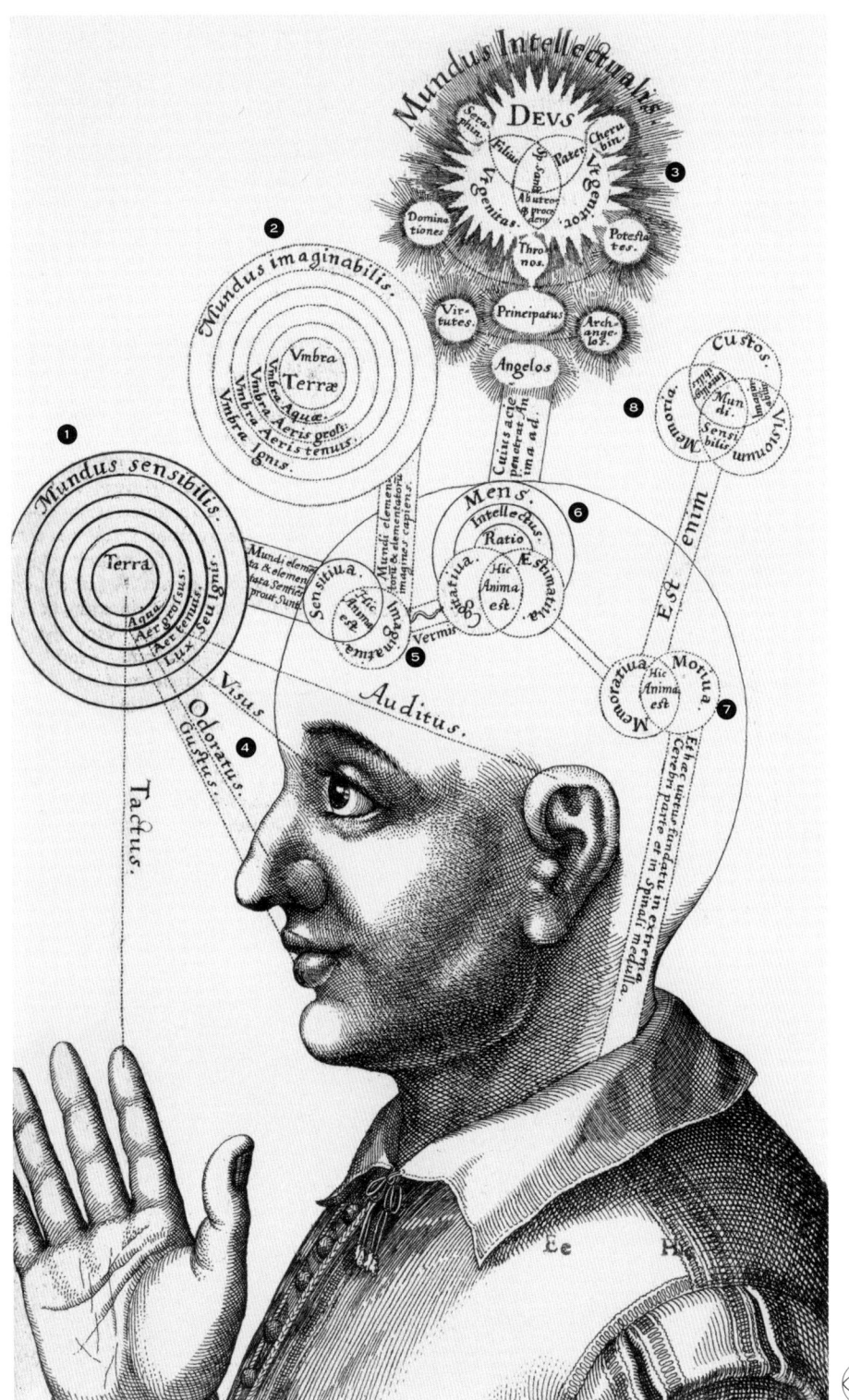

INTRODUCTION — *As Above, So Below*

Cornelis Bloemaert, after Giovanni Angelo Canini, *Oedipus Solving the Riddle of the Sphinx*, 1652

Oedipus is depicted solving the riddle of the Sphinx, the malevolent creature of Greek mythology with the head of a woman and the body of a winged lion. This engraving forms the frontispiece to Athanasius Kircher's Oedipus Aegyptiacus *(1652–54), which, in addition to Kircher's theories about Egyptian hieroglyphs, discusses Jewish and Saracenic Kabbalah.*

between God, man and nature, encompassing natural philosophy, psychology and religion, with an underlying message of the unity of the cosmos. Agrippa's collection of occult material from a wide variety of sources, although it was fiercely resisted by the Dominican Inquisitors, has been of inestimable influence on occult thinkers and practitioners over the centuries and continues to be an important work of reference in the present day.

Agrippa and subsequent writers on magic, including the Italian scholar, polymath and playwright Giovanni Battista della Porta (1535–1615) and the Italian Dominican friar, philosopher, magus and mathematician Giordano Bruno (1548–1600), each present a cosmopolitan lineage of 'learned' practitioners, including Persian magi, Greek philosophers, Latin wise men, Indian Brahmans, Egyptian priests, Jewish Kabbalists, Babylonian Chaldeans and Celtic druids. Occult philosophy appears as an extensive – ultimately Christian – religious philosophy and cosmology resting on Neoplatonic, Hermetic and kabbalistic foundations.

The Latin term *scientiae occultae* (occult sciences) also appeared during this period, an early example being in a work on secret writing, *Traicté des chiffres, ou Secrètes manières d'escrire* ('Treatise of Ciphers, or Secret Ways of Writing', 1586), by the French cryptographer and Christian Cabalist Blaise de Vigenère (1523–96). Johannes Trithemius and Giovanni Battista della Porta were also deeply interested in steganography, the practice of concealing data within a non-secret message, and cryptography, the art of writing and deciphering codes.

Although the rise of mechanical philosophy during the 17th-century Scientific Revolution, and the conviction that truth should be found through experiment based on empirical sensory experience, and the rationalism of the 18th-century Enlightenment are sometimes considered to have sounded the death knell for occult philosophy, this was not the case. Occult philosophy did not vanish in the face of rejection in some institutions of learning but, rather, withdrew from the public eye, surviving, for example, in the privacy

William Stewart Watson, *The Inauguration of Robert Burns as Poet Laureate of the Lodge*, 1846
Burns became a Freemason in 1781. This is a painting of his inauguration as Laureate of Lodge Canongate Kilwinning No. 2 in Edinburgh in 1787. This Lodge, which dates from 1736, is the oldest purpose-built Masonic meeting room in the world.

of Masonic lodges. Freemasonry had its origins in medieval stonemasons' guilds, but gradually developed into a 'gentlemen Freemasonry'. This transition took place in England and Scotland in the 17th and early 18th centuries, with the traditional founding date of the Premier Grand Lodge in London being given as 1717. The biblical account of the construction of the Temple of Solomon and its architect Hiram Abiff was one of the foundation stories of Freemasonry, which, depending on the nature of the specific lodge, augmented this with esoteric doctrines and symbolism from a wide range of sources, including alchemy and Kabbalah, the lore of ancient Egypt and legends of the medieval Knights Templar. In the Masonic lodges, occult thought persisted, at times undergoing periodic revivals, reconfigurations and even reinventions, co-existing and interacting with new scientific developments. Famous representatives of 'modern' science, including Robert Boyle (1627–91) and Isaac Newton (1642–1727), are known to have practised alchemy. The persistence of occult forms of thought is found, for example, in the collected works of the German theosopher Jacob Boehme (1575–1624), with their impressive illustrations

◁ Dionysius Andreas Freher, *The True Principles of All Things*, from William Law's *The Works of Jacob Behmen, The Teutonic Theosopher* (1764–81)
This illustration represents God the Father, God the Son and the Created Universe.

▷ Dionysius Andreas Freher, *Figure 12 of 13*, from William Law's *The Works of Jacob Behmen, The Teutonic Theosopher* (1764–81)
C stands for Christ and A is for Adam, while M and U represent the angels Michael and Uriel, respectively.

by Dionysius Andreas Freher (1649–1728) and Jeremias Daniel Leuchter. Two particularly important pioneers of occult thought at this time were the Swedish scientist and mystic Emanuel Swedenborg (1688–1772), who wrote extensively about his dreams and psychic visions, and the German physician Franz Anton Mesmer (1734–1815), who developed the practice of 'mesmerism', the forerunner to hypnotism.

The relentless materialism spawned by the Industrial Revolution inadvertently provoked a countervailing resistance to the rationalist eclipse of magical thinking, which sociologist and historian Max Weber (1864–1920) called the 'disenchantment of the world'. This response combined an interest in the wonders of modern science with a resurgence of interest in occult philosophy, emerging in the 19th century with a new name, occultism. The term first appeared in Jean-Baptiste Richard de Radonvilliers' *Enrichissement de la langue française: Dictionnaire des mots nouveaux* ('Enrichment of the French Language: Dictionary of New Words', 1842), where it is defined as 'occult system, of occulticity'. Works published over the next decade helped to establish the term, including

Henri Delaage's *Le monde occulte* ('The Occult World', 1851) and Jean-Marie Ragon's *Orthodoxie Maçonnique* and *Maçonnerie occulte* ('Masonic Orthodoxy' and 'Occult Masonry', both 1853). However, the wider dissemination of the word is most likely due to one of the most famous magicians of the time, Alphonse Louis Constant (1810–75), better known as Éliphas Lévi, who spoke of 'occultism' in his *Dogme et Rituel de la Haute Magie* and reinvigorated interest in magic. The French occult revival continued in works by the next generation of occultists, who often supported one another in the founding of new esoteric orders. Some of the most influential writers were Papus (the pseudonym of Dr Gérard Encausse, 1865–1916), Stanislas de Guaita (1861–97), and the French novelist and Rosicrucian Joséphin Péladan (1858–1918), whose *L'Amphithéâtre des sciences mortes* ('The Amphitheatre of Dead Sciences') of 1892–94 included volumes on how to become a fairy, a mage or an artist.

In 1875, the Russian occultist Helena Petrovna Blavatsky (1831–91) co-founded the Theosophical Society in New York. Among its objectives was the desire to oppose materialism and theological

Annie Besant and C. W. Leadbeater, *Music of Gounod*, from *Thought-Forms* (1901)
This is an example of a thought-form produced by the music of French composer Charles Gounod, with the book's text explaining: 'this music is not so much a thread of murmurous melody as a splendid succession of crashing chords'.

Annie Besant and C. W. Leadbeater, *Music of Wagner*, from *Thought-Forms* (1901)
The second example shows a thought-form produced by Wagner's music, with the book's text pointing out the marked difference between the two types of music that occur in it: 'one producing the angular rocky masses, and the other the rounded billowy clouds which lie between them'.

William Preston, *Eye of Providence*, 18th century
This illustration shows a symbol often associated with Freemasonry: the all-seeing eye of God, the Great Architect of the Universe. Preston was a Masonic lecturer, and the symbol appears in his lectures in various places and forms.

dogmatism, and to demonstrate the existence of occult forces unknown to science, and the presence of psychic and spiritual powers in man. It was Blavatsky who most likely introduced the notion of occultism to English-speaking audiences in an article published in the *Spiritual Scientist* that same year, in which she discusses Rosicrucian and Oriental Kabbalah, Eastern and American spiritualism, as well as magic and alchemy. Also in 1875, the French physiologist Charles Richet (1850–1935) became one of the first scientists to publish about occult phenomena – specifically, somnambulism – in a scientific journal. He was later president of the Society for Psychical Research, a London organization founded in 1882 to investigate paranormal phenomena. In 1884, the first German Theosophical Society was established, which was a catalyst for a German occult revival. Austria quickly followed suit and founded its own Theosophical Society in 1887, with two particularly influential members, the medical doctor Franz Hartmann (1838–1912), who was an author of works on alchemy, astrology and occult medicine, and the clairvoyant and social reformer Rudolf Steiner (1861–1925), who was eventually to found the esoteric spiritual movement called the Anthroposophical Society in 1912.

The 19th century was witness to new initiatory societies with occultist orientations, descendants of the Freemasonary of the previous century. In 1888 the Kabbalistic Order of the Rose-Cross was founded (by De Guaita and Péladan), with a particular focus on the practice of Christian Cabala in order to gain deeper insights into holy scripture. The same decade saw the establishment of the mystical Christian Martinist Order by Papus and the French journalist and historian Augustin Chaboseau (1868–1946). Around the same time three Freemasons, William Wynn Westcott, William Robert Woodman and Samuel Liddell MacGregor Mathers, all members of the Societas Rosicruciana in Anglia (SRIA), formed the Hermetic Order of the Golden Dawn in England. Although only active in its original form for little more than a decade, the Golden Dawn was ahead of its time in being open to men and women from all levels of society. It attracted a number of celebrities and was one of the most influential of all British initiatory societies. At the beginning of the 20th century, Theodor Reuss (1855–1923) was a key figure in establishing the Ordo Templi Orientis, a secret science research lodge in which initiates studied and practised a system of sex magic, later led by the notorious magician Aleister Crowley (1875–1947), who had also been a member of the Golden Dawn.

These individuals and societies often displayed a far broader range of interests than their medieval and early modern predecessors, adding new elements to the occult repertoire: cartomancy and the tarot or an interest in Eastern, mostly Indian forms of religious wisdom, a new orientation towards parapsychology and psychical research, animal magnetism, hypnosis, spiritualism and spiritism, disincarnated or ascended Masters, and an increasing emancipation from (or antagonism towards) Christianity. Much of this continues to the present day, with the advent of the New Age, the broad-spectrum category of the occult, courtesy of Colin Wilson's 1971 bestseller *The Occult: A History*, which embraces anything from vampires and UFOs to parapsychology, and the more recent confluence of the occult and popular culture in what has come to be known as 'occulture'.

John William Waterhouse, *Study for The Magic Circle*, 1886

Waterhouse presents a Pre-Raphaelite vision of a sorceress, with a snake coiled around her neck. She draws a fiery magic circle with the wand in her right hand, and the crescent-shaped sickle in her left hand links her with the moon and Hecate. A cauldron stands at the centre, while ravens and a toad watch from outside the circle.

CHAPTER ONE
FOUNDATIONS

ASTROLOGY — 1

ALCHEMY — 2

KABBALAH — 3

/faʊnˈdeɪʃən/ noun
The basis or groundwork of anything.

METTRATON
AMBRIEL
ASMODEL
MALCHIDAEL
BARCHIEL
GAMBIEL
HANAEL
ADVACHIEL
BARCHIEL
ZVRIEL
HAMALIEL
VERCHIEL
MVRIEL
ZAPKIEL
CAMAEL
RAPHAEL
HANIEL
GABRIEL

'The position of this or that star in the Sky [must] have an influence on the child who is born, who enters by the very fact of his birth into the universal harmony of the sidereal world.'

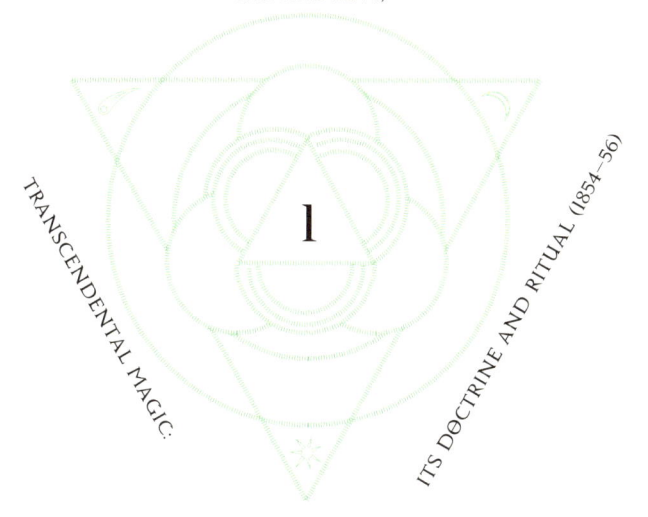

ÉLIPHAS LÉVI, *TRANSCENDENTAL MAGIC: ITS DOCTRINE AND RITUAL* (1854–56)

ASTROLOGY

Astrology presupposes a link between the positions and movements of the sun, moon and planets – against the backdrop of the constellations – and life on earth. Practitioners believe that knowledge of this relationship can be beneficial for human life. Astrologers perform divinatory activities based on the calculation of horoscopes to provide insights into an individual's life or world events.

page 34
Anonymous, *Mountain of the Philosophers*, from a manuscript (1943) of the 18th-century *Geheime Figuren der Rosenkreuzer*
To reach the top of the mountain, which holds the philosophers' stone, one must pass fierce beasts, the lion and dragon, the raven and eagle – all symbols of alchemy. The naked man guarding the cave sits in what is symbolically the fire-place of the athanor or alchemical furnace.

page 36
Jean Thenaud, *Influx of the Angelic or Celestial World*, from *Introduction to the Kabbalah*, dedicated to King Francis I (1536)
This illustration features the divine name YHVH in Hebrew at the top, surrounded by choirs of different orders of angels in a large triangle of light that reaches down to the centre of the cosmos. Its point touches the earth, which is encircled by the orbits of the planets and the signs of the zodiac.

Let us start with astrology, from the Greek words *astron* ('star') and *logos* ('study'), one of the most enduring pillars of occult philosophy, even if nowadays it is so familiar to us from the horoscope sections in magazines, newspapers, a myriad of websites and smartphone apps that many modern astrologers would contest it being considered 'occult' at all, in the hidden sense of the term.

Observation of the movements of the planets and stars in the heavens, and the belief that they have an influence on earthly events, has played a significant role in many cultures for thousands of years, with the worship of the stars as deities believed to have existed in Mesopotamia (modern-day Iraq) as early as the second millennium BCE. The *Enuma Anu Enlil*, a collection of approximately seventy cuneiform tablets on the subject of Babylonian astrology, produced in this region from the second millennium BCE, is the oldest known written record. The tablets contain around 7,000 celestial omens concerning the king and state, based on observations of the rising and setting of the moon and sun in relation to the planets and stars, lunar haloes, and solar and lunar eclipses. The earliest known horoscope, in the sense of a chart representing the positions of the planets and stars at the time of someone's birth, is also Babylonian, dating from approximately 410 BCE.

Elements of this knowledge may have passed to the Egyptians after the Persians conquered Babylonia in 539 BCE and then Egypt in 525 BCE. Babylonian horoscopes were calculated solely for the ruler and empire, but this began to change in Egypt during the Hellenistic period, following Alexander the Great's conquest of the country in 332 BCE, when interest in horoscopes and predictions for individuals grew. In Alexandrian Egypt, astrologers adopted the Babylonian system, observing the sun's circular path through the sky throughout the course of a year and dividing its 360-degree circuit into twelve zodiac signs, each representing a 30-degree section. They then subdivided these signs into 10-degree intervals, creating thirty-six 'decans' to mark the rhythm of the year and aid in calculating the rising and setting of stars. This gave rise to horoscopic astrology, the Greek word

Ceiling relief, Temple of Hathor, Dendera, Qena, Egypt, *c.* 54 BCE

This ceiling relief from the large pronaos (vestibule) at the Temple of Hathor depicts Egyptian zodiac signs. The top image shows Sagittarius and Scorpio, the central section represents Capricorn, and at the bottom Taurus and Aries can be seen.

PROFILE
THE ZODIAC

In a system that originated in ancient Babylon, the circle of the astrological zodiac is divided into twelve signs, each 30 degrees, according to the earth's annual orbit around the sun. The signs are traditionally arranged according to the progress of the year from the first day of spring, beginning with the first degree of Aries and ending with the last degree of Pisces. Each sign is related to a constellation, and the date ranges can vary slightly from year to year. The signs represent different elements (fire, earth, air, water), as well as different

♈ ARIES
(21 March–19 April)
Aries is symbolized by the ram. Classed as male, Aries is a fire sign and its quality is cardinal. It is ruled by Mars.

♉ TAURUS
(20 April–20 May)
Represented by the bull and ruled by Venus, Taurus is thought of as a female sign. Taurus's modality is fixed, and its element is earth.

♊ GEMINI
(21 May–21 June)
The symbol for Gemini is the twins. Traditionally a male sign, Gemini is mutable and ruled by Mercury, and its element is air.

♋ CANCER
(22 June–22 July)
Symbolized by the crab and ruled by the moon, Cancer is one of six female signs. It is a water sign and its quality is cardinal.

♌ LEO
(23 July–22 August)
The symbol for Leo is the lion and its element is fire. A fixed sign that is classed as male, Leo is ruled by the sun.

♍ VIRGO
(23 August–22 September)
Embodied by the maiden and thought of as female, Virgo is an earth sign. Virgo is ruled by Mercury and is mutable.

modalities; those that in theory initiate activity are cardinal, those that sustain activity are fixed, and those that modify it are mutable. Six are traditionally classed as male, six as female. Each sign is ruled by a different planet; some rulerships were modified with the discovery of new planets. Many representations of the zodiac can be found in medieval manuscripts. This series is from the 12th-century *Hunterian Psalter*. Rather than simply a goat, here Capricorn is depicted as a mythical Sea-Goat, sometimes associated with the god Pan.

♎ *LIBRA*
(23 September–22 October)
Symbolized by the scales, Libra is an air sign that is cardinal. Libra is classed as a male sign and is ruled by Venus.

♏ *SCORPIO*
(23 October–22 November)
Scorpio is a female sign and its element is water. Represented by the scorpion, it is ruled by Mars/Pluto and its modality is fixed.

♐ *SAGITTARIUS*
(23 November–21 December)
Sagittarius is embodied by the archer and is ruled by Jupiter. Tied to fire as its element, Sagittarius is a male sign and mutable.

♑ *CAPRICORN*
(22 December–19 January)
The symbol for Capricorn is the goat and it is an earth sign. Ruled by Saturn, Capricorn is thought of as a female sign and is cardinal.

♒ *AQUARIUS*
(20 January–18 February)
The water-bearer, Aquarius is traditionally male and is an air sign. Aquarius's modality is fixed and it is ruled by Saturn/Uranus.

♓ *PISCES*
(19 February–20 March)
Represented by the fish, Pisces is a water sign. A mutable sign, Pisces is ruled by Jupiter/Neptune and is thought of as female.

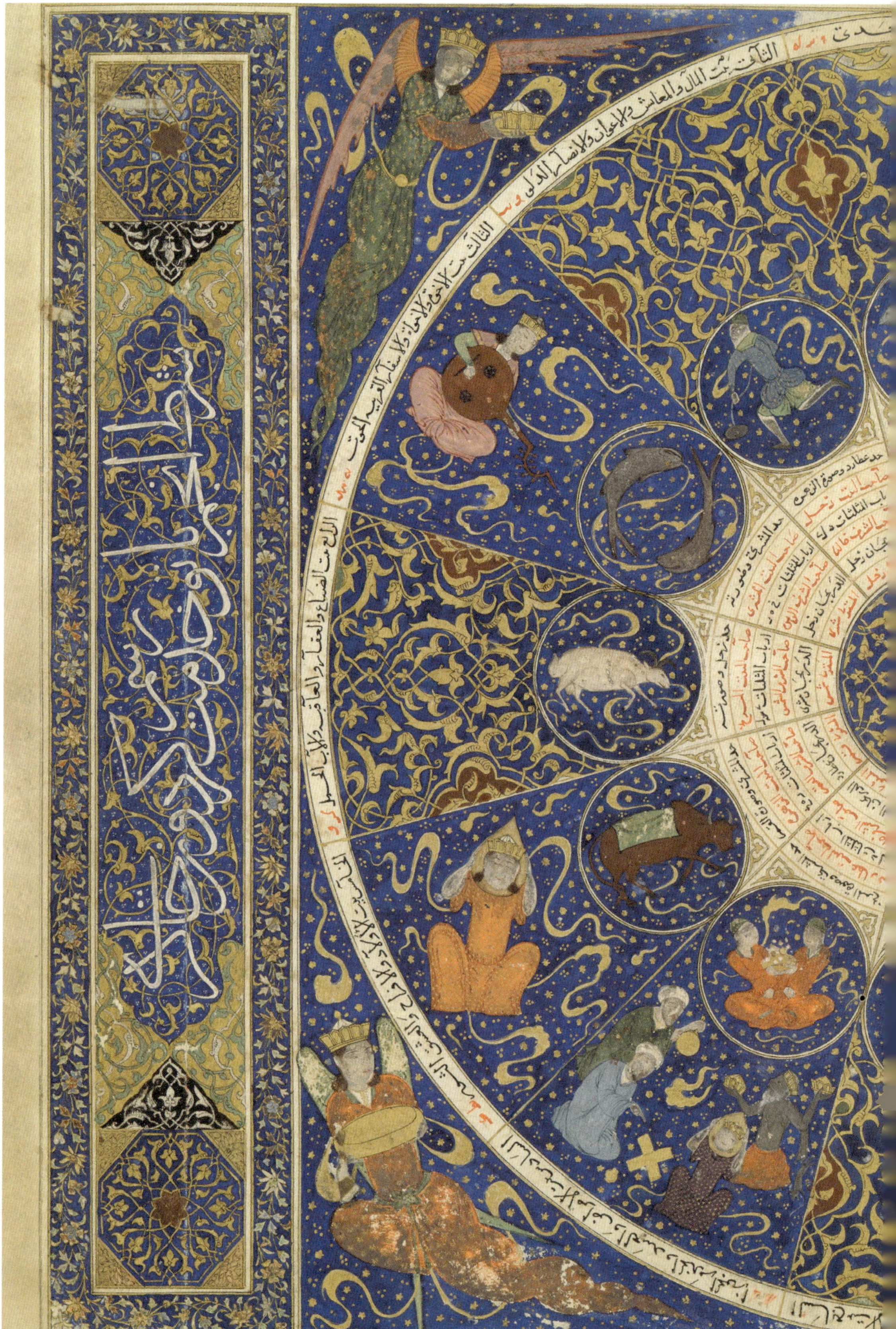

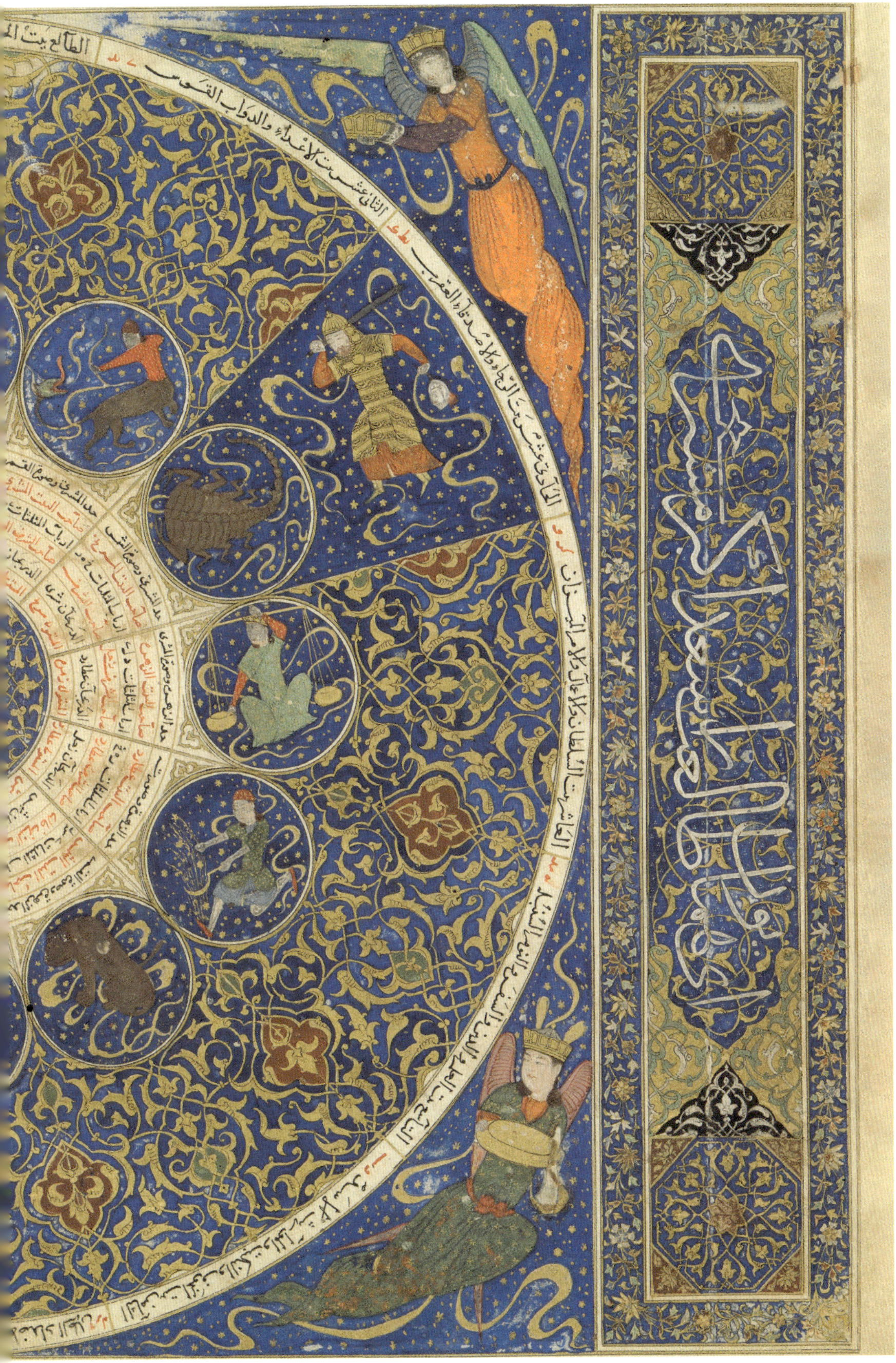

pages 42–43
Horoscope of Sultan Iskandar, from *Kitab-i viladat-i Iskandar* (1411), the 'Book of the Birth of Iskandar'
Iskandar was the grandson of the Turkmen-Mongol conqueror and founder of the Timurid dynasty, Tamerlane. In 1415, ten years after Tamerlane's death, he was executed following a failed rebellion.

The Nebra sky disc, c. 1600 BCE
Discovered in Germany in 1999, this 3,600-year-old bronze disc - decorated with inlaid gold symbols of the sun, the moon and the stars - is believed to be the world's oldest map of the heavens.

Celestial planisphere
This fragment of a Neo-Assyrian clay tablet depicts the night sky of 3–4 January 650 BCE over the ancient city of Nineveh. It would have been used for astrological calculations.

horoskopos being the Ascendant or zodiac sign rising on the eastern horizon at the time of a person's birth, its degree representing the cusp or beginning of the first celestial house of the birth chart. Over the centuries, horoscope has come to mean the complete diagram of the heavens calculated at the time of birth. The earliest personal horoscope from Hellenistic Egypt dates from the last decades of the 1st century BCE. The Hellenistic period also saw the development of collections of astrology related to medicine in the *Iatromathematica* of the Egyptian sage Hermes Trismegistus. This was used to identify individual susceptibilities towards certain ailments indicated in a birth chart and to recommend an appropriate diet, preventative sanitary regimen and so forth, for the preservation of health.

The Graeco-Roman astrologer Claudius Ptolemy (*c.* 100–*c.* 170 CE), who lived in Alexandria, was an important figure in the development of horoscopic astrology. His *Tetrabiblos* ('Four Books'), a compilation of traditional Egyptian astrological knowledge, adapted to the natural philosophy of Aristotle, was to become an influential source for the Western astrological tradition. The *Tetrabiblos* is a manual of genethlialogy (natal astrology or birth charts), with detailed discussions of the zodiac signs, the seven classical planets (those visible with the naked eye from earth – Mercury, Venus, Mars, Jupiter and Saturn – as well as the Moon and the

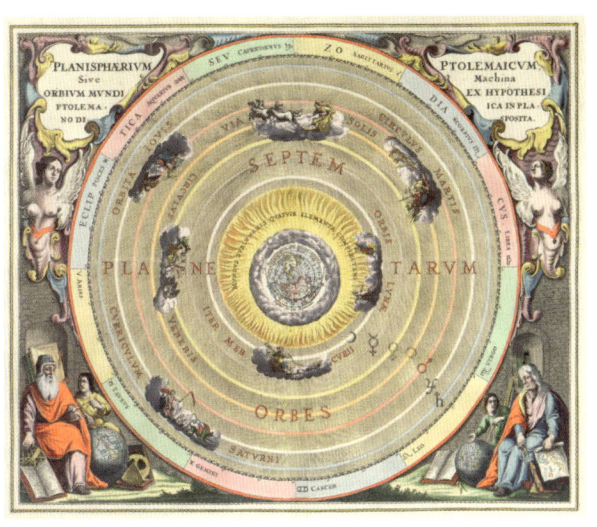

Justus van Gent, *Portrait of the Greek Astronomer Claudius Ptolemy*, c. 1475
The famous astronomer Ptolemy holds an armillary sphere, a three-dimensional model of the cosmos with the earth at the centre, surrounded by rings. The widest ring represents the ecliptic, on which the constellations of the zodiac were often inscribed.

Andreas Cellarius, *Geocentric System of Ptolemy*, from *Harmonia Macrocosmica* (1660–61)
This illustration shows the orbits of the planets around the earth, according to the cosmological theories of Claudius Ptolemy.

Sun), and the fixed stars (which do not seem to move and were believed to be attached to the most distant heavenly sphere of the Firmament) forming the patterns of the constellations, and explanations of how to interpret the favourable and unfavourable angular distances (or 'aspects') between the planets and other parts of the horoscope such as the Ascendant and Midheaven. Ptolemy instructs his readers about which planets are benign (Moon, Venus and Jupiter) and which are malign (Saturn and Mars). Using this information, the novice astrologer could learn how to construct charts for both natural and judicial astrology, by calculating the positions of the planets and stars for a specific date, time and place. Natural astrology, based on the observation of seasonal phenomena, is concerned with general predictions about terrestrial events, such as outbreaks of plague or famine, and includes astrometeorology, the art of astrological weather prediction of storms, floods or droughts. While natal astrology uses a person's birth chart to draw conclusions about their character and life, judicial astrology takes this a step further and attempts to predict future possibilities by tracing the continuing movement of the planets (known as transits) through the person's horoscope. This form of predictive astrology that forecasts events in an individual's future provoked fierce polemic,

DECODING
ZODIAC MAN

The *Homo Signorum* ('Man of Signs') or melothesia, the practice of associating the influence of the constellations on the human body, originated in Greek antiquity and became a common image of iatromathematics or medical astrology in the Middle Ages. The Zodiac Man appears not only in medical and philosophical works, but also in calendars and books of hours. The twelve signs are approximately mapped onto the human body, with the first sign, Aries, associated with the head and the twelfth sign, Pisces, linked with the feet. This 15th-century example from the Wellcome Collection, London, is in a folding almanac, an astro-medical physician's calendar or girdle book, which was attached to the belt as an early portable information source.

1. *Aries* — head
2. *Taurus* — neck
3. *Gemini* — shoulders
4. *Cancer* — chest
5. *Leo* — sides
6. *Virgo* — belly
7. *Libra* — buttocks
8. *Scorpio* — groin
9. *Sagittarius* — thighs
10. *Capricorn* — knees
11. *Aquarius* — shins
12. *Pisces* — feet

‹ The Zodiac Man opposite forms part of this folding almanac.

tione i capitevl i sa
nam capitale. Taurus
m collo vl' i guttu
venam i illis loas.
i latione i humeris
bue i manibus
na m hijs loas.
ab m latione
vl' collis + a
stomach
ms ner m
arteri a
nam q
splen
rigit.

ne neruoy + a lesione
des i loso p apicionem
Virgo. Caue ne i scin
nec m loas o vulnis i
ne llandat. whuis m
op yte ventris nec apr
phias ibi ventosam
lione restiau og + am
redulle ner j sudas
nere. Sagittar. Caue ab
i noy nec i scaidas
ris exertentes. Capri
tis tu gemb; + ab ita
m hijs loas. Aquari
m ib; uel uerius cor
Pisces. Caue
bis.

47   FOUNDATIONS — 1 — *Astrology*

Zakariyā' al-Qazwīnī, miniature of the seven classical planets from his *Aja'ib al-Makhluqat wa Ghara'ib al-Mawjudat*, 13th century
Translated as 'Wonders of Creation and the Unique Phenomena of Existence', this work by the Persian cosmographer, geographer and natural historian Zakariyā' al-Qazwīnī is divided into two parts: the first deals with the heavenly bodies, the second with the terrestrial world. The watercolour above, from the first part, shows the seven classical planets personified.

however, from the 1st century CE onwards, from anti-astrological theologians and church fathers, such as John Chrysostom, archbishop of Constantinople (d. 407), about the dangers of astral determinism and was at times perceived as a denial of the Christian doctrine of free will, resulting in it being the form of astrology most commonly condemned by the Church.

Another branch of horoscopic astrology is represented by horary astrology, which works on the assumption that the heavens contain the answer to any question at the exact moment in which it is asked. The position of the fast-moving moon, which passes through each zodiac sign in approximately 2.5 days in its cycle, and the subject matter of the question determine the celestial house in which the astrologer will find the answer. If the 'interrogation' (i.e. question) were about wealth or material possessions, for example, the astrologer would examine the second house of the chart and the planet ruling that house; if it concerned partners or partnerships, he would look at the seventh

Illustrations of zodiac signs by Qanbar ʿAlī Naqqāš Šīrāzī, *c.* **1300**
The pages below are from a 15th-century Egyptian manuscript of the Kitāb al-Mawālīd *or 'Book of Nativities' by the 9th-century Persian astrologer Abū Maʿshar (Jaʿfar ibn Muhammad al-Balkhī), known in the West as Albumasar. The illustration on the left depicts the zodiac sign of Leo, while the one on the right represents Capricorn.*

house; if the question was about the querent's profession, the answer would be sought in the tenth house. Related to this is electional astrology, in which an individual chooses the most auspicious moment to carry out an activity, such as a journey, a marriage, the purchase of a house, a coronation or even the founding of a city. The Greek physicians Hippocrates (*c.* 460–370 BCE) and Galen (129–216 CE) believed that anyone working in the medical field ought to be familiar with astrology and its role in determining the appropriate times for purgations, phlebotomies, and the preparation and administering of medicine.

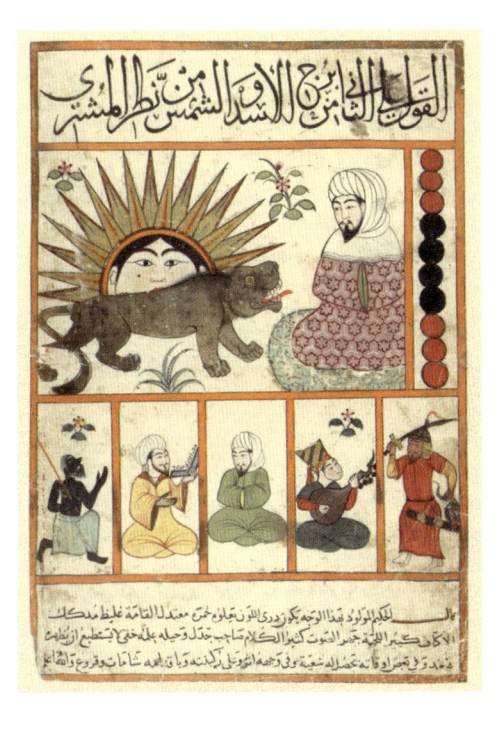

New developments were to come following the rise of Islam in the 7th century and the development of Islamicate astrology, which integrated knowledge from many astrological traditions, including Indian and Chinese. Two of the most influential astrologers during this period were the Arab polymath Al-Kindi (*c.* 801–873) and the Persian Abū Maʿshar (787–886). The former promoted a mixture of astrology and magic, most notably in his *De radiis* ('On Rays'), where he wrote not only of the influence of stellar rays on all things, but also of the emission of rays from every material object, even from words, which radiated outwards to influence the cosmos. Abū Ma'shar is famed for his promotion of mundane astrology and his doctrine of the Great Conjunctions, a form of astrological history or chronosophy in which the conjunctions or coming together of the two slowest-moving and outermost planets of the Ptolemaic cosmos, Jupiter and Saturn, were tied to major world events, including the rise and fall of kingdoms, dynasties and even religions. This was adopted by Jewish astrologers seeking to predict the coming of the Messiah and likewise Christians in an attempt to anticipate the second coming of Christ, closely connecting astrology with apocalypticism. The Bohemian astrologer Cyprian Leowitz (1524–74) promoted a science of 'natural prophecy' based on observations of the stars and careful comparison of data from historical records of great conjunctions, eclipses and comets from the preceding 1,600 years, in the conviction that from knowledge of past events he would be able to hypothesize about the future, aligning his findings with biblical prophecies in the Book of Daniel.

In the Christian West, there were few developed textbooks on either astronomy or astrology in the Middle Ages; indeed, detailed observations of the heavens appear to have been rare in Europe until the 12th century. It was only with the 12th-century Renaissance translation of Arabic treatises into Latin that Christian thinkers gained access to essential reading for the theory and practice of astrology, with the Latin translation of Ptolemy's *Tetrabiblos* in 1138, which became one of the most popular astrological manuals of the Middle Ages. By the end of the century, astrology was practised in almost all monasteries, with interest spreading from the clergy to the aristocratic courts and other layers of society. The Platonist philosopher Bernardus Silvestris's *Cosmographia* (c. 1147–48), which is divided into two parts – *Megacosmus* and *Microcosmus*, concerning, respectively, the formation of the universe and the creation of man – became one of the most important

Constellation of Pegasus, from the *Astronomical-Astrological Codex of King Wenceslaus IV*, 1401

The constellation of the winged horse Pegasus is one of the largest constellations in the heavens and was first catalogued as one of forty-eight constellations by Ptolemy. The mythical Greek hero Bellerophon rode Pegasus to defeat the fire-breathing Chimera, but then angered the gods by trying to fly to Mount Olympus. Zeus sent a gadfly to sting Pegasus, who threw his rider and entered the heavens on his own.

51   FOUNDATIONS —1— *Astrology*

PROFILE
CHILDREN OF THE PLANETS

For centuries the classical cosmos, as described by the 2nd-century astronomer-astrologer Claudius Ptolemy, was populated by seven planets (πλανήτης, *planētēs*, literally 'wanderers'): the two luminaries, the sun and the moon, and the five planets visible to the naked eye. New planets in the solar system were only added later. In Western astrology, these planets have the names and symbolic qualities of the Roman gods. These images

☽ *MOON*
The moon is associated with intuition, receptiveness, emotions and feelings, the unconscious, memory, moods, and the ability to react and adapt to surroundings.

☿ *MERCURY*
Mercury represents communication, thinking, reasoning, intelligence, adaptability, variability, wit, information gathering, education and learning.

♀ *VENUS*
Venus signifies the desire for harmony, beauty, refinement, affection, love, romance and sex, that which brings people together, including fashion and the arts.

♂ *MARS*
Mars is connected with assertion, aggression, the fighting spirit, that which makes us distinct, energy, strength, ambition, the competitiveness of sports and physical activities in general.

♃ *JUPITER*
Jupiter signifies energies of growth, expansion of one's horizons (spiritual, mental or physical), higher education, philosophy, religion, law, as well as prosperity and good fortune.

♄ *SATURN*
Saturn is associated with career, self-discipline, authority figures, commitment, stability, productiveness, endurance, long-term planning, and facing one's anxieties and fears.

are from *Sphaerae coelestis et planetarum descriptio* ('A Description of the Heavenly Sphere and the Planets'), a 1491 manuscript based on Johannes de Sacrobosco's 13th-century *De sphaera mundi* ('On the Sphere of the World'). Pictured opposite, the sun (symbol: ☉) represents the personal motivating power behind all activities, the light one casts in the world, individuality, creativity, vitality and life force.

Pages from *The Guild Book of the Barbers and Surgeons of York*, 1486
Melothesia or Zodiac Man can be seen on the left-hand page, opposite a rotating volvelle to predict the best time for medical treatment.

works of the High Middle Ages for its adaptation of Abū Ma'shar's ideas to a Christian context. In the trilogy *Liber introductorius* ('Introductory Book'), the Scottish scholar and mathematician Michael Scot (1175–1232), court astrologer to the Holy Roman Emperor Frederick II, presents his readers with a history of astrology stretching back to the Persian prophet and inventor of ritual magic Zoroaster. By the mid-13th century, astrology had been incorporated into the standard philosophical curriculum of Western universities, as part of the four liberal arts of the quadrivium (alongside mathematics, music and geometry); and by the 15th century, it was firmly allied with medicine, with chairs of astrological medicine in Italy, France and Poland. Many of the popes were patrons of astrologers, despite the Church's concerns about judicial astrology. Opinion was divided among the leading lights of the Protestant Reformation. Its most prominent voice, Martin Luther (1483–1546), denounced astrology as an illicit pagan art, indeed a dangerous

Baldassarre Peruzzi, fresco of Venus in Capricorn, Villa Farnesina, Rome, *c.* 1511
This fresco, representing the planet Venus in the zodiac sign Capricorn, forms part of Peruzzi's astrological painting on the ceiling of Villa Farnesina's Loggia di Galatea representing the horoscope of the Renaissance banker Agostino Chigi.

game with the Devil. Luther's friend and collaborator, the German theologian Philipp Melanchthon (1497–1560), considered it a science with potential in many spheres of life, valuable for the study of nature as well as for understanding the history and fate of mankind. The French reformer John Calvin (1509–64), meanwhile, although rejecting judicial astrology, accepted natural astrology related to medical prognosis.

The Rosicrucians, whose ideology of universal reform (of society, religion, medicine and the sciences) flourished in Protestant Europe during the 17th century, were fascinated by astronomical phenomena. In fact, their two manifestos, the *Fama Fraternitatis* ('Rumour of the Brotherhood', 1614) and *Confessio Fraternitatis* ('Confession of the Brotherhood', 1615), mention the 'new' stars detected in the constellation of Cygnus in 1600 and the supernova observed by Emperor Rudolf II's mathematician Johannes Kepler (1571–1630) in the constellation of Serpentarius (the 'serpent bearer') in 1604. The supernova also made a powerful impression on the Italian philosopher Tommaso Campanella (1568–1639), who supported astrology as a Christian activity with reference to the three magi who followed the star to bear witness to the newborn Jesus. Campanella, like many others, was excited by the grand conjunction of Jupiter and Saturn in the fiery sign of Sagittarius in 1603, which he believed indicated a 'revolution' of the

Pages from Theophilus Schweighardt's *Speculum Sophicum Rhodo-Stauroticum*, 1618
The title page (left) features personifications of physiology and theology, while the illustration on the right shows the College of the Brotherhood of the Rosicrucians. Schweighardt was one of the pseudonyms of the astronomer and mathematician Daniel Mögling.

birth of Christ – that is, the two planets occupied the same place in the heavens that they had at the time of Christ's birth, which presaged, for him, a renewal of Christianity, the return to an age of innocence. In Britain, William Lilly (1602–81) – arguably the most famous English astrologer of the 17th century, best known for his prediction of the overthrow and possible execution of King Charles I in *The Starry Messenger* (1645), as well as the Great Plague and the Fire of London (1666) – published a large compendium, the first of its kind to be printed in English, explicitly calling itself *Christian Astrology* (1647).

It is only in the 18th century that we really begin to see a division between astronomy and astrology. Previously the two words were often interchangeable. With the coming of the Enlightenment, a split began to form between the quantitative study of the laws of the stars (the literal meaning of the Latin word *astronomia*), which was considered rational and scientific, and the qualitative interpretations of astrology, which were dismissed as non-rational or superstitious. Despite falling out of favour at universities and in aristocratic courts as the Scientific Revolution took hold, interest in astrology continued in other circles, sustained over the next two centuries by members of esoteric societies such as the Rosicrucians, Freemasons and theosophists. On a popular level, astrology weathered the 18th and 19th centuries in almanacs, such as *Vox Stellarum* or *Old Moore's Almanack* and Raphael's *Prophetic Almanac*, offering agricultural, commercial and astrological information each year.

One of the most influential astrological theorists of the 20th century, the English theosophist Alan Leo (William Frederick Allan, 1860–1917) is considered the father of modern astrology. Like many in the Theosophical Society, Leo was deeply interested in Indian philosophy and studied *Jyotisha*, traditional Hindu or Vedic astrology, and integrated notions of karma and reincarnation into his thought. In works such as *Esoteric Astrology* (1913), he turned away from an external, event-orientated astrology and initiated an 'interiorizing trend' in modern Western astrology that took the subject in new directions, arguing that the planets and zodiac signs symbolized levels of spiritual existence and stages of spiritual evolution. Inspired by these ideas, the American theosophist

Matthaeus Merian (engraver), *Astrologers Preparing a Horoscope*, from Volume 2 (1619) of Robert Fludd's *Utriusque Cosmi Historia*

Two men are seated at a table bearing astronomical instruments, including a celestial globe and dividers for measuring distances. The figure on the left is entering planetary positions in a horoscope (which were square then, but nowadays are circular). In the background we see the sun, the moon and stars, towards which the astrologer is pointing, indicating direct observation of the heavens.

Dane Rudhyar (Daniel Chennevière, 1895–1985) reformulated astrology, moving away from the notion that stars exerted influences on human life towards the concept of synchronicity first proposed by the Swiss depth psychologist Carl Jung (1875–1961). In books such as *The Astrology of Personality* (1936) and *Occult Preparations for a New Age* (1975), Rudhyar promoted both a humanistic, psychologically orientated, 'person-centred' astrology to facilitate self-understanding and a transpersonal astrology, which regarded astrology as a spiritual path. The individual's task, according to Rudhyar, is to integrate with the higher, spiritual cosmos and become a vehicle for the coming of the new astrological Age of Aquarius (see p. 224) and the second coming of the Christ consciousness that leads to an experience of one's higher self.

Astrology enjoyed a revival in the counterculture of the 1960s and '70s, becoming emblematic of the New Age in such influential works as Liz Greene's *Relating: An Astrological Guide to Living with Others on a Small Planet* (1977) and Stephen Arroyo's *Astrology, Karma & Transformation* (1978). During the first quarter of the 21st century, psychological astrology integrated various forms of depth, humanistic and transpersonal psychology. These approaches are often strongly influenced by the writings of the Swiss psychiatrist Carl Jung, who was known for studying his patients' horoscopes in order to gain insights into the unconscious dynamics of their psyche, writing in *The Spirit of Man, Art and Literature* (1971) that 'astrology represents the sum of all the psychological knowledge of antiquity'. The psychosynthesis approach of Italian psychiatrist Roberto Assagioli (1888–1974) has also embraced astrology in the guise of the Astrological Psychology Institute founded in Zurich in 1968 by Swiss astrologer and psychologist Bruno Huber (1930–99). Such astro-psychological notions enjoy a strong following in popular culture – in particular, those dealing with behavioural dispositions and personality traits – alongside numerous versions of mundane astrology, including financial astrology to predict fluctuations in the stock market, and astrological gardening, planting and harvesting according to the stars.

Dane Rudhyar,
Creative Man, 1948

This painting appeared on the cover of Rudhyar's The Astrology of Transformation: A Multilevel Approach *(1980). Rudhyar describes this image as an archetypal structure based on the interplay of forces within the human body.*

The chapiter folowyng convenient for a clerk
Shewith the counsels of the subtile werk

'Alchemy, the Most Ancient, Certain, Wisest, Holiest…. Most Wonderful and Wonder-working Art of Arts…either finds a man Holy, or makes him Holy!'

ATTRIBUTED TO THOMAS AQUINAS, IN PETRUS BONUS, PRETIOSA MARGARITA NOVELLA (1546)

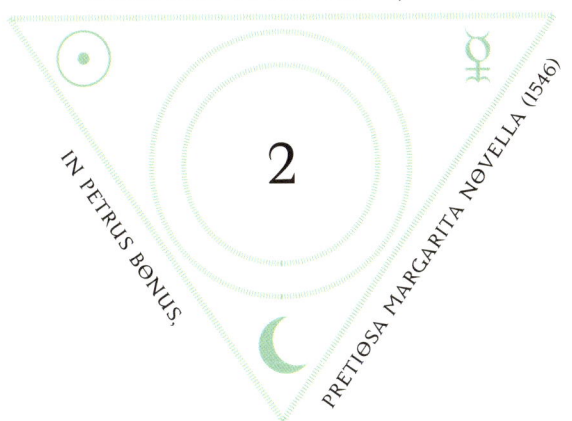

2

ALCHEMY

Alchemy is the belief that the investigation of the properties of earthly matter leads to an intimate knowledge of how natural matter – plants, minerals and metals, in particular – are formed by nature. Historically, alchemists tried to replicate these processes in their laboratories in diverse ways, often in the hope of transmuting base metals into silver or gold, but also to create alchemical medicines to treat diseases or prolong life – both directions involved in a quest for the elixir or philosophers' stone.

The oldest historical texts that form the basis of Western alchemy date to around the 3rd century CE and were discovered in Egypt. These are recipes written in Greek on papyrus, instructions on how to imitate precious materials, make copper look like silver, or silver like gold, and create artificial gemstones. Although we do not find the idea of the transmutation of base metals (copper, iron, tin, lead, mercury) into noble metals (silver, gold), we nevertheless encounter the notion of transformation of matter. Similar material can be found in a text called *Physika kai mystika* ('Natural and Secret Things'), which is believed to date from around the 1st century CE but survives only in later manuscripts. It adds, however, a completely new dimension to the story, with an account of how the author's master died before revealing all his secrets. The student summons his master's spirit from Hades but, being obstructed by a daemon, receives simply a message that 'the books are in the temple'. A search proves unsuccessful, but during a feast in the temple a column suddenly breaks open, revealing the master's hidden book!

The earliest alchemical works tend to have mythical or legendary authors. In one, for example, Isis reveals the secrets of *chrysopoeia* (gold-making) to her son Horus. In another, attributed to Cleopatra the Alchemist (*c.* 3rd century CE) – not to be confused with the Egyptian queen – symbols and drawings related to gold-making include what was to become a popular alchemical image of the ouroboros and one of the earliest depictions of alchemical apparatus, resembling a *kerotakis*, a piece of equipment used to subject a sample of metal to vaporized sulphur or mercury, in the hope of transmutation.

It is important to note, however, that alchemy is far more than the aspiration to create gold. Etymologically, the Latin words *alchemia* and *alchymia* are said to be derived from the Arabic *al-kīmiyā*, itself from the Persian *kimia* ('elixir'), with its origin in the Greek *khymeia*, from the base *kheō* ('to pour' or 'to melt'), related to either *khuma* ('that which is poured out or flows' or 'an ingot') or *khumos* ('juice of a plant'), which alchemists extract with their art; the prefix 'al' is

⟨ *page 60*
Thomas Norton,
Ordinall of Alchimy, 1477
An alchemist is seated at his work table in the laboratory, with two assistants tending the apparatus in the foreground.

Python, from an *Alchemical and Rosicrucian Compendium*, c. 1760

The image originally appeared in Giovanni Battista Nazari's Della tramutatione metallica sogni tre *(1599), where the creature is introduced as a dangerous dragon. Its winged boots indicate that it is Mercury, the messenger of the gods, or here the alchemical metal. The three figures above represent the moon, sun and Mercury (silver, gold and quicksilver).*

PROFILE
OUROBOROS

One of the oldest symbols in alchemy is the ouroboros, the image of a dragon or serpent devouring its own tail. The symbol first appears in an alchemical context in the *Chrysopoeia* ('Gold-making') of Cleopatra the Alchemist, representing the oneness of all things. Arguably its most famous representation is in a Byzantine collection of Greek alchemical works copied by Theodoros Pelecanos in the 15th century. For some alchemists, it came to be understood as a symbol of the circular nature of the process of distillation and redistillation. It was to become a popular symbol, often appearing with wings, to symbolize its volatility (as quicksilver or mercury), as well as a variant in which a winged and wingless serpent or dragon devour each other's tail. In the image opposite, from the 15th-century *Aurora Consurgens* ('Rising Dawn'), an alchemist mixes the ingredients of the philosophers' stone on the left, while, on the right, a glass vessel sitting in flames contains a large, blue, winged mercurial ouroboric dragon with four feet, on whose tail perches a blue eagle, symbolizing volatile spirit, and a small black bird, symbolizing the calcination or burning taking place.

TUTANKHAMUN OUROBOROS
The symbol first appeared in the 13th century BCE on a shrine in the tomb of the Egyptian pharaoh Tutankhamun, where it alludes to cyclical time, which flows back into itself, such as the rising and setting of the sun or the annual flooding of the river Nile.

ALCHEMICAL OUROBOROS
The *Chrysopoeia* of Cleopatra depicts an ouroboros that is half dark with spines and half pale and scaled, said to represent body and soul. Within its circle is the Greek *Hen to pan* ('The One [is] the All'), indicating the unity of all things. This is a 10th- or 11th-century reproduction.

BYZANTINE OUROBOROS
Possibly the best-known version of the ouroboros is this 1478 drawing by Theodoros Pelecanos. It displays a dragon with four feet, a red back and a pale green belly, interpreted as a symbol of the primal matter, containing the four elements, the union of which became the philosophers' stone.

FOUNDATIONS —2— *Alchemy*

DRAGON AND SERPENT
This 17th-century manuscript, the *Clavis Artis* ('Key of the Art'), shows a winged, four-footed dragon above (representing volatile spirit) swallowing the tail of a wingless serpent below (symbolizing fixed body), which in turn swallows the dragon's tail. Each digests, purifies and perfects the other.

SQUARE OF ELEMENTS
This illustration, from a manuscript that translates as 'A Week of Weeks, Containing the Secret Mysteries of the Kabbalists, Magicians, Brachmans, and all the Ancient Wise' (*c.* 1600), shows a winged green ouroboros intertwined with the square of the four elements.

DRAGONS AND HEXAGRAM
Between a dragon and what is described as a wingless dragon is a hexagram of a red fiery triangle and a blue watery triangle, their combination symbolizing 'Heaven' or the 'Quintessence'. At the centre are the symbols for sulphur, mercury and salt, the three Paracelsian components of matter.

65 FOUNDATIONS — 2 — *Alchemy*

Sulphur and cinnabar crystals
The image on the left shows fiery sulphur, which was believed to be one of the two ingredients of the philosophers' stone in medieval alchemy – the second ingredient being watery mercury. Cinnabar, on the right, is a compound of fiery sulphur and watery mercury.

simply Arabic for the definite article. Alchemy is an investigation into the properties of matter, the attempt to bring matter to a state of perfection, whether that meant gold as the perfect metal, the elixir or tincture as the perfect medicine, or the philosophers' stone as the ideal universal agent of transformation, capable of altering the nature of substances, especially metals and stones. With this in mind, historians of Western alchemy speak of *chymiatria* or *spagyria*, both forms of alchemical medicine; of theoalchemy and mythoalchemy, expressed by (and sometimes claiming to find new insights into) mythology or religion; of emblematic alchemy, revealed through visual images; and, in modernity, of spiritual, psychological or philosophical alchemy. One way or another, each of these approaches engages with ideas of metamorphosis, transmutation, transformation, even transfiguration.

Alchemical traditions also exist in China and India, with somewhat different goals. Chinese alchemy sought to produce the *jindan* or 'golden elixir', related to cinnabar, the red crystalline mineral form of mercuric sulphide, from which mercury was extracted. It differs from Western alchemy in having both an internal (*neidan*) form, in which the alchemist engages in mental exercises to create an immortal spiritual body, and an external (*waidan*) form, in which the alchemist works on natural substances in a crucible. Both forms of Chinese alchemy involve the creation of elixirs and the quest for immortality. Indian alchemy, *Rasaśāstra* ('science of mercury'), dating from the 5th century CE,

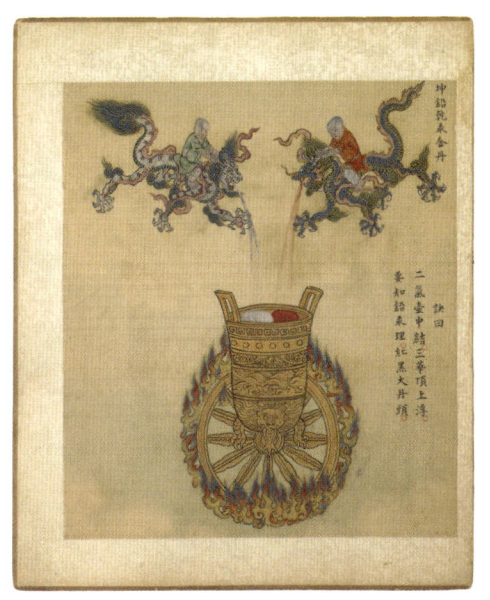

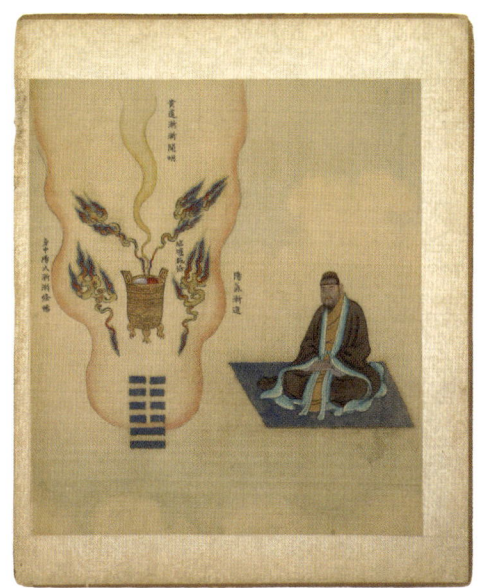

Chinese silk paintings of Taoist alchemy, 17th century

These are from an early Qing dynasty (1644-1911) guide to produce a golden elixir for immortality. The image on the left shows a white female tiger and a blue/green male dragon, which represent, respectively, yin, earth and lead, and yang, heaven and mercury. In the right-hand image a Taoist alchemist contemplates the mixture of ingredients. The combination of six broken and unbroken lines, bottom left, indicates Hexagram 19 ('Approach') from the ancient divination text I Ching, or Book of Changes – a positive indicator of great change.

is connected with Ayurveda ('science of life') and is the general term for combining purified metals and minerals with herbs for treating illnesses; more specifically *Rasāyana* ('the way of mercury') is concerned with long life, rejuvenation and invigorating the body, as well as heightening cognitive power, increasing virility and even gaining magical powers. Like Chinese Taoist alchemy, it also involves the preparation of forms of cinnabar or mercury and the use of other metals, together with herbs, salts and a range of other substances.

Western alchemy is by no means monolithic; there are many variants. Over the centuries, some practitioners have combined alchemy and astrology. Others have tried to interpret highly ambiguous alchemical works using different approaches – for example, texts found in Jewish Kabbalah and Christian Cabala. Some have communicated in words, others using a combination of word and image, and occasionally just images.

Zosimos of Panopolis, who lived in Upper Egypt around 300 CE, is the first alchemist about whose existence we can be relatively confident. He wrote about laboratory apparatus and furnaces, and about metallic transmutation, but he is best known today for

PROFILE
TWO PRINCIPLES, OR THREE

In medieval alchemy, the two ingredients of the philosophers' stone were considered to be fiery sulphur and watery mercury, their union symbolized by the conjunction of the sun and the moon and, in later manuscripts, by the image of the hermaphroditic Rebis. In alchemical theory, masculine sulphur fixes changeable female mercury, so that it does not evaporate in the fire. This combination of substances was a suitable symbol for the red philosophers' stone because they chemically combine to form the red mineral cinnabar. In the 16th century, the Swiss alchemist Paracelsus introduced a third ingredient: earthy salt. These *tria prima* or 'three principles' respectively represented, for him, the soul, spirit and body of metals and minerals, indeed of all things. According to Paracelsus, when wood burns, what burns is sulphur; the volatile smoke is mercury, and the remaining ash is salt. This triad was not to be understood as the literal chemical substances, but as modalities of matter: flammability, fusibility and incombustible fixity.

LION AND LIONESS
The 16th emblem in Michael Maier's *Atalanta fugiens* ('Atalanta Fleeing', 1617/18) depicts sulphur and mercury as a wingless lion and a winged lioness. The earth-bound male can be seen preventing the lioness from taking flight. This represents the power of 'fiery' sulphur to fix volatile 'watery' mercury, preventing it from evaporating, so that it survives the fire to become the greatly desired philosophers' stone.

ADAM, EVE AND THE SERPENT
Adam, Eve and the Serpent in the 15th-century *Das Buch der heiligen Dreifaltigkeit* ('Book of the Holy Trinity'), which connects alchemy with the three protagonists in the book of Genesis. Here a female serpent pierces Adam's chest with a spear. Adam represents the body of the philosophers' stone, while the serpent is the mercurial spirit whose subtle venom penetrates the body. Eve represents the soul of the stone.

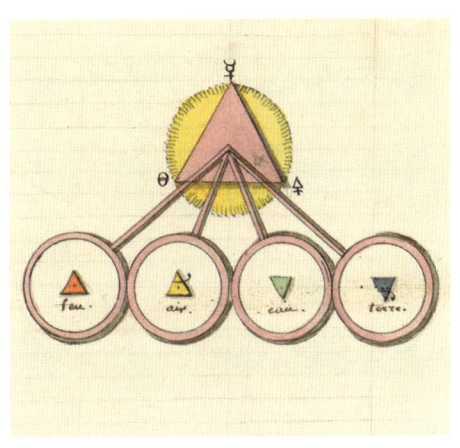

TRIANGLE OF THE PRINCIPLES
In this illustration from *L'alchimie du maçon* ('The Mason's Alchemy', c. 1812), François-Nicolas Noël presents a radiant circle, representing primal matter, within which stands the triangle of the three principles, their 'hieroglyphs' standing at each vertex, with mercury, often considered the most important, at the apex. From this triangle emanate the four elements, fire, air, water and earth.

LION DEVOURING THE EAGLE
In *De Tinctura Physicorum* ('On the Tincture of the Natural Philosophers'), Paracelsus describes the creation of the alchemical tincture or elixir as the coagulation of the rose-coloured blood of the lion and the white gluten of the eagle. This symbolism reappears in the *Liber Azoth* (1613), attributed to the fictitious cleric and alchemist Basil Valentine, where we see the sulphurous lion devouring (i.e. fixing) the eagle.

THREE FACES
In a manuscript of the *Rosarium Philosophorum* ('Rose-Garden of the Philosophers', 1550), we find a stone basin in a lush green landscape. Above, there floats a cloud containing three faces, out of whose mouths liquid pours down like rain, collected in the basin, which then drips from a spout into a small glass vessel. The three faces are identified in Latin as the spirit (*spiritus*), soul (*anima*) and body (*corpus*) of matter.

SECRET OF THE PHILOSOPHERS' STONE
The 21st emblem of *Atalanta fugiens* depicts the secret of the philosophers' stone: 'Make a circle from the male and female, then a square, from this a triangle, make [another] circle, and you will have the philosophers' stone.' The inner circle is primal matter, the man and woman are sulphur and mercury, the square represents the elements, the triangle the body, spirit and soul of matter, and the large circle the stone.

George Anrach,
Praetiosissimum Donum Dei,
c. 1473

Nine stages from the magnum opus *(Great Work) are represented, each involving an alchemical process inside a glass vessel. The illustrations show male and female figures 'conjoining' to conceive the philosophers' stone and the content of the vessels undergoing colour changes to produce a white elixir (queen) and red elixir (king).*

the *way* he wrote, presenting his alchemical knowledge through dream sequences using a mixture of religious, mystical and metallurgical language. In several visions he describes a flight of fifteen steps leading to a bowl-shaped altar; a priest who sacrifices and is also chopped to pieces with a sword; a white-haired old man called Agathodaimon (Good Spirit), a leaden man, who is transformed into a pillar of fire, undergoing torment; a man of bronze who becomes a man of silver, and finally a man of gold, in a spring within a temple guarded by a dragon. Zosimos introduced the highly allegorical style that would become a hallmark of alchemical communication.

Much of what we know of Greek alchemy, and its transmission from Alexandria to Byzantium, is found in later manuscript compilations or anthologies, such as the 11th-century codex *Marcianus graecus* 299 at the Marciana Library in Venice. As well as the writings of Zosimos, this manuscript includes works by the 6th-century pagan alchemist Olympiodorus and the 7th-century Stephanus of Alexandria, who combines mystical Christianity and Pythagorean ideas, presenting alchemy as an intellectual and spiritual endeavour, with transmutation of base metal into gold as a symbol of the perfection of the human spirit.

By the late 8th and early 9th centuries, Greek alchemical material was available in Arabic translation, with the Arabs and Persians also producing their own works. The 8th century saw, for example, influential works attributed to the Persian alchemist Abū Mūsā Jābir ibn Ḥayyān (*c.* 721–815), who became famous for his sulphur–mercury theory of metals, based on the Aristotelian notion of two exhalations from the earth – one dry and smoky (fiery sulphur), the other wet and steamy (watery mercury). He argued that gold is the perfect combination of the finest, most densely packed sulphur and mercury, while the other metals have different ratios of these two substances, with impurities and imbalances. In order to arrive at gold, the alchemist basically had to follow in the footsteps of nature, combining sulphur and mercury in the correct way, but speed up the process in the laboratory.

DECODING AN ALCHEMICAL LABORATORY

This scene from the title page of Lazarus Ercker's *Beschreibung allerfürnemisten mineralischen Ertzt, vnnd Berckwercks Arten* ('Description of the Most Distinguished Mineral Ore and Mining Arts', 1574) displays some of the apparatus in a laboratory working with minerals and metals. The alchemist is busy checking the contents of the glass vessels in the small ovens heated by the athanor, while his assistants are maintaining the fires in several furnaces and a junior assistant appears to be washing a glass vessel.

1.
ATHANOR
An 'oven of digestion' filled with charcoal or coal providing a continuous fire.

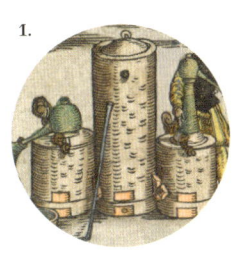

2.
CUCURBIT AND ALEMBIC
A two-piece glass vessel containing the alchemical ingredients.

3.
CRUCIBLE
A three-footed crucible encircled by fire to provide indirect heat, for melting silver and other metals.

4.
WIND-OVEN
A shaft kiln, with natural draft (without bellows), providing a milder fire.

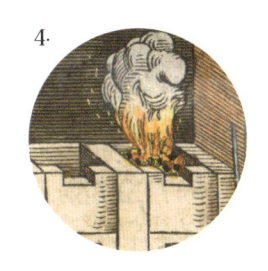

5.
ALEMBIC AND RECEIVER
Distilled liquid pours through the spout of the glass helm into the big glass receiver.

6.
RETORT
A cucurbit and alembic combined into one, also known as a Horn of Hermes, seated on a fiery tripod.

7.
CEMENTATION FURNACE
An oven used for calcining or reducing metals into a subtle powder with corrosive salts.

8.
ASSAY FURNACE
An oven in which the nobler metals (silver and gold) are tested and refined.

Hermes, *Alchymia Naturalis Occultissima Vera*, 18th century
The illustration on the left shows personifications of the three Paracelsian principles of matter in a hot-tub (i.e. the alchemical vessel): White Queen as salt, Red King as sulphur, with Multicoloured Mercury in the centre. The illustration on the right depicts the 'dissolution' of the sun and moon - their death symbolized by the black bird and in the background, mythologically, by the Fall of Icarus.

Mercury and sulphur were also considered to be the base ingredients of the elixir or philosophers' stone. Jābir discussed the preparation of elixirs not only from minerals but also from organic matter, from plant and animal substances, by breaking down the raw material into the four elements (earth, water, air, fire). He also introduced the idea that the elixir could be a panacea both for curing human diseases and for healing 'sick' metals by bringing their qualities into the perfect equilibrium of gold. He even believed that the alchemists' knowledge of nature gave them the potential to create artificial life, such as the homunculus or 'miniature human'.

Two styles of writing can be found in Islamicate alchemical works of this period – one accessible, the other coded. In his *Book of Secrets*, the Persian alchemist and physician Rhazes (865–925) communicates in clear, straightforward language. Muḥammad Ibn Umail (*c.* 900–960), on the other hand, in his *Book of the Silvery Water and the Starry Earth*, uses 'cover names' to conceal important information. An 'eagle' is used to represent evaporated volatile substances, for example, and a 'raven' to

Painting of a statue of a wise man in a temple, 14th century
This illustration is taken from a manuscript (1339) of the Book of the Silvery Water and the Starry Earth *by the 10th-century Egyptian alchemist Muḥammad ibn Umail. It is generally considered to represent Hermes Trismegistus holding his alchemical* Emerald Tablet.

symbolize putrefaction of matter and the colour black. Variations and combinations of these two styles of communication led to a diverse range of alchemical genres, from recipes and instructional dialogues to allegories, enigmas and didactic poems.

From the same period we have the earliest known version of the *Emerald Tablet*, a short text attributed to the legendary figure Hermes Trismegistus. The *Emerald Tablet* is one of alchemy's foundational texts and was cited by many authorities over the ages, including Isaac Newton. It is famous for the statement 'That which is Above is like that which is Below, and that which is Below is like that which is Above', and the idea that the goal of the alchemical 'operation of the Sun' – i.e. (depending on the alchemist's interpretation of the text) the creation of gold, the elixir or the stone – has the Sun as its father and the Moon as its mother; the Wind carried it in its belly, and its nurse is the Earth.

As with astrology, alchemy reached Europe relatively late, in the 12th century, through the translation of Arabic works into Latin. The West's initiation into

PROFILE
THE REBIS

The Rebis ('Two-Thing') symbolizes the conjunction of opposites: the ingredients of the philosophers' stone, male sulphur and female mercury, often represented as the sun and the moon. In the Rebis above, from the *Buch der heiligen Dreifaltigkeit* ('Book of the Holy Trinity'), the male wing is golden (sun) and the female is blue (moon); he holds a coiled snake (fixed sulphur), she holds three snakes in a chalice (volatile mercury); he stands on sulphur, she on mercury; on his side is the plant *Solaria*, on hers *Lunaria*. Underneath is an amphisbaena, a dragon with a head at both ends, signifying quicksilver or mercury. The eggshell on its back alludes to the alchemical egg, which contains all things needed for the creation of the elixir or philosophers' stone.

THREE-LEGGED REBIS
In the *Aurora Consurgens* ('Rising Dawn'), a blue eagle, symbolizing mercury, unites the sun and moon. At their feet are small blue eagles produced from their union. She holds a bat, a night creature; he holds a hare, symbol of the sun/day. The Latin *lepus* ('hare') is perhaps also a pun for the philosophers' *lapis* ('stone').

RED- AND WHITE-WINGED REBIS
In the *Splendor Solis* ('Splendour of the Sun'), the colours of the Rebis's wings allude to the red solar and white lunar stones. He holds the earthly macrocosm with rings of the four elements; she holds the microcosm of the philosophical egg, from which the Bird of Hermes is born.

BURNING REBIS
Michael Maier's Rebis is titled 'The Hermaphrodite, lying like a dead man in darkness, wants fire'. The fire turns the Rebis white like the lunar stone, then red like the solar stone: the female is made male, while the text alludes to men like the prophet Tiresias, who changed from male to female and back again.

PHILOSOPHICAL EGG REBIS
This Rebis from *Liber Azoth* (1613) sits in the outline of a philosophical egg. He holds a compass, she a square – the tools of divine creation. Below, a fire-breathing dragon (alluding to sulphur and mercury) crouches on a sphere, created by the compass, with a triangle (body, spirit, soul) and square (four elements).

ALBERTUS MAGNUS WITH REBIS
The Dominican bishop Albertus Magnus (1200–80) pointing at the Rebis in Michael Maier's 1617 *Symbola aureae mensae* ('Symbols of the Golden Table'). The Rebis holds the letter Y, symbolizing one root (primal matter) from which spring male and female (sulphur and mercury).

FIRST PRINTED REBIS
This Rebis, featured in the 1550 *Rosarium Philosophorum* ('Rose-Garden of the Philosophers'), is clearly influenced by the 'Book of the Holy Trinity', but now the male holds the chalice with the snakes, while the female holds the coiled snake. The Rebis stands on a moon and there is only one alchemical plant.

FOUNDATIONS — 2 — *Alchemy*

Illustrations from a manuscript of the *Aurora Consurgens*, 15th century

The top image depicts the volatile spirit of mercury, which is dangerous and poisonous, especially when volatile. A winged demon holding a sword and arrow stands beside a vessel containing a winged blue eagle and wingless white eagle, which represent volatile and fixed substances respectively. The black woman in the bottom image, a volatile (winged) spirit of the moon, is showing the philosophers' stone in her womb.

the alchemical mysteries is thought to have begun in 1144 with the *Book of the Composition of Alchemy*, a translation of instructions on how to make the philosophers' stone, given by the Christian monk Morienus to the Umayyad prince Khālid ibn Yazīd (*c.* 668–704/9). The work is presented in, at times, highly allegorical language, which leaves open the possibility that there are various levels of interpretation at play, for example the assertion that the matter needed to create the philosophers' stone 'comes from you, who are yourself its source'. The translator introduces it as a book that is 'divine and most full of divinity', as 'perfect proof of the Old and New Testaments', with the text talking of the 'transfiguration of metals'. There are two great secrets of alchemy: the first, the identity of true primal matter; the second, how to prepare it to make the stone.

Given the highly visual nature of alchemical metaphors, it was only a matter of time before a new genre of alchemical imagery emerged. Particularly beautiful examples from the Late Middle Ages include the *Aurora Consurgens* ('Rising Dawn') and *Buch der heiligen Dreifaltigkeit* ('Book of the Holy Trinity'), both early 15th century. In addition to the standard correlation between the 'higher astronomy' of the planets above and the 'lower astronomy' of the metals below – the sun and moon representing gold/sulphur and silver/mercury, respectively – we start to see new imagery, the two substances being substituted by more elaborate pairings: a king and a queen, a red man and a white woman, a cockerel and a hen, or a lion and a griffin. Gradually a whole menagerie of creatures was introduced, including various birds to symbolize the different colour changes taking place in alchemical processes: burning, washing, evaporation and condensation. The age of print saw the publication of works with sequences of images, one of the most famous being the *Rosarium Philosophorum* ('Rose-Garden of the Philosophers', 1550), which features twenty woodcuts – from a mercurial fountain, standing for alchemical primal matter, to the image of Christ stepping out of the tomb, as a symbol of the perfection of the philosophers' stone.

◁ **Glass alchemical apparatus, Middle East, 10th to 12th centuries**
The cucurbit (bottom) and alembic (top) are iridescent after being buried in the earth.

▷ **Ivory mortar and pestle, possibly 16th or 17th century**
The mortar is carved with cherubs busy in a laboratory, and a snake is curled around the pestle. These were used to grind vegetable and mineral ingredients - for example, for the distillation of medicines.

While the main focus of alchemy in the Middle Ages was on the transmutation of base metals into the precious 'noble' metals silver and gold, there were exceptions. The popular *Book on the Consideration of the Quintessence of All Things* (1351–52), by the French Franciscan Jean de Roquetaillade, known as John of Rupescissa (c. 1310–62), promoted the distillation of quintessences of many substances, including the preparation of alcohol distilled from wine, to produce the paradoxical 'fiery water' of the alchemists, extremely useful for preserving substances, as well as for extracting active ingredients from plants. He even argued that alchemy was useful against the Antichrist. The Italian Pietro Antonio Boni of Ferrara (fl. c. 1323–30), known as Petrus Bonus, added a new dimension in his *Pretiosa margarita novella* (*New Pearl of Great Price*, c. 1330), with the claim that alchemy was natural, supernatural and divine, and that a knowledge of the philosophers' stone enabled pagan philosophers to predict the virgin birth of Christ, leading him to declare that alchemy 'either finds a man Holy, or makes him Holy'. Alchemy was useful not only for the conversion of metals, but also of unbelievers.

The 16th century saw a major change in the direction of alchemy in the West: a move, by some, from the goals of transmutational alchemy to the search for chemical medicines. This was promoted in particular

Oil painting after Maarten de Vos, date unknown
This allegorical painting depicts a young woman, perhaps Prudentia, warning an alchemist of the dangers of the art of fire. It is based on a print by the 16th-century Flemish painter Maarten de Vos - originally one work in a set of four representing the elements - and the alchemical equipment we see in the foreground is typical of the period.

by the Swiss physician and iatrochemist Paracelsus (the pseudonym of Philippus Aureolus Theophrastus Bombastus von Hohenheim, 1493–1541), who argued that the true goal of alchemy was the preparation of Hermetic medicines, not from simple plant mixtures, as was the case with traditional academic medicine, but instead from more potent substances like metals and minerals, as highly refined essences or 'arcana' (secret remedies), through processes of analysis and resynthesis. As such he is often seen as a forefather of homeopathy. Paracelsus also argued that metals (indeed all matter) were not simply composed of mercury and sulphur, but contained a third element (or 'principle', the word used by Paracelsus to describe these three ingredients): incombustible, non-volatile salt – a grouping more suited to his Trinitarian Christian worldview. His approach became popular among physicians dissatisfied with the existing classical

82   FOUNDATIONS — 2 — *Alchemy*

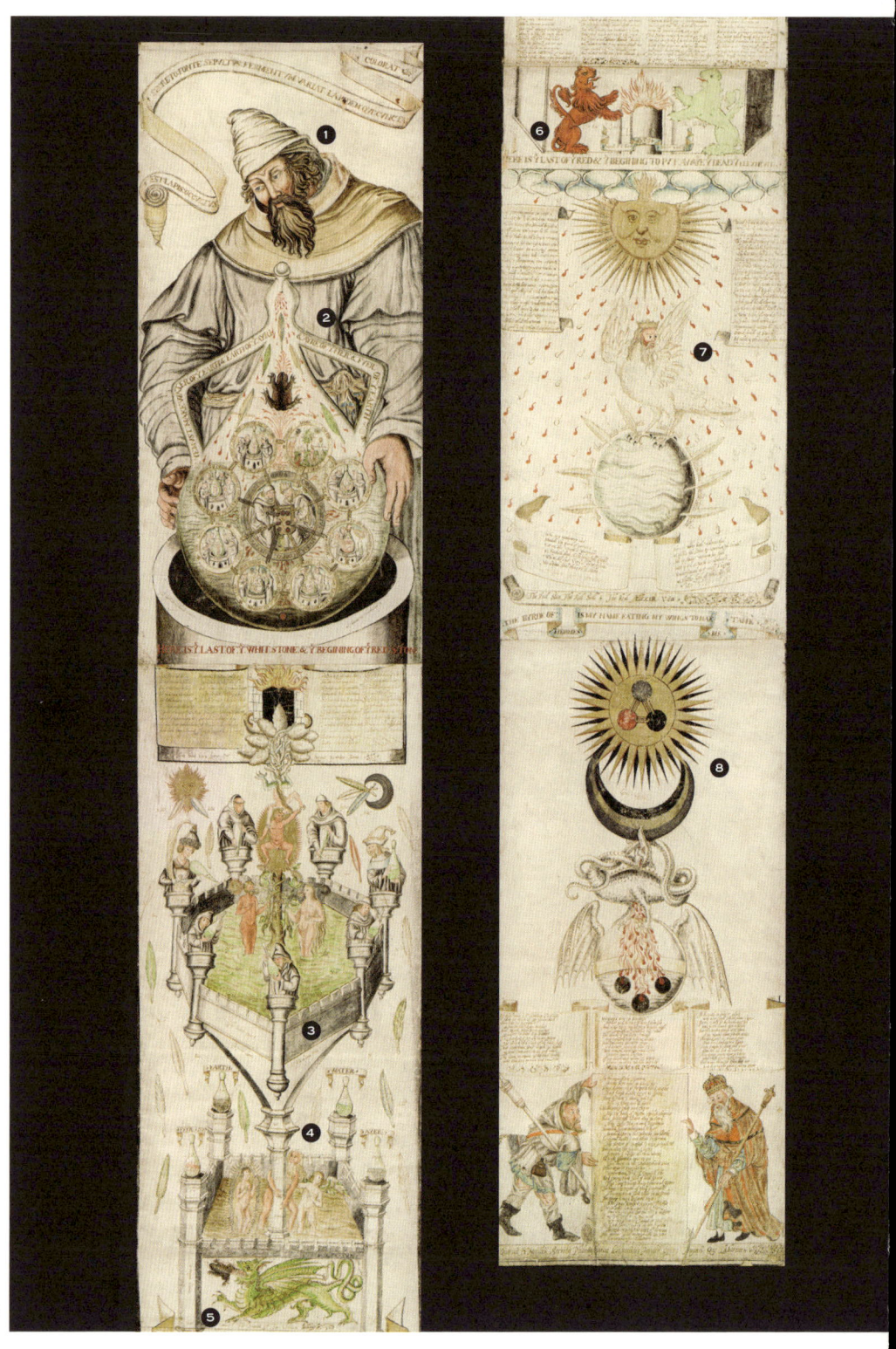

DECODING THE RIPLEY SCROLL

The *Ripley Scroll* exists in various versions, the earliest dating from the 15th century and attributed to the English Augustinian Canon George Ripley (*c.* 1415–90). This particularly beautiful example dates from the second half of the 16th century and is over 3 metres (10 feet) long. At the foot of the scroll stand a scribe and a bishop.

ALCHEMIST
The Alchemist with the words: 'The Stone is hidden, buried in a secret fountain. The Ferment changes the Stone which colours all things.' He holds a large glass pelican.

PELICAN
The glass pelican displays the processes for the creation of the white stone. It contains a toad, a book with seven seals, and eight circles with monks looking at human figures in glass vessels.

FOUNTAIN
Seven philosophers pour liquid into a fountain, which contains the ingredients for the red stone: a red man and white woman (labelled 'Body'), a reptilian Mélusine ('Spirit') and a child ('Soul').

MAN, BOY AND GIRL
An old man ('Earth'), a winged boy ('Spirit') and a girl in a blaze of light ('Soul') stand at the base of the fountain, surrounded by the four elements in sealed glass vessels.

DRAGON AND TOAD
A green dragon is depicted with a toad coming from its mouth – two reptiles often symbolizing poisonous alchemical primal matter, i.e. quicksilver.

LIONS
At the bottom of the furnace stand two lions, the famous alchemical red and green lions, which are sometimes identified as the 'fiery' substances sulphur and vitriol.

BIRD OF HERMES
'The Bird of Hermes is my name eating my wings to make me tame.' By consuming its feathers it is no longer volatile, but becomes fixed, stable in the alchemical fire.

SUN WITH SPHERES
Three spheres in a sun – a white (lunar) stone, red (solar) stone and black elixir of life – form one philosophers' stone. The sun and crescent moon are held up by a wyvern.

83   FOUNDATIONS — 2 — *Alchemy*

David Teniers the Younger, *Alchemist in his Workshop*, c. 1650

Alchemy was a popular subject in 17th-century art, and Teniers often painted alchemists studying or experimenting in their laboratories. The crocodile suspended from the ceiling was a symbol of alchemy's ancient Egyptian origins and particularly significant for alchemists, who make use of images of alchemical serpents, dragons and other reptiles, which lay (alchemical) eggs.

medicine of Galen and Hippocrates that was taught at the universities. Paracelsian 'spagyric' medicine (a refining process of separation and recombination of materials, in order to remove impurities and toxicity) was promoted by the Rosicrucians, in their early 17th-century manifestos, as part of their philanthropic aim of treating the sick for free.

Although the 17th century began to see a bifurcation of alchemy and chemistry, the publication of important collections of texts, such as the six-volume *Theatrum Chemicum* ('Chemical Theatre', published between 1602 and 1661), sustained interest in succeeding centuries among theosophers and Freemasons in particular. During the Age of Enlightenment, which dominated European society in the 18th century and celebrated science and reason over religion and tradition, alchemy's reputation declined. The development of more refined laboratory equipment and procedures led to some of its theories being tested and rejected, which gave rise to a popular view that transmutational alchemists were fraudsters. Nevertheless, enthusiasm continued, especially in

The Bird of Hermes, from Elias Ashmole's *Theatrum Chemicum Britannicum* (1652)
This engraving, which appears in a compendium of English poems about alchemy compiled by Ashmole from his collection of medieval manuscripts, depicts a two-headed dragon representing both the sun and the moon, with a mercurial spirit as a bird uniting them. The words list the qualities necessary for an alchemist, such as prudence and patience.

Germany, in organizations such as the Order of the Golden and Rosy Cross, whose members were expected to practise alchemy, in ways that later influenced the Hermetic Order of the Golden Dawn in England.

There had already been some intimations of spiritual alchemy in the 17th century, in circles influenced by the theosophy of Jacob Boehme, but this was to flower in the 19th century with the renewed fascination with occult practices in Victorian Britain. One notable example is *A Suggestive Inquiry into the Hermetic Mystery* (1850) by the English writer Mary Anne Atwood (1817–1910), in which alchemy is presented as a work of self-knowledge, self-purification and self-transformation, with man being the true laboratory of the Hermetic art. A few years later, the American General Ethan Allen Hitchcock (1798–1870), military adviser to President Lincoln, published *Remarks upon Alchemy and the Alchemists* (1857), which likewise argued that man was the subject of alchemy, and his perfection the real goal. Such seeds were to find fertile ground in the circles of theosophists and spiritualists, as well as later in the works of the Austrian psychoanalyst Herbert Silberer (1882–1923) – an early participant in Freud's Viennese circle – and the depth psychologist Carl Jung.

1. CHAOS
Unformed matter made of the four elements, from Genesis 1:2: 'the earth was without form, and void'.

2. FOUNTAIN OF THE PHILOSOPHERS
The Sun and the elemental symbols, fire △, air △, water ▽ and earth ▽.

3. GREEN LION
The occult virtue of nature or Paracelsian Archaeus, producing and healing all things.

4. FEMININE, MOTHER AND MATTER
The Moon, pregnant with solar and lunar children.

5. HEAVENLY WATER
A flask of heavenly water, also labelled eagle's gluten or mercury of the philosophers.

6. MEDICINAL POTABLE GOLD
Symbols for sulphur ♄ and gold ☉. Described as an incombustible oil.

7. CLOSED DOOR OF THE PHILOSOPHERS
An alchemical furnace, with symbols for the four elements: △, △, ▽ and ▽.

8. SILENCE OF THE WISE
Also called green gold of gold. Trees with symbols for gold ☉, silver ☽ and water, i.e. mercury.

9. PRACTICE
Labelled 'Few are chosen'. Alongside 'Theory' ('many are called'), it forms Jesus's words in Matthew 22:14.

10. SILVER OF THE PHILOSOPHERS
An imperial eagle with antimony ♁, sulphur ♄, salt ⊖ and mercury ☿.

11. DEAD HEAD SKULL
A skull labelled 'Fiat lux' ('Let there be light'), representing unwanted residue from an experiment.

12. ULTIMATE MATTER
Skeleton as matter, with the words 'I live and you will live', the ultimate end-product of alchemy.

DECODING VIRGIN SOPHIA

This is the Virgin Sophia, the personification of God's wisdom, mediator between the human and the divine, mother of the new man reborn from God's wisdom. The illustration is from an 18th-century Masonic manuscript of the *Geheime Figuren der Rosenkreuzer* ('Secret Symbols of the Rosicrucians'), which has been called the 'last Hermetic manifesto in the Age of Enlightenment' by Carlos Gilly. The twenty-five spheres in the lower part represent different aspects of alchemical creation.

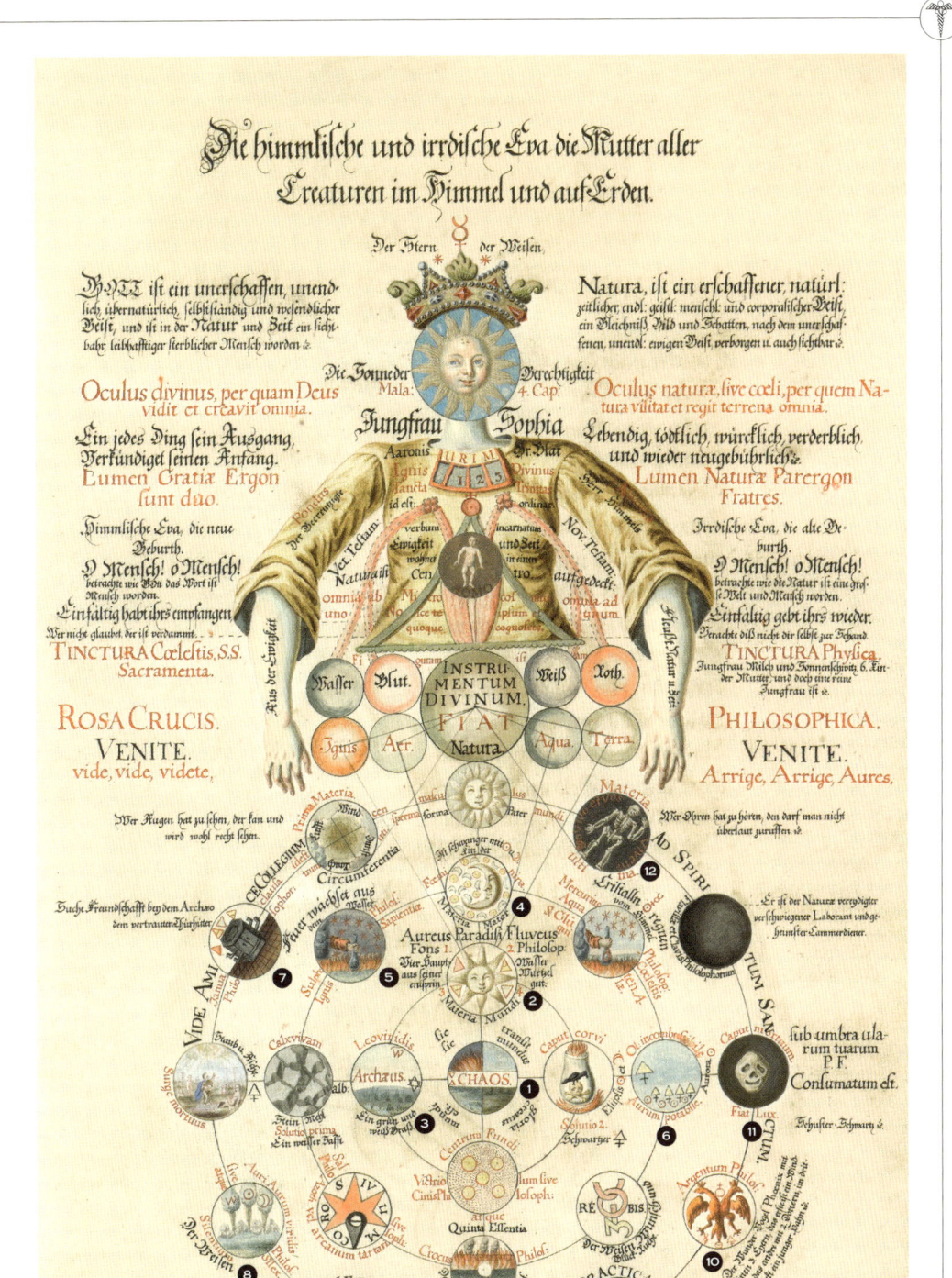

Die himmlische und irrdische Eva die Mutter aller Creaturen im Himmel und auf Erden.

This is not to say that practical laboratory alchemy was abandoned. In France, alchemy was a beneficiary of the occult revival, a famous, fin-de-siècle exponent being Albert Poisson (1868–93), who carried out experiments in the laboratories of the Faculty of Medicine in Paris, as well as writing several books on the subject, including *Théories et symboles des alchimistes* (published in English as *Theories and Symbols of Alchemy*, 1891), *L'Initiation alchimique* ('Alchemical Initiation', 1900) and a text about the 14th-century alchemist Nicolas Flamel. In England, the Hermetic Order of the Golden Dawn placed emphasis on the knowledge and practice of alchemy, one of its main promoters, the British writer Arthur Edward Waite (1857–1942), engaging with (or vacillating between) practical and spiritual notions of the art in his voluminous work. In London, in 1912, Waite was one of the founding members of the Alchemical Society for the study of alchemy from philosophical, historical and scientific perspectives.

Although many others could be mentioned, let us conclude with the enigmatic French alchemist Fulcanelli (fl. 1920s), author of *Le Mystère des cathédrales* (*The Mystery of the Cathedrals*, 1926), who claimed that the Gothic cathedrals of the Middle Ages, Notre-Dame de Paris in particular, were preservers of alchemical knowledge, the secrets of the Great Work – the quest for the philosophers' stone – having been carved into their stones in plain sight. Many curious stories surround him, such as the account of him asking the chemical engineer and member of the French resistance Jacques Bergier (1912–78) to warn French atomic physicist André Helbronner (1878–1944) about the dangers of nuclear weapons. Fulcanelli's identity remains a mystery and he vanishes from the historical record; the practice of alchemy, however, persists, sometimes in the laboratories of historians of science attempting to decode recipes and reproduce experiments from old books and manuscripts; sometimes in the homes of occult practitioners seeking personal insight into the properties of matter or themselves.

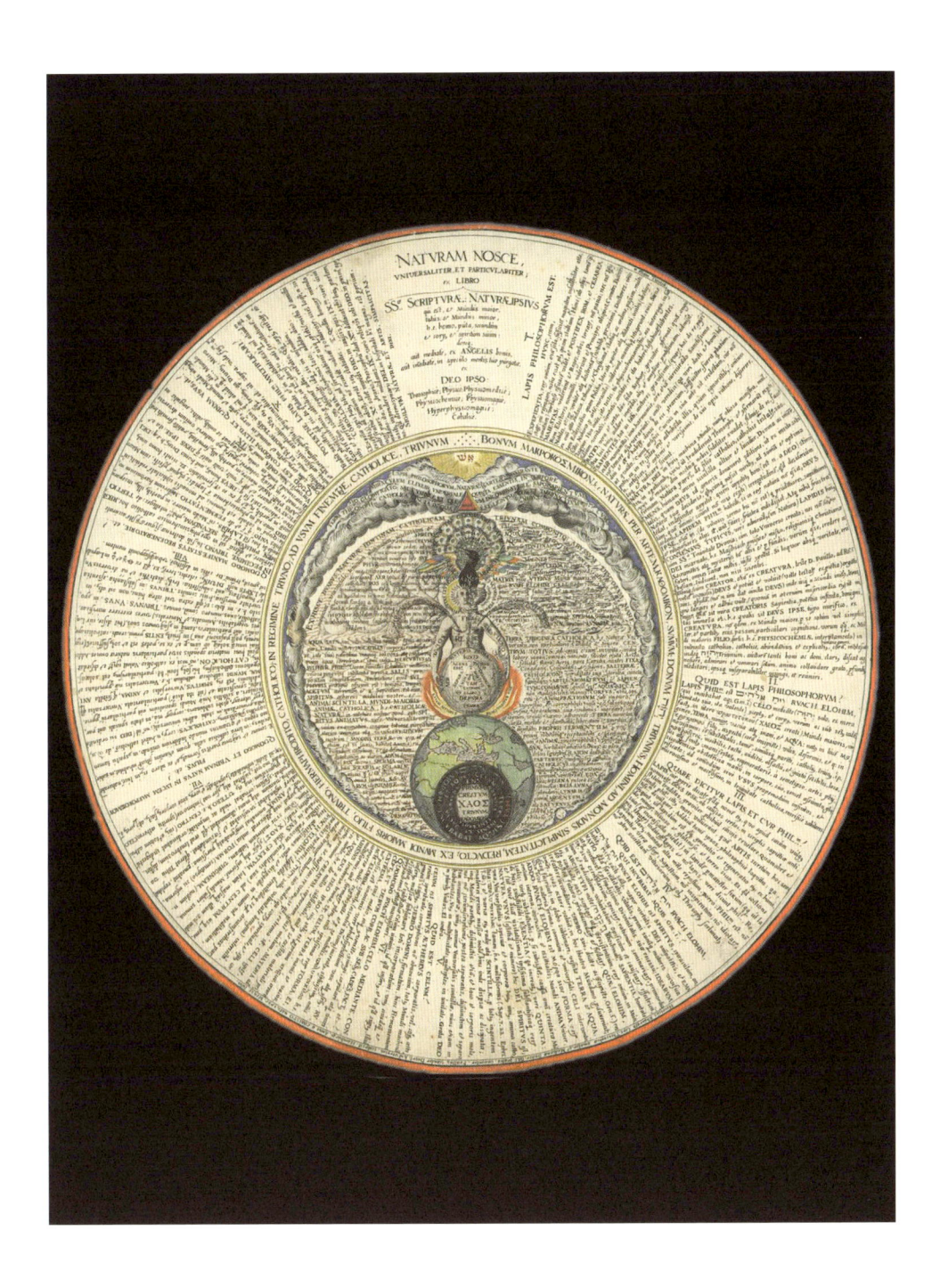

Paulus van der Doort of Antwerp (engraver), *The Alchemical Rebis or Hermaphrodite*, from Heinrich Khunrath's *Amphitheatre of Eternal Wisdom* (1595)

The Alchemical Rebis represents the conjunction or compounding of the ingredients required for the philosophers' stone. It is hermaphrodite because it is the union of male sulphur and female mercury, represented as a king and queen. The bird on the Rebis's head is a composite of various alchemical birds representing the colour changes that take place in the Great Work.

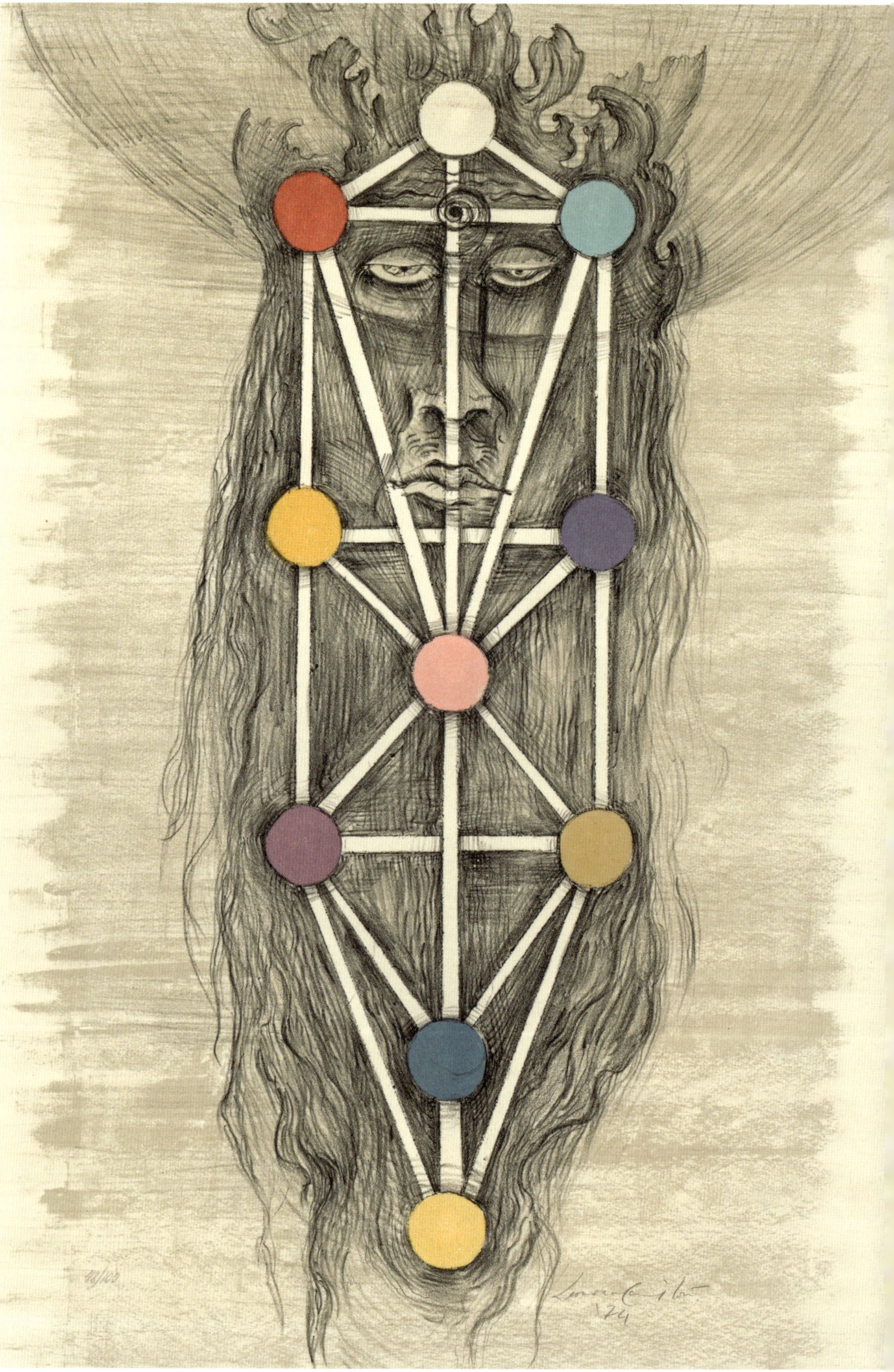

'With 32 mystical paths of Wisdom
engraved Yah the Lord of Hosts….
And He created His universe.'

3

SEFER YETZIRAH: BOOK OF FORMATION

KABBALAH

Kabbalah is a form of medieval Jewish mysticism that first appeared in Provence and northern Spain, though with claims to Moses' reception of a two-fold revelation during his encounter with Jehovah on Mount Sinai. There – in addition to the Ten Commandments – Moses is believed to have received a secret teaching that was transmitted orally over generations, developing into theosophical, prophetic and practical Kabbalah, and later Christian Cabala.

Kabbalah has its origins in the Middle Ages, for it is in 12th-century France that we find the first historical stages of this form of Jewish mysticism. The Hebrew term *kabbalah* is generally translated as 'reception', 'received lore' or 'doctrine received by oral tradition', and refers to a series of revelations stretching back to Moses, Abraham or Adam that were preserved as a secret oral tradition and passed down over the generations from master to disciple. In Christian Cabala the most common account was of a twin revelation on Mount Sinai when Moses received the Ten Commandments, revealed to everyone, and a secret teaching, passed on only to the chosen few.

Although there are earlier, late-antique works that are important to Kabbalists, such as the *Sefer Yetzirah* (*Book of Formation*), possibly dating from the 5th or 6th century CE, the first text generally considered a work of Kabbalah is the *Sefer ha-Bahir* (*Book of Illumination*), its earliest surviving manuscript dating from the late 12th or early 13th century. The *Bahir* presents itself as a series of dialogues between master and disciples, with commentaries on the first chapters of the Book of Genesis, on the hidden significance of the letters of the Hebrew alphabet, on statements from the *Sefer Yetzirah*, and so forth. It introduces for the first time the concept of the *ilan* or tree with ten branches, a system of divine emanations, the ten *sefirot*. These *sefirot* had already been described in the *Sefer Yetzirah* as ten fundamental 'numerations', but it was in the *Bahir* that they first came to be regarded as divine attributes, powers emanating into creation from the unknowable mystery of the Godhead.

At the end of the 13th century in Spain, there appeared the *Sefer ha-Zohar* (*Book of Splendour*) by Moses ben Shem Tov de León (1240–1305), who claimed to be drawing from pre-existing manuscript material reaching back to the 2nd-century rabbi Shimon bar Yochai. The *Zohar* is a huge collection of texts that present the reader with commentary on the Torah (the first five books of the Hebrew Bible), detailing the nature of God and the structure of the cosmos, the primordial man, the emanation

< *page 90*
Leonora Carrington,
Janan, 1974
This is one of a series of prints illustrating a play based on Jewish folklore, The Dybbuk, or Between Two Worlds, *written c. 1914 by S. Ansky. Leah is possessed by the spirit of a dead lover, Janan, who had knowledge of practical Kabbalah from the Book of Raziel. In the end he is exorcised from Leah's body, but rather than marry another, she joins him in death. Here we see Janan behind the kabbalistic Tree of Life.*

Jean Thenaud, *Man and the Macrocosm*, from *Introduction to the Kabbalah* (1536)

Man stands in the midst of three rings: the lowest, the four elements of earth, water, air and fire; the middle, the planetary spheres; the highest, heaven, with the Hebrew words for Father, Son and Holy Spirit. In one hand he holds the Star of David, which symbolizes the union of fire and water, and in the other a winged ouroboros.

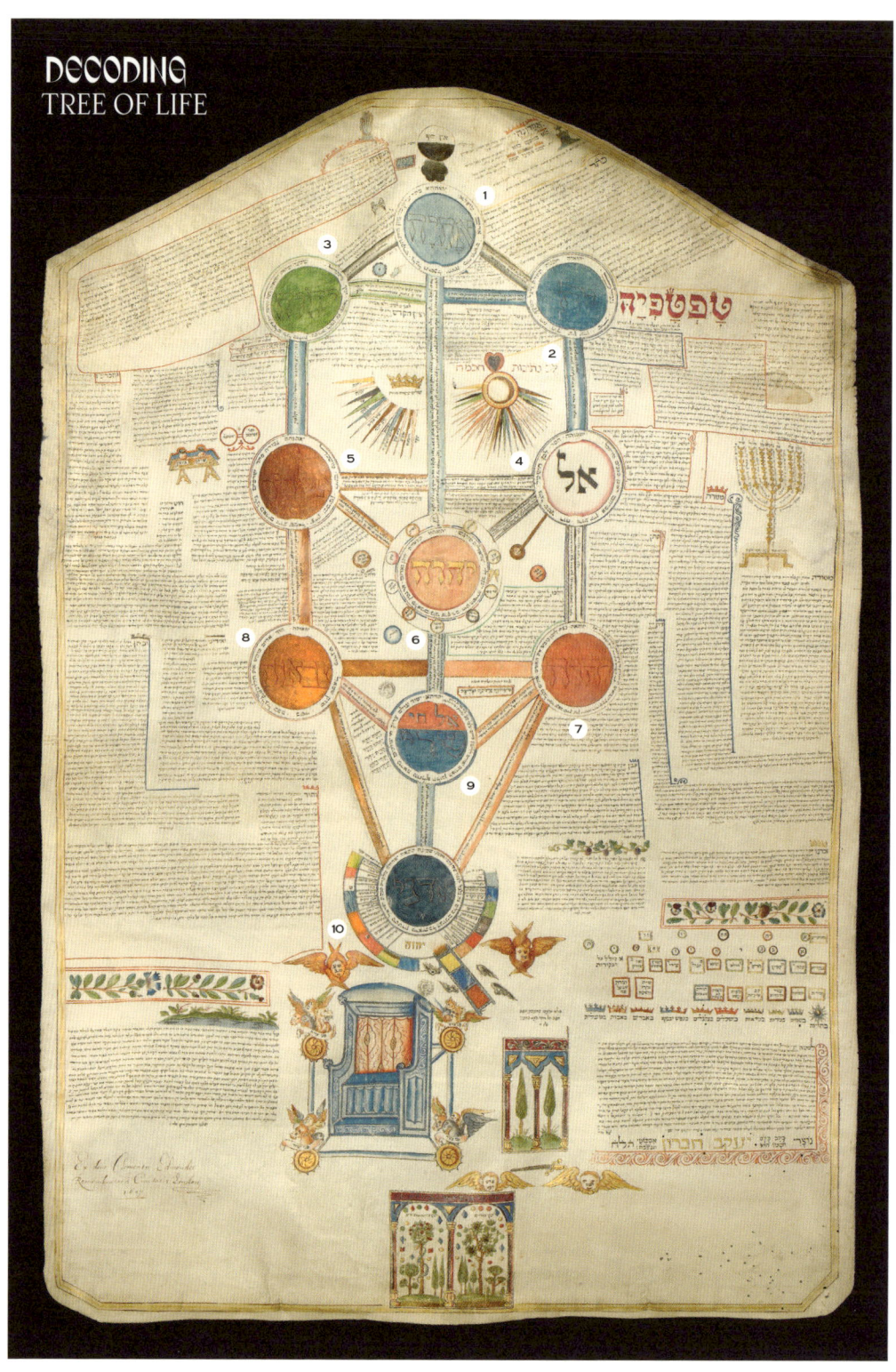

DECODING
TREE OF LIFE

94 FOUNDATIONS — 3 — *Kabbalah*

1.
KETHER (Crown)
Divine name: Ehieh

2.
CHOCHMAH (Wisdom)
Divine name: Yah

3.
BINAH (Understanding)
Divine name: YHVH

4.
CHESED (Mercy)
Divine name: El

5.
GEBURAH (Strength)
Divine name: Elohim

6.
TIFERETH (Beauty)
Divine name: YHVH

7.
NEZAH (Victory)
Divine name: YHVH

8.
HOD (Splendour)
Divine name: Tsabaoth

9.
YESOD (Foundation)
Divine name: El Chai
and Shaddai

10.
MALCHUTH (Kingdom)
Divine name: Adonai

This Tree of Life was made by James Bonaventure Hepburn (1573–1620) in 1606–7. It displays the ten *sefirot* symbolizing the emanation of divine powers into the world. Each *sefira* is linked to a divine name. The highest, Kether (Crown) is the most subtle, closest to the Godhead, and the lowest, Malchuth or Kingdom, represents the Shekinah or female aspect of the Godhead, closest to humanity. The Tree is divided into pillars: the right-hand male Pillar of Mercy, headed by Chochmah (Wisdom), the left-hand female Pillar of Severity, headed by Binah (Understanding), and the Middle Pillar of Balance or Harmony.

Henry More, *Ezekiel's Vision of the Chariot*, two pages from *Visionis Ezechielis sive Mercavae Expositio* (1679)
In the illustration on the left, the prophet Ezekiel kneels on the ground and sees the vision of the Merkavah *(Chariot) and the angels with the likeness of four living creatures. Each creature has four faces – human, lion, ox and eagle – and four wings, depicted in more detail in the illustration on the right.*

of the four worlds, the nature of souls, the notion of redemption, the counterparts to the *sefirot* (the forces of evil known as *klifot*), and how the individual practitioner relates to God and the rest of creation. In Kabbalah, the primordial man (Adam Kadmon), has been variously explained as the first *sefira*, the entire *sefirotic* system, or the personification of the first world created by infinite God when he withdrew, in a process called *Tzimtzum* (contraction), in order to make space within himself for creation. Adam Kadmon is imagined as a figure of light with a human form, through which four spiritual worlds are created, from the most subtle, *Atzilut* (world of emanation), down through *Beri'ah* (world of creation) and *Yetzirah* (world of formation) to the physical world in which we exist, *Asiyah* (world of action). Two major points of focus involve *Ma'aseh Bereshit* ('Work of Creation'), based on the interpretation of Genesis chapters 1 and 2, and *Ma'aseh Merkavah* ('Work of the Chariot'), visions and speculations involving the throne or 'chariot' of God as described in the first chapter of Ezekiel.

In the wake of the expulsion of the Jews from Spain in 1492 and then from Portugal in 1497, these kabbalistic works and ideas spread throughout Europe, so much so that the *Zohar* became the authoritative text for most Jewish Kabbalists. Three major models

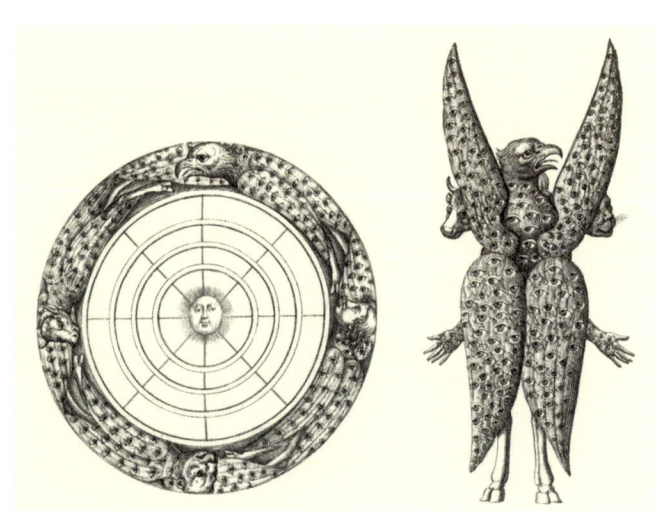

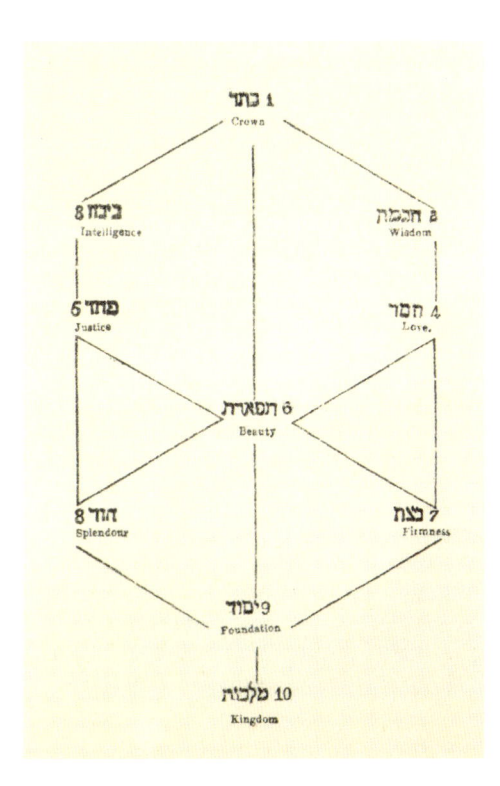

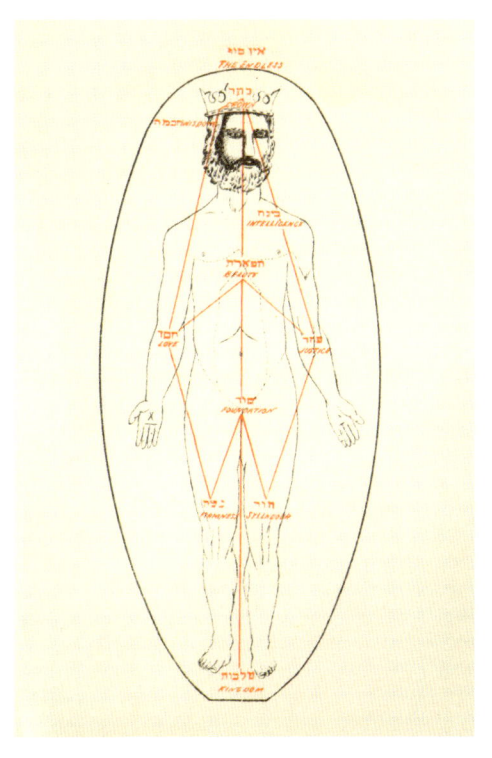

Christian David Ginsburg, *Adam Kadmon*, two pages from *The Kabbalah: Its Doctrines, Development and Literature* (1865)

The sefirot of the Tree of Life, in the diagram on the left, are represented on the right in human form as primordial man (Adam Kadmon).

of Kabbalah flourished: the ecstatic or prophetic Kabbalah of the school of Abraham Abulafia (1240–91), with its emphasis on the permutations of the *shemot* (divine names) for possible union with the divine; the theosophical-theurgical Kabbalah, promoted by Menahem Recanati (1250–1310), with its focus on the *sefirot* on the Tree of Life; and the astromagical Kabbalah favoured by Yohanan Alemanno (c. 1435–c. 1504). Each of these represents different combinations and considerations of the balance between speculative and practical Kabbalah, between scriptural interpretation and religious action.

The person generally considered to be the father of Christian Cabala – the first Christian by birth to introduce Kabbalah into Christian circles – was the syncretic Italian philosopher Count Giovanni Pico della Mirandola. In 1486 Pico published 900 theses, with plans for a debate in Rome before the Pope and leading theologians and scholars of his day. In this work Pico introduces many of the themes that were adopted by later Christian Cabalists, such as the vital significance of the Hebrew letters and their connection to the *sefirot*, as well as the privileged status of the Hebrew language with relation to magic. Pico proposes correspondences between Judaism and Christianity, but also highlights their relations with Platonism, mysticism and magic. The provocative nature of Pico's statements regarding Kabbalah ensured a widespread interest in this mystical Jewish tradition.

Pico's contemporary Johannes Reuchlin (1455–1522) was the first German scholar to promote the study of Jewish Kabbalah, writing two highly influential books, *De Verbo Mirifico* ('On the Wonder-Working Word', 1494) and *De Arte Cabalistica* (*On the Art of the Kabbalah*, 1517). In these works Reuchlin compares Kabbalah to the philosophy of Pythagoras (*c.* 570–495 BCE), defining it in Pythagorean terms as 'symbolic theology': both traditions, Reuchlin argues, communicate their mysteries through symbols, signs, adages and proverbs, numbers and figures, letters, syllables and words, with Reuchlin comparing the symbolic similarities between the most powerful Hebrew divine name, the four-letter Tetragrammaton – the Hebrew name for God revealed to Moses on Mount Sinai, consisting of the four consonants YHVH – and the Pythagorean triangular figure of ten points in four rows, the *Tetraktys*.

One of the main reasons why Christians such as Pico and Reuchlin were fascinated by the potential for new insights from Kabbalah was its novel techniques of textual interpretation and a radically new concept of language. The Jewish method of reading and interpreting scripture was fundamentally different from Christian methods in that it reshaped and transformed the text itself, discovering significance in the very forms and parts of individual letters, thus generating an almost infinite variety of new meanings in scriptural material. This was accomplished by three main techniques: *gematria* (a system of assigning numerical values to the letters of the Hebrew alphabet), *notarikon* (the manipulation of letters into acronyms and acrostics), and *temura* or *tseruf* (substituting letters

An illustration from the *Portae Lucis* (1516) by Joseph Gikatilla

The illustration above adorns the title page of a Latin translation of the 13th-century Sha'arei 'Orah or Gates of Light by the Spanish Kabbalist Joseph Gikatilla. It was translated by Paolo Ricci, a German Jewish convert to Christianity, and published as the Portae Lucis in 1516. It is the earliest printed version of the Tree of Life in a work aimed at Christian readers.

The Pythagorean *Tetraktys* and a three-dimensional hexagram or star, from *Cabala* (c. 1700)
This manuscript collection of drawings and paintings by an anonymous author contains thirteen illustrations of sacred geometry, with no accompanying text. It formed part of a substantial collection of rare books and manuscripts about alchemy and esotericism belonging to the 20th-century Canadian author and Freemason Manly Palmer Hall.

in words according to various permutations of the alphabet, such as the *Atbash* cipher, where the first letter of the alphabet *aleph* is replaced by the last *tav*, the second *beth* with the penultimate *shin*, and so forth; hence AtbBaSh, i.e. A[leph], T[av], B[eth], Sh[in]).

In the Hebrew alphabet, every letter possesses an inherent numerical value; therefore every letter, word or phrase has a mathematical significance by which correspondences can be found with other words. Take, for example, the thirty-two 'wondrous paths of wisdom' mentioned at the start of the *Sefer Yetzirah*. The thirty-two paths are made up of the ten *sefirot* and the twenty-two paths that connect them, corresponding to the twenty-two letters of the Hebrew alphabet. The number 32 can be written with the Hebrew letters *lamed* (which represents the number 30) and *beth* (the number 2), which combine to form the Hebrew word *leb*, meaning 'heart'. These two letters are also the first and last letters of the Torah, the five books of Moses: the *beth* of *Bereshit* ('In the beginning'), the first word of Genesis 1:1, and the *lamed* of *Israel*, the last word of Deuteronomy 34:12. Thus the five books of Moses constitute the 'heart' of the Kabbalah, together with the ten *sefirot* and the twenty-two letters of the alphabet that form all the *shemot* or divine names. These

Ceiling of Saint Nicholas in Castro, Carisbrooke Castle, Isle of Wight, UK, early 20th century
The interior of this chapel, which was rebuilt in 1904 as a memorial to Charles I, features an ornate sunburst emblazoned with the Tetragrammaton, or four-letter name of God YHVH.

Hebrew names of God (including *Ehieh, Yah, El, Elohim, Eloha, YHVH, Shaddai, Adonai*) refer to different aspects or activities of the Godhead. The first of these, *Ehieh*, for example, is the name that God revealed to Moses when he spoke from the burning bush in Exodus 3:14 '*Ehieh eser Ehieh*, I will be he who will be'.

One of the influential examples of *gematria* provided by both Pico and Reuchlin relates to the most powerful Jewish name for God, the ineffable Tetragrammaton יהוה YHVH (Yahweh). When the numerical value of this name is calculated simply, the four letters add up to the total 26. However, by cumulatively adding up the values of these letters when they are written in four rows, aligned according to the ten points of the Pythagorean *Tetraktys* – that is, by adding י *Yod* (10), on the top row 1, to יה *Yod-He* (10 + 5), on row 2, to יהו *Yod-He-Vav* (10 + 5 + 6), on row 3, to יהוה *Yod-He-Vav-He* (10 + 5 + 6 + 5) on the bottom row – we reach the symbolically significant number 72, associated, for example, with 72 psalmodic verses and related angelic powers, or the 72-letter name of God, the *Shem HaMephorash* (the 'explicit' name). Reuchlin is fascinated with kabbalistic ideas concerning the multiple names of God. The main thrust of *De Verbo Mirifico* reveals his interest in proving the supremacy of the Christian Cabalist Pentagrammaton or five-letter name of Jesus, YHSVH, the 'true Messiah', over the Jewish four-letter YHVH. In *On the Art of the Kabbalah* he mentions the creation of a golem after a Kabbalist studied and meditated on divine names in the *Sefer Yetzirah*.

The first author known to have written of a specifically 'Christian' Cabala is the French Franciscan Jean Thenaud (*c.* 1480–1542), chaplain to King François I, whose manuscript *Traicté de la Cabale* ('Treatise of the Cabala, *c.* 1521) summarizes some of the earlier Latin works. The first published work, however, to explicitly describe itself as 'Christian Cabalist' is the *Amphitheatrum Sapientiae Aeternae* ('Amphitheatre of Eternal Wisdom', 1595/1609) by the German theosopher Heinrich Khunrath, who forcefully asserts that Kabbalah, magic and alchemy must of necessity be practised together. Khunrath informs his reader that Christian Cabala's goal is the union of man with Christ, whom he calls the 'Son of the Microcosm', while the goal of alchemy is the creation of the 'Son of the Macrocosm', the philosophers' stone.

Matthew Jaffe,
Der Golem, 2020
Jaffe's work in pastel depicts one of the best-known accounts of the Golem, a creature of Jewish folklore that is usually made of clay and earth. Here the 16th-century rabbi of Prague, Judah Loew ben Bezalel, is seen inscribing the Hebrew word emet (truth) on the Golem's forehead to bring it to life. Although he creates the Golem as a protector, the rabbi ends up having to destroy the creature when it becomes harmful, inactivating it by removing the first letter of emet to leave the word met (dead).

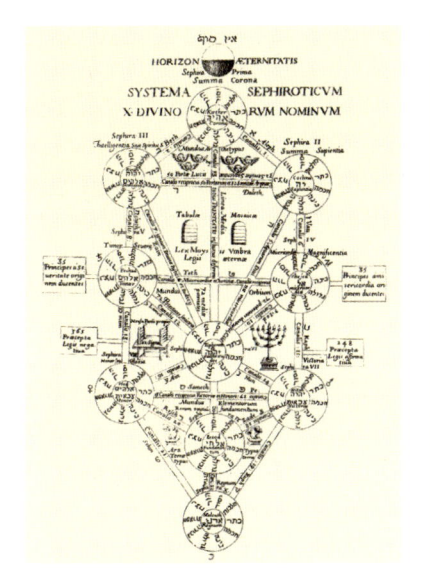

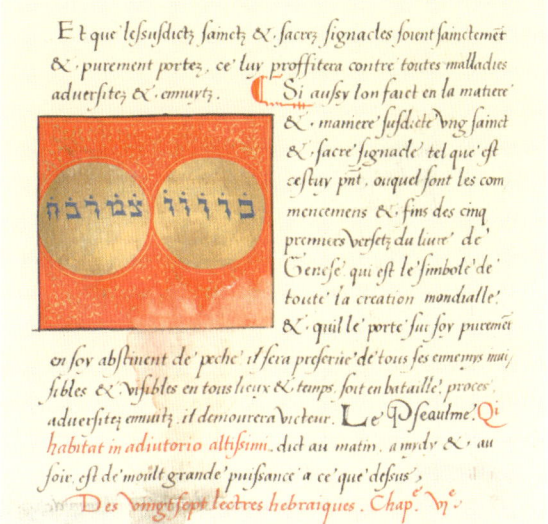

< The Tree of Life, from Athanasius Kircher's *Oedipus Aegyptiacus* (1652–54)
This extremely baroque version divides the Tree into four different worlds in descending order: Archetypal, Angelic, Sidereal and Elemental.

> Kabbalistic magical seal, from Jean Thenaud's *Introduction to the Kabbalah* (1536)
One side uses the initial letters of the first five verses from the Book of Genesis; the other uses the final letters from the same verses. The bearer is said to be free from all mischiefs of men and evil spirits.

The 17th century saw the publication of two major esoteric works that engaged with Jewish Kabbalah. The first, *Oedipus Aegyptiacus* by the ever-industrious Jesuit polymath Athanasius Kircher, covers many subjects, including Egyptian hieroglyphs, and devotes hundreds of pages to the presentation of the Kabbalah of the Jews, as well as the 'Cabala Saracenica', a Kabbalah of the Arabs and Turks. Kircher's beautifully illustrated book provides a great deal of information of value for understanding occult philosophy, much of it taken from his predecessors Pico, Reuchlin and Agrippa, and contains arguably the best-known image of the Tree of Life, a highly baroque representation of the four kabbalistic worlds, described by Kircher as Archetypal, Angelic, Celestial and Elemental.

The second of these important works was a compilation of kabbalistic texts entitled *Kabbala denudata, seu doctrina Hebraeorum transcendentalis et metaphysica atque Theologica* (*The Kabbalah Unveiled*). The first volume was published in Sulzbach in 1677–78 by the German Christian Cabalist, Hebraist and alchemist, Christian Knorr von Rosenroth (1636–89), in collaboration with the Flemish physician and alchemist Frans Mercurius van Helmont (1614–98), and dedicated, somewhat curiously, to 'the lover of

William Blake, *The Whirlwind: Ezekiel's Vision of the Cherubim and Eyed Wheels,* c. 1803–5

This is a particularly powerful depiction of Ezekiel's vision of the four living creatures that came out of the whirlwind of cloud and fire. It shows the angel as a human fourfold man, standing within circular forms with eyes, which represent the angels called ophanim (wheels). Ezekiel is seen lying on a rock at the very bottom of the illustration.

Hebrew, Chymistry and Wisdom'. This compilation was superior to anything that had previously been published on Kabbalah in a language other than Hebrew, providing a non-Jewish readership with translations of authentic texts that were to be the principal source for Western literature on Kabbalah until the end of the 19th century. The first volume featured a key to the divine names of the Kabbalah, as well as works by, or inspired by, the originator of the modern school of kabbalistic thought, Isaac Luria (1534–72), including a detailed Lurianic explanation of the Tree of Life. It also contained a summary of a Jewish alchemical treatise, the *Esch Mezareph* ('The Refiner's Fire'), suggesting correspondences between the *sefirot*, planets and metals.

A second volume begins with a systematic resumé of the doctrines of the Aramaic *Zohar*, to which is added a Christian interpretation with passages drawn from the New Testament, to show the intimate relations between Jewish and Christian traditions. There we read of kabbalistic ideas about spirits, angels and demons, as well as various states and transformations of the soul, including the theory of metempsychosis (the transmigration of the soul of a human being or animal on death into a new body of the same or a different species). Several texts promote the magical creative power of language – the presentation of the Hebrew letters as building blocks of the universe, for example, or the ability of pious men to create angels and spirits through prayer. We also find the new Lurianic doctrine of *Tzimtzum*, the idea that God as the Infinite withdraws into Himself in order to provide room into which his creative light could beam, and related doctrines of how the sefirotic vessels of the Tree of Life were first emanated in a straight line, with the lower vessels shattering, because they were unable to contain all the influx of divine energy. The better known representation of the Tree of Life with three columns or 'pillars' is a more stable structure, which is reinforced or weakened by the pious or impious actions of believers, each of whom plays a vital part in the process of *tikkun* or restoration – human actions

DECODING PRINCESS ANTONIA'S KABBALISTIC ALTARPIECE

The small Church of the Holy Trinity in Bad Teinach, Germany, is home to this large, impressively detailed *Lehrtafel* or teaching panel, created in 1663 for Princess Antonia of Württemberg (1613–79). The painting's central panel is rich in kabbalistic symbolism, with

1. **HUMAN SOUL**
Representing the human soul, a woman holds the flaming heart of charity. Her hand rests on the anchor-cross of faith and hope.

2. **TEMPLE**
The two pillars at the entrance imply that this represents Solomon's temple and its pillars Jachin and Boaz (3 Kings 7:21).

3. **HIGHEST SEFIROT**
Three crowned women represent Kether (Crown), Chochmah (Wisdom) and Binah (Understanding).

4. **MIDDLE SEFIROT**
On the right pediment sits Chesed (Mercy), on the left is Geburah (Strength), and in the centre is Tifereth (Beauty).

5. **NEZAH (VICTORY)**
The lowest triad has Nezah (Victory) holding what looks like a palm leaf on the right, at the base of the pillar Boaz.

6. **HOD (SPLENDOUR)**
Hod (Splendour), the second of the lowest *sefirot* triad, plays the harp on the left, at the base of the pillar Jachin.

7. **YESOD (FOUNDATION)**
Between Hod and Nezah, in the centre, is Yesod (Foundation) standing on a crescent moon.

8. **CHRIST RESURRECTED**
The tenth *sefira*, Malchuth (Kingdom), is represented by a statue of Christ holding his cross and trampling a serpent.

9. **CHRIST'S PEDESTAL**
The Hebrew for 'I am' alludes to 'I am the way, and the truth, and the life. No man cometh unto the Father, but by me.' (John 14:6)

10. **TWELVE FIGURES**
The figures surrounding Christ represent the twelve tribes of Israel and, possibly, the signs of the zodiac.

11. **MATTHEW AND JOHN**
On the left of the temple sit Matthew and John, with symbols linked with Ezekiel's vision: the man and the eagle.

12. **LUKE AND MARK**
On the right are Luke with the lion and Mark with the bull. Together, the four evangelists emphasize a Christian message.

13. **JEWISH ELEMENTS**
At the top is Elijah with his sword, Moses and the burning bush, and Enoch with the book of mysteries given by the angel Raziel.

14. **JEREMIAH AND DANIEL**
In the left outer portico are Jeremiah and Daniel, two major prophets of the Old Testament.

15. **EZEKIEL AND ISAIAH**
In the right outer portico are the two other major prophets of the Old Testament, Ezekiel and Isaiah.

16. **THRONE OF GOD**
Above the dome is a depiction of the vision of the twenty-four elders around the throne of God from Revelation 4:4.

17. **ANGELS AND SATAN**
In the sky we see angels singing praises to God and battling Satan, who takes the form of a dragon.

18. **'FIRE' (ESCH)**
On the pediment of the sanctuary stand two obelisks: on the left is one of 'fire' (*Esch*).

19. **'WATER' (MAYIM)**
The right obelisk is 'water' (*Mayim*). Together, *Esch* and *Mayim* constitute the Hebrew for 'heaven' (*Schamaim*).

20. **SUN ANGEL**
Next to the water obelisk stands the angel with a face 'like the sun' from Revelation 10:1.

21. **NEBUCHADNEZZAR'S VISION**
Nebuchadnezzar's dream of gold, silver, bronze and iron from Daniel 2:31–33.

Jewish and Christian elements. It is particularly interesting for its inclusion of female figures as personifications of nine of the ten *sefirot*. The story goes that Princess Antonia requested that her heart be interred in the wall behind her painting.

Anselm Kiefer, *The Breaking of the Vessels*, 1990
Lead books and broken panes of glass fill the shelves of a bookcase, which also represents the Tree of Life, above which are written the Hebrew words Ain Soph Aur *(Light without End)* in a semicircular pane of glass. The title of this work refers to a doctrine of Lurianic Kabbalah in which the first time the sefirot were created, they couldn't hold God's light and shattered, their shards falling down to be trapped in matter. It also recalls Kristallnacht (the Night of Broken Glass) in November 1938 when the windows of synagogues and Jewish-owned stores were shattered in an anti-Jewish pogrom.

by which souls, trapped among the shards of the shattered vessels, can be reunited with the divine light. The *Kabbala denudata* contains an impressive set of fold-out *ilanot* (the plural form of *ilan*) or 'maps of God', providing detailed instruction on many aspects of Kabbalah.

In the same period, Princess Antonia of Württemberg (1613–79), one of the daughters of the alchemist and occultist Frederick I, Duke of Württemberg, devoted herself to the study of Holy Scripture and the Cabala, having a particular interest in the *sefirot* and *Zohar*. In 1673 she donated a painting to the Church of the Holy Trinity at Bad Teinach in southwest Germany: a cabalistic *Lehrtafel* (teaching panel), planned by the princess but executed by the court painter, full of motifs from Jewish and Christian Cabala. The painting so impressed the German theologian and theosopher Friedrich Christoph Oetinger (1702–82) with its scholarly erudition and artistic detail that he wrote a description and analysis of it in 1763. This followed the publication of a collection of sermons about the painting in 1759, in which Oetinger drew parallels

Leonard Nimoy, *Shekhina*, 2002
One of a series, this arresting photograph features in a book by the American actor exploring the feminine aspect of the divine, the Shekhina, the glory or radiance, literally the dwelling of the divine presence on earth.

between the theosophy of Jacob Boehme and the philosophy of Isaac Newton.

As previously mentioned, kabbalistic ideas were enthusiastically adopted in the French and English occult revivals of the 19th century, forming the basis of new kabbalistic orders. An influential figure in the Hermetic Order of the Golden Dawn, Samuel Liddell MacGregor Mathers (1854–1918), published *The Kabbalah Unveiled* (1887), his translation of parts of Knorr von Rosenroth's *Kabbala denudata*, accompanied by notes and commentary. In the introduction, which also includes references to the *Bhagavadgita* (an episode recorded in the Sanskrit epic poem, the *Mahabharata*, which appeared in its present form around 400 CE) and Friedrich Max Müller's *Sacred Books of the East* (a set of fifty volumes of religious texts published between 1879 and 1910), he makes the familiar claim that Qabalah is the key to unlocking the meaning of obscure passages in the Bible, and provides detailed examples of four kinds of Qabalah discussed in the *Kabbala denudata*: 'Practical Qabalah', dealing with talismanic and ceremonial magic; 'Dogmatic Qabalah', consisting of Qabalistic literature; 'Literal Qabalah',

DECODING KHUNRATH'S SEAL OF GOD

This is the *Sigillum Dei* (Seal of God) of the theosopher Heinrich Khunrath, which first appeared in his *Amphitheatre of Eternal Wisdom* (1595; second edition 1609). It is an early example of a Christian-Cabalist diagram, showing Christ at the centre of concentric rings containing significant kabbalistic material. The person meditating on this image can either move inwards from the Ten Commandments towards Christ at the centre of the cosmos, or contemplate Christ's influence radiating outwards through the universe.

110 FOUNDATIONS —3— *Kabbalah*

CHRIST RESURRECTED
Around Christ are the words 'Truly this was the Son of God' (Matthew 27:54) and 'In hoc signo vinces' ('In this sign you shall conquer'), from the dream vision of the first Christian Emperor Constantine the Great (c. 272–337).

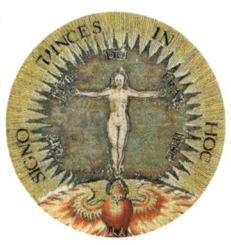

1.

SEFIROT
Inside a band of clouds, alongside the two black spheres of *Ein Soph* and *Emet* are ten blazes of light. Each blaze of light bears one of the names of the ten kabbalistic emanations of the *sefirot*.

5.

PHOENIX/FIERY DOVE
Beneath Christ is a fiery bird, either a phoenix, symbolizing Christ's resurrection, or a fiery dove, a symbol of the Holy Spirit. In Genesis 8:8–12, a dove signals the end of the flood, and when Jesus was baptized, the Holy Spirit descended as a dove.

2.

CIRCLE OF HEBREW ALPHABET
The 22 letters with which God created the universe, according to the ancient *Sefer Yetzirah*, or *Book of Formation*. Above is a Latin verse from the Jewish *Shema* prayer from Deuteronomy 6:4 and Leviticus 19:18.

6.

PENTAGRAM
A fiery pentagram of five large flames, each bearing a letter of the Christian-Cabalist Pentagrammaton or five-letter name of Jesus יהשוה (YHSVH). The ring of fire contains ten *shemot* or divine names from Jewish Kabbalah.

3.

TEN ANGELIC ORDERS
These groups of angels are, in order of their positions (from highest ranking): Tarshishim or Chayoth ha-Kadosh, Ophanim, Aralim, Chashmalim, Seraphim, Malachim, Elohim, Bene Elohim, Cherubim and Aishim.

7.

SPHERES
Above Christ is a sphere with the words אין סוף (*Ein Soph*), meaning 'Infinite' – 'without' (*Ein*) 'limit' or 'end' (*Soph*). Below is another sphere, with the word אמת (*Emet*) – 'Truth' – representing Jesus as the knowable counterpart to an unknowable, infinite God.

4.

PYTHAGOREAN TETRAKTYS
Superimposed on the Pythagorean *Tetraktys* is the most powerful Jewish divine name, the four-letter Tetragrammaton יהוה (YHVH). Encircling the seal on either side of the *Tetraktys* are the Ten Commandments.

8.

FOUNDATIONS — 3 — *Kabbalah*

concerned with the use of letters and numbers; and 'Unwritten Qabalah', which refers to knowledge of the way the symbol-systems are arranged on the Tree of Life.

Another influential Golden Dawn member was the British psychotherapist Violet Mary Firth (1890–1946), better known as Dion Fortune. A pioneer of Qabalah as a key to the Western mystery tradition, she went on to found her own esoteric order, the Fraternity (later Society) of the Inner Light, established in Glastonbury in 1924. Over the years she published a number of works that have had a significant impact on modern occultism, including *Sane Occultism* (1929), *Psychic Self-Defence* (1930) and *The Cosmic Doctrine* (the material for which was 'channelled' in the 1920s, although the book was not published until 1949). Her most famous work, *The Mystical Qabalah* (1935), was initially written as an introduction to the Tree of Life and presents Qabalah very much from the viewpoint of Western mysticism, calling it 'the Yoga of the West' and in many places displaying the influence of Madame Blavatsky's *Isis Unveiled* (1877) and *The Secret Doctrine* (1888). Fortune's method has been described as an alchemical Qabalah, going far beyond traditional Jewish mysticism and often couched in the language of Eastern philosophy. In *The Mystical Qabalah*, students are introduced to the *sefirot* in the four worlds, the interconnecting paths on the Tree of Life, with information on related magical images that can be used, text from the *Sefer Yetzirah*, associated names of God, archangels, angelic orders, yogic chakras, spiritual experiences, virtues to be cultivated, vices to be avoided, correspondences with the microcosm, related tarot card, and so on, each forming part of the symbolism of the astral paths and serving as landmarks for anyone travelling in spirit-vision – that is, in an altered state of consciousness, having a visionary experience of the astral plane.

Christian Cabala and modern Qabalah have often deviated widely from their Jewish progenitors, but the ideas espoused by Pico della Mirandola and his successors have had an undeniable influence on the story of esotericism and occultism in the West.

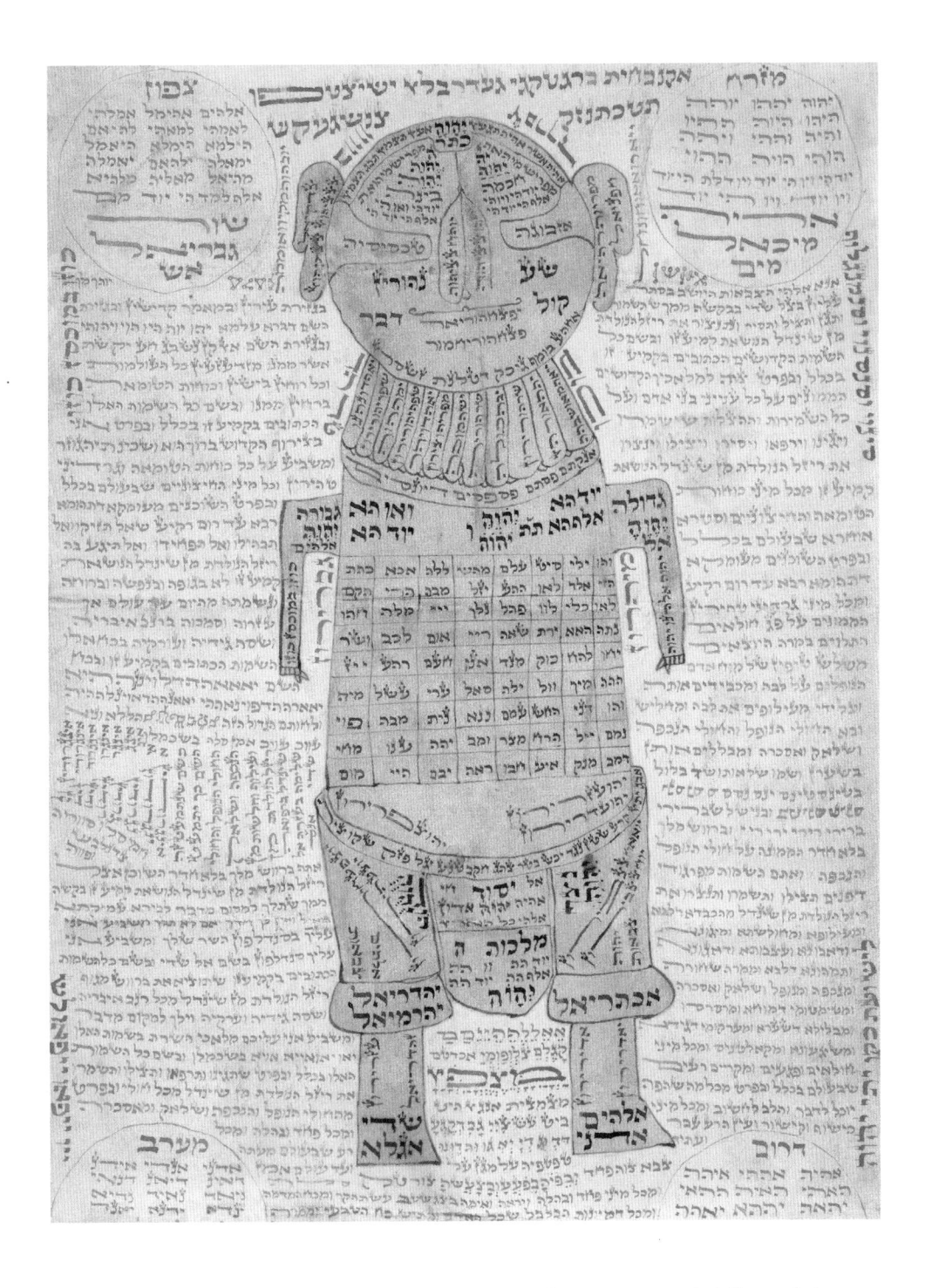

Amulet for exorcising a dybbuk (a malevolent spirit), date unknown

A Jewish exorcism to treat a case of spirit possession involved efforts to obtain the name of the spirit, threats of excommunication, fumigations of burning sulphur, blasts of a shofar (ram's horn trumpet), and an amulet to be written and hung on the victim, to prevent them from being repossessed by the exorcised spirit.

FOUNDATIONS — 3 — *Kabbalah*

Anzug des Operateurs bei der magischen Beschwörung.

CHAPTER TWO

OCCULT PHILOSOPHY

NATURAL MAGIC — 1

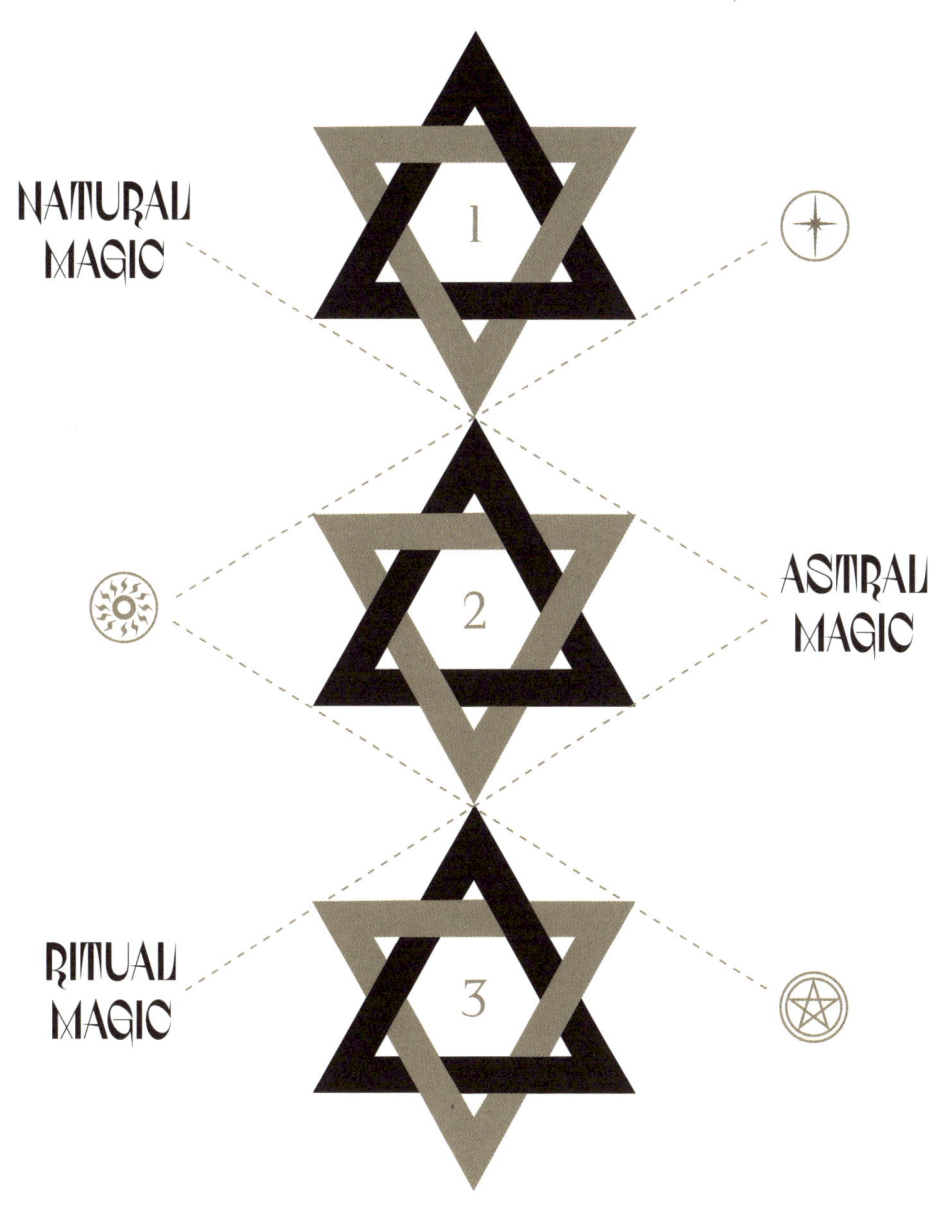

ASTRAL MAGIC — 2

RITUAL MAGIC — 3

/fɪˈlɒsəfi/ noun
The study of the fundamental nature of knowledge, reality and existence.

Xilocaracta. grece latini
uero carabia. aut car
nubium a. lignum cor
nutu uocant.

Ypericon. fuga demonum.
perforata.
herba. sci. Johis.

Doropip. qd latin.
piperastrum dicit.

> 'Magic comprises the most profound contemplation of the most secret things, their nature, power, quality, substance and virtues, as well as the knowledge of their whole nature.'
>
> HEINRICH CORNELIUS AGRIPPA, THREE BOOKS OF OCCULT PHILOSOPHY (1533)

NATURAL MAGIC

Natural magic focuses on discovering the secrets of nature, the occult properties of the animals, vegetables, minerals and stones of the sublunary world. Natural magicians considered the sympathies and antipathies in physical objects and how they could be used in a practical way for the benefit of mankind. Knowledge of nature's secrets enabled the magus to produce marvels that looked like miracles but were achieved without any supernatural aid.

As with astrology and alchemy, magical literature in the Latin West was profoundly influenced by an influx of new learning in the 12th and 13th centuries, by which it inherited a rich variety of magical practices from the classical world and benefited from significant Islamicate and Jewish developments in the field.

An interest in the occult properties of the animals, vegetables and minerals of the natural world had existed since antiquity, with Pliny the Elder (23–79 CE) compiling vast amounts of information about the wonders of nature from a wide range of authors in the thirty-seven books of his encyclopedic *Natural History*. There he wrote of the *anancitis* (compulsive stone) used in divination by means of water to conjure up divine apparitions, and the *synochitis* (holding stone) used to hold the shades of the dead when they have been summoned from below; the legendary echeneis fish, which was said to latch on to ships and hold them back, and the shocking power of the torpedo or crampfish, with its ability to numb fishermen; and the fabled phoenix, dying in fire and rising from the ashes. The *Kyranides*, attributed to Hermes Trismegistus, provided information about the medicinal and magical virtues, or properties, of animals, stones and plants. Another natural magical work in his name, the *Liber de quatuor confectionibus ad omnia genera animalium capienda* ('Book of the Four Preparations for Catching all Kinds of Animals'), included details of incense offerings and prayers to the spirits of animals in order to gain their obedience, with recipes using animal and plant ingredients. A long poem, *Lithika* ('On Gems'), believed to be by the mythical musician Orpheus, defended the practice of magic, describing the properties of twenty-eight stones.

It was the Bishop of Paris, William of Auvergne (c. 1180–1249), who first coined the term *ars magica naturalis* in c. 1230 to describe the knowledge of surprising natural wonders that are accomplished without the aid of supernatural beings, stating that this natural magic was practised in India. Natural magic enabled human beings to know and make use of the occult virtues of natural things – the properties of

< *page 114*
Magician preparing to do a summoning, from *Compendium rarissimum totius Artis Magicae* (c. 1775)
With the skull and crossbones motif on the magician's clothing, it is likely that necromancy is involved.

< *page 116*
Page from the *Tractatus de herbis* (c. 1440)
St John's Wort (Hypericum perforatum) is among the plants depicted in this beautifully illustrated treatise on medicinal herbs, which is thought to have originated in Italy. It was recommended for wound-healing and as a cure for snakebites, but also for protection against demons since it was believed to drive away evil spirits.

Hermes, Father of Philosophers, from *Ashburnham 1166*, c. 1470

Here Hermes Trismegistus is depicted in Arabic costume, wearing a turban and a royal crown. The illustration is from an alchemical miscellany known as Ashburnham 1166, after its former owner Bertram Ashburnham, a Victorian bibliophile. The manuscript, which originated in Italy, is now held by the Biblioteca Medicea Laurenziana, Florence.

stones, metals, plants and animals, the sympathies and antipathies existing in the whole of nature – without risk of manipulation by demons. This somewhat paradoxical concept of a magic that was a combination of the natural and the extraordinary gained traction, with a gradual move from purely negative connotations of paganism and idolatry in the Early Middle Ages to a new understanding of magic as a discipline, however potentially perilous, of use to humanity.

This regard for the wonders of nature flourished in the medieval lapidary and bestiary traditions. Medieval lapidaries are books about the properties and virtues of precious and semi-precious gems and minerals, as well as mythical stones. In one such book, a widely read compendium of mythological gemlore called the *Liber lapidum* ('Book of Stones') by the French bishop Marbode of Rennes (*c*. 1035–1123), the author lists the medicinal and magical qualities of many stones: a sapphire will prevent the wearer from being deceived and keep them free of physical infirmities, beryl cures pains in the liver, amethyst works well against intoxication, an emerald can be used to foretell future events, coral repels tempests, and moonstones are powerful aids to winning love. Just as the lodestone was a source of wonder for its ability to attract iron and infuse its virtue into the metal, so too jet and amber – made from fossilized wood and tree resin, respectively – were admired for sharing the occult

Three magical gems depicting the moon goddess Hecate, Mediterranean Basin, 2nd–3rd century CE
Among the decoration is a triform figure with three heads and three bodies, alluding to the waxing, full and waning phases of the moon. Made of red jasper, these gems were probably created as protection against evil spirits, but also as aids for menstruation, pregnancy and childbirth.

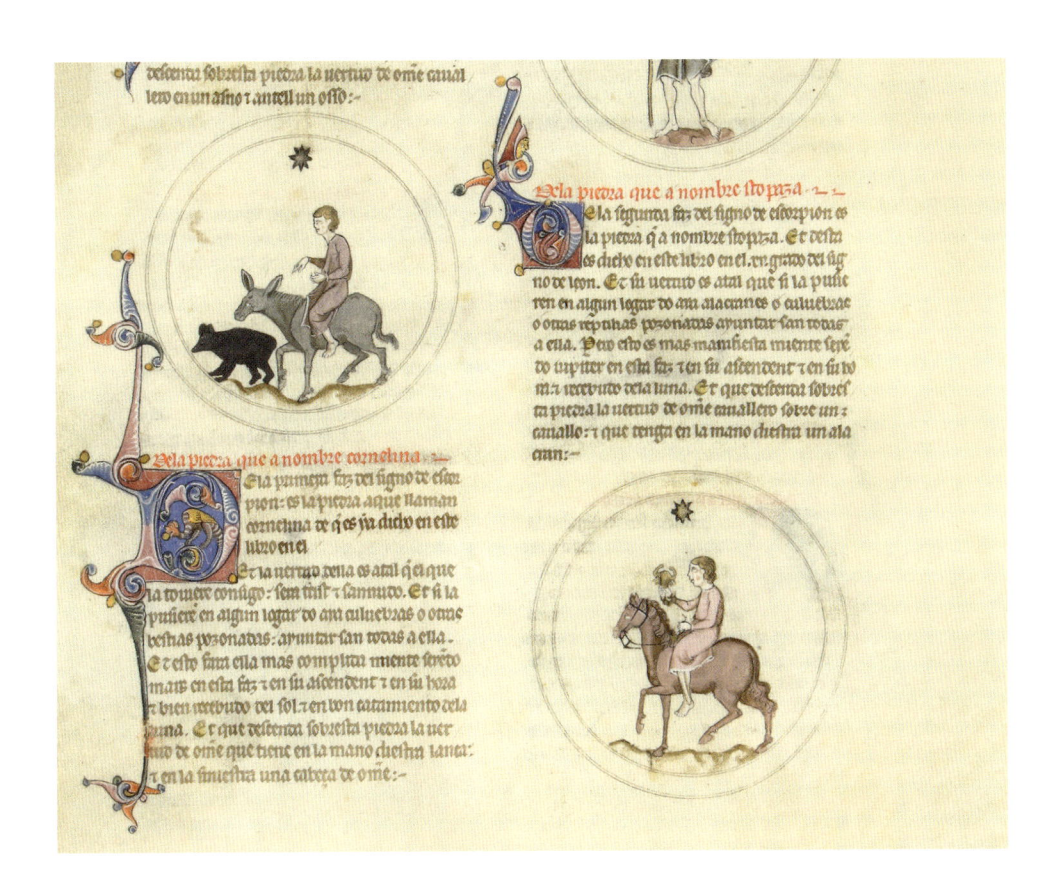

Illustrations from the *Lapidario* (*c.* 1250) of Alfonso X 'The Wise', King of Castile and León
The text describes the properties of the emery stone, which is associated with fornication and song, symbolized by a knight riding on a donkey, with a bear. The figure riding the donkey is an image for the third decan of Libra. The figure on the horse is for the first decan of Scorpio.

power of inducing an electric charge when rubbed, such that they could pick up pieces of straw or chaff; Marbode noted the same of chalcedony when warmed by the sun, comparing it to the faithful who do good works in secret.

The German Dominican friar and natural philosopher Albertus Magnus (*c.* 1200–80) acknowledged the possibility of natural magic in *De animalibus* (*On Animals*) and wrote of the occult powers of stones in *De mineralibus* (*Book of Minerals*). His contemporary Alfonso X 'the Wise', King of Castile and León, and a well-known patron of the translation of works on magic, sponsored the *Lapidario* (*c.* 1250), a collection of four lapidaries in which stones were listed not only with their physical descriptions and virtues, but also their correspondences with specific planets, with the twelve signs of the zodiac and with the thirty-six astrological decans. The diamond, for

A pelican feeding its young from the *Bestiaire d'amour rimet* (1275–1325), based on Richard de Fournival's *Bestiaire d'amour* (c. 1250)
The 'Rhyming Bestiary of Love', by an unknown author, features intricate, full-colour miniatures. In the example below, a pelican pecks its own breast to revive its chicks from death with blood. This became a symbol of Christ's self-sacrifice to redeem mankind.

example, is described in one of the lapidaries as the stone of the sun and he who wears it when the sun is in Aries and well aspected with the moon, will be feared by any who see him; one of the other lapidaries associates the diamond with the sign of Taurus, describing it as 'the stone which breaks all others', which seems suitable for the sign of the Bull; in a third lapidary, it is also with the third decan of Gemini, where we read that whoever wears a diamond will love hunting and be good at it. Medieval bestiaries provided fantastic descriptions and illustrations of a variety of real and fabled creatures, mammals, birds and fish. Some of this material originated in the *Physiologus*, a didactic Christian text written in Greek by an unknown author and dating from 2nd-century Alexandria, which itself drew information from Aristotle, Pliny and others, with the addition of allegorical Christian interpretations. The *Physiologus* tells of the pelican reviving its dead chicks with its own blood after pecking its chest, a symbol of Christ's sacrifice to redeem humanity; of another symbol of Christ, the unicorn, whose horn can detect poison and render it harmless; of the cold salamander

A salamander from a medieval bestiary, *c.* **1270**
Salamanders were believed to be able to live in fire. This one, by an unknown artist, is unusual in having wings and bearing no resemblance to our conventional understanding of a lizard.

that can live in fire, a symbol of righteous people like Shadrach, Meshach and Abednego (in the account of the biblical prophet Daniel 3:8–25) who survived being thrown into King Nebuchadnezzar's fiery furnace. Much of this worldview survived in Renaissance emblem books and hieroglyphica.

Probably the most widespread medieval treatise on natural magic was the *Experimenta*, frequently attributed to Albertus Magnus, and later known as the *Liber aggregationis seu secretorum de virtutibus herbarum, lapidum et animalium* ('Book of Collection or of Secrets about the Virtues of Plants, Stones and Animals'). A whole culture of popular books of secrets developed, containing collections of *secreta*, *experimenta* and recipes, predominantly concerned with practical recipes for producing cosmetics or dyeing textiles, preparing drugs or brewing beer. The 13th-century pseudo-Aristotelian *Secretum Secretorum* ('Secret of Secrets'), which is sometimes described as the most popular book in the Middle Ages, is filled with material from the occult sciences, from alchemy, medical astrology, and lapidaries and herbals. Herbals, needless

DECODING ROBERT FLUDD'S 'MIRROR OF NATURE'

This engraving, from Robert Fludd's *Utriusque Cosmi Historia* (1617–21), depicts a geocentric cosmos, with a series of concentric rings. At the circumference stands the empyrean heaven, followed by a ring of stars; next occur the rings of the sun, moon and planets, followed by the elements of fire and air. In the outer central section, we find the animal, vegetable and mineral realms and a landscape labelled 'Elements of water and earth', on which stands Nature personified. She is the assistant of God, who appears above her as a cloud. Nature's companion, the ape, represents Art. The four innermost rings show the liberal arts and the three modes of art, illustrating the power of human invention in relation to Nature.

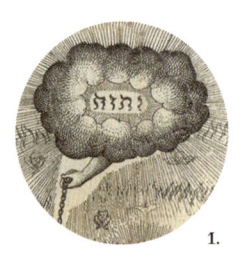

1. GOD
From a cloud labelled with the four-letter Hebrew name of God, *YHVH*, emerges a hand holding a chain, bound at the other end to the wrist of a woman.

2. NATURE PERSONIFIED
With one foot on land and one on water – symbolizing the alchemical conjunction of sulphur and mercury – Nature's body features stars and moons, and her breasts radiate heat and rain down moisture.

3. ART PERSONIFIED
A chain links Nature to 'her Ape, which we call Art', symbol of humankind's ingenuity. The ape holds a pair of compasses and a sphere, in imitation of divine creation.

4. ART SUPPLANTING NATURE IN THE ANIMAL REALM
Fludd shows Art supplanting Nature, through bee-keeping, raising silkworms, incubating eggs and preparing medicines.

5. ART ASSISTING NATURE IN THE VEGETABLE REALM
Fludd demonstrates the second mode of Art with illustrations of tree-grafting and cultivation of the earth.

6. ART CORRECTING NATURE IN THE MINERAL REALM
The third mode of Art is represented by alchemical distillation with cucurbit and retort.

OCCULT PHILOSOPHY —1— *Natural Magic*

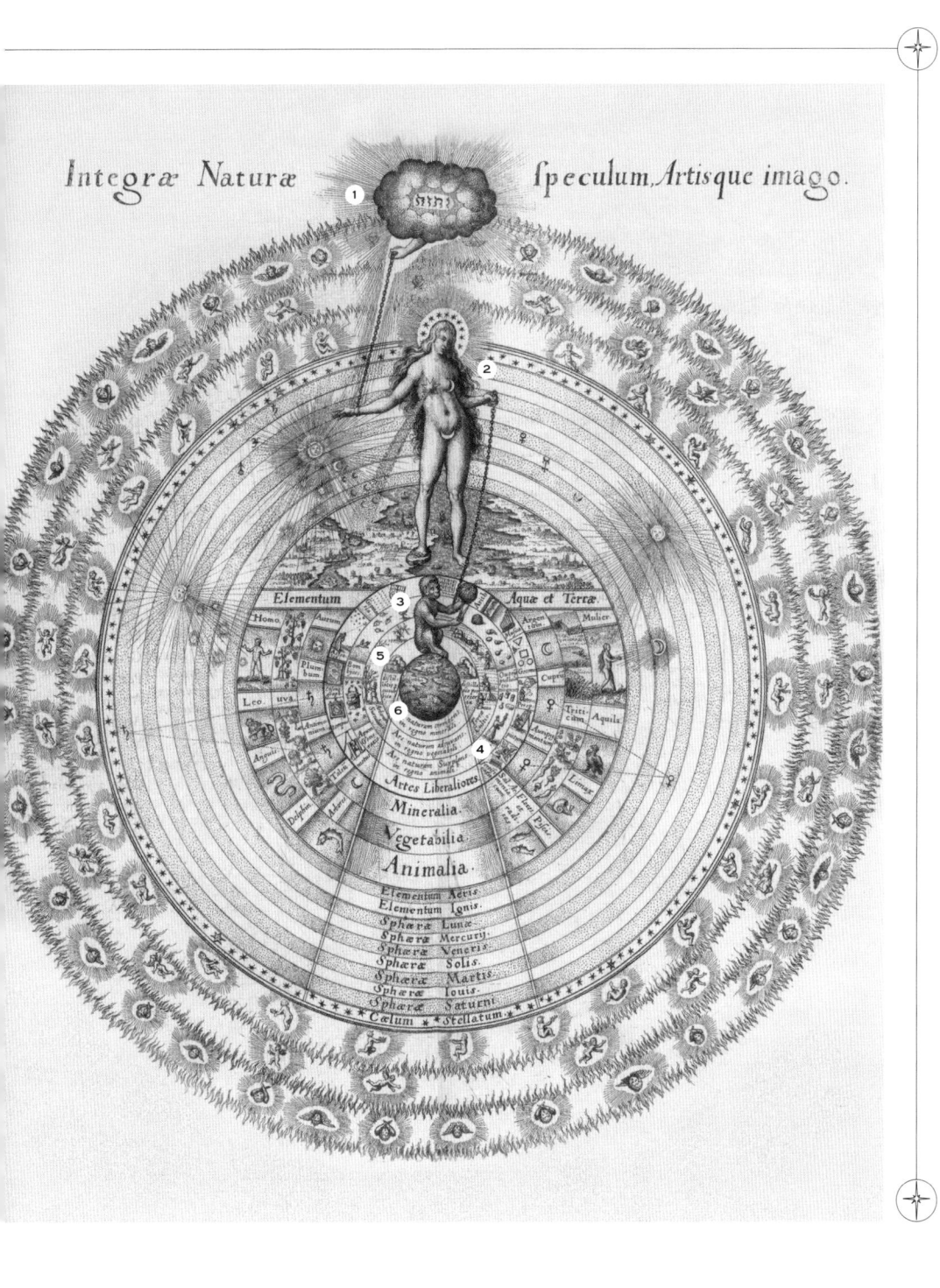

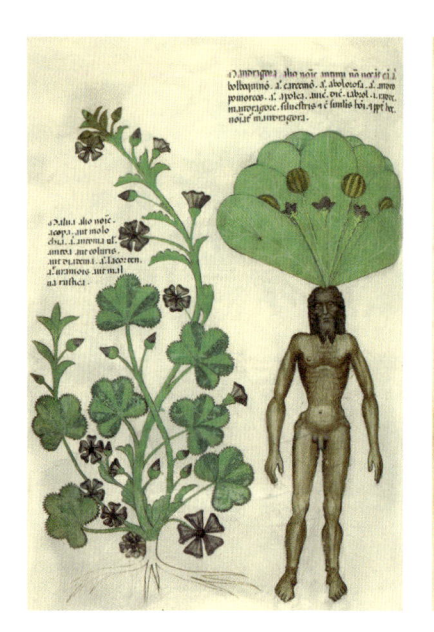

Page from the *Tractatus de herbis* (c. 1440)
The roots of the mandrake, shown on this page from a herbal, were considered particularly magical if they resembled a human figure.

A man harvesting mandrake, from a manuscript (c. 1400) of Ibn Butlān's *Tacuinum sanitatis*
A man ties the mandrake to a dog, which pulls it up, while he covers his ears to avoid being killed by the mandrake's scream. The illustration features in a Latin translation of the Tacuinum Sanitatis, an 11th-century medical treatise by the physician Ibn Butlān from Baghdad.

to say, were not without their curiosities, one of the most famous being the magical mandrake, the root of which was seen to resemble the human form. Although it has a long history of being used for medicinal purposes, its hallucinogenic and narcotic qualities led it to be associated with magic. As a generation of *Harry Potter* readers and students of folklore know, the root is said to scream so violently when dug up that it kills anyone nearby. This gave rise to a popular belief that a mandrake should be unearthed by tying a dog to the root and walking away. When the faithful dog attempted to follow its master, it would pull up the root and die, leaving its wretched master with a safe mandrake root.

During the Renaissance the Italian astrologer Marsilio Ficino would write in his *Three Books on Life* of the true magician being like a farmer, a husbandman of nature, a cultivator of the world, who 'fittingly subjects earthly things to heaven that they may be fostered'. His younger contemporary Giovanni Pico della Mirandola also compared the magician to the farmer in his *Oration on the Dignity of Man*: 'as a farmer marries elm to vine, so a magus joins earth to heaven, linking things below to properties and powers of those

Bezoar stone with case and stand, 17th century
Bezoar stones, found in the digestive tracts of animals, were believed to detect toxins in food and drink, and provide an antidote to poison. Some were even made into drinking bowls. The example below is a Goa stone, a manmade bezoar of organic and inorganic materials, gilded in mercury.

above'. Furthermore, they believed that the natural magician should follow the example of the farmer not only for earthly benefits, but also for the more lofty goals of reconstituting broken correspondences in nature caused by Adam and Eve's disobedience, as well as restoring man's relationship to nature by recovering knowledge lost after the Fall. Although there were many voices who condemned supernatural magic, the idea of a purely natural magic had some support in the biblical story of King Solomon, who had received knowledge of natural things from God in a dream.

In the 16th century, Heinrich Cornelius Agrippa included natural magic as the first of his *Three Books of Occult Philosophy*, in which he focused on the most licit form of magic, that connected with the objects and creatures of the sublunary or elementary world. Agrippa engages with such fundamental themes of natural magic as the elements, the spirit and soul of the world, planetary correspondences, and the attraction of celestial virtues, the energies of the planets and stars. He starts with the four elements and their qualities, then moves on to the compounds of the four kinds of perfect bodies, each dominated by a particular

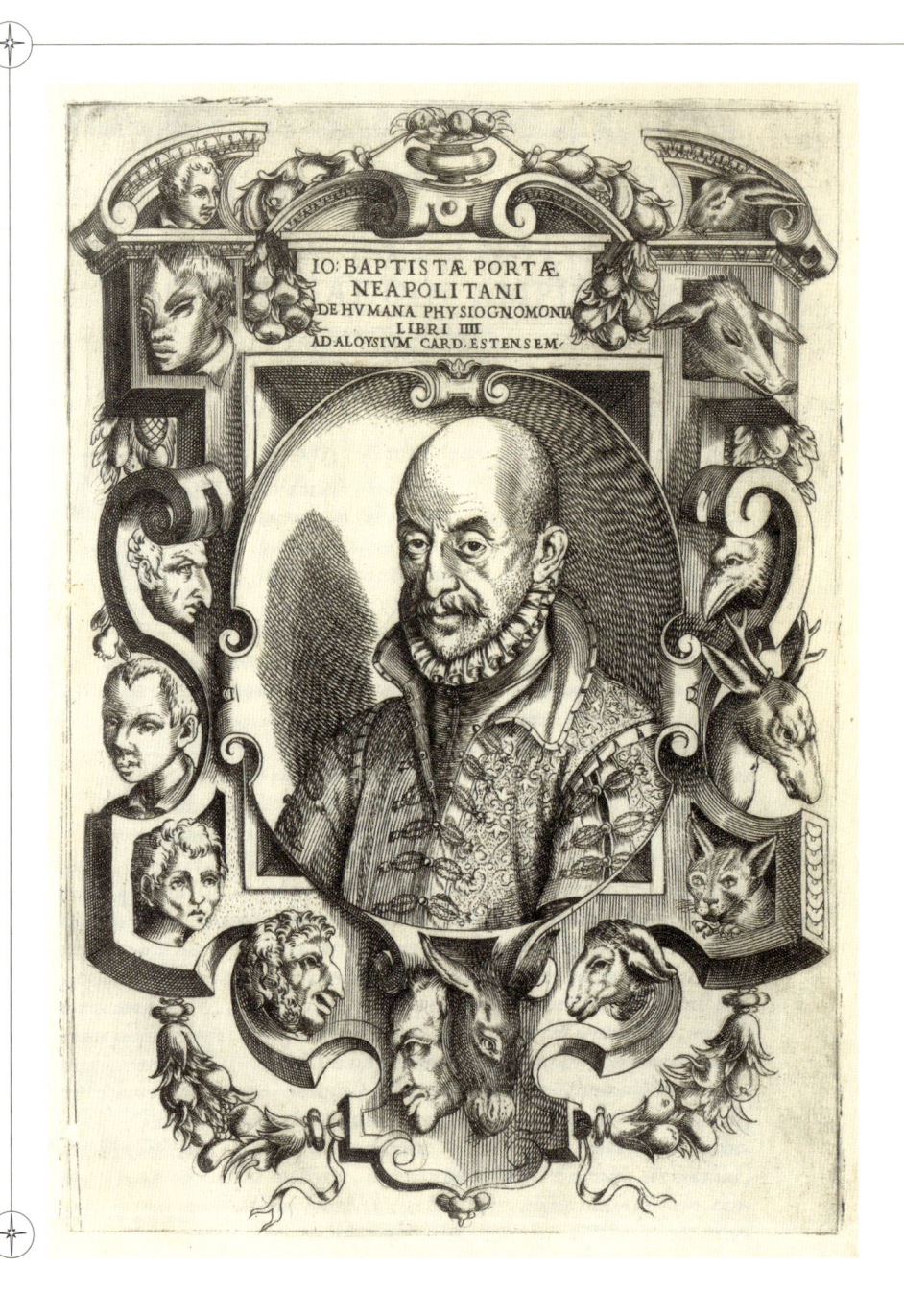

PROFILE
PHYSIOGNOMY

Natural magic included the arts of character reading, ways of gaining insights into an individual's character (and fate) based on aspects of their outer appearance. They were considered one of the more acceptable forms of divination because they were based on natural observation. Physiognomy is the practice

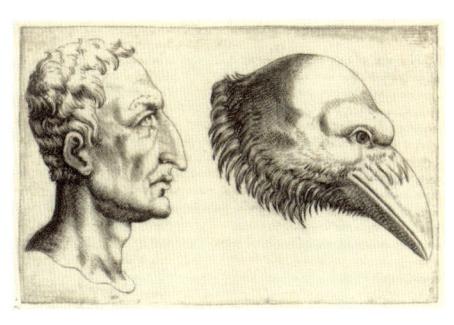

CORVINE
Someone with features like a crow will be clever but impudent.

AQUILINE
A person who has features like an eagle will be magnanimous, far-sighted and regal.

BOVINE
Anyone unfortunate enough to resemble a bull will be slothful, stolid and ignorant.

ASININE
Anyone with a forehead like an ass will be foolish and recalcitrant.

LEONINE
Someone with the features of a lion, however, was considered magnanimous and courageous.

CANINE
A broad brow like this dog (and next to it, Plato) indicates good senses and vigour, with gentleness.

of discerning a person's character from their face and involves comparison of human faces with those of other creatures in the world, including birds and mammals. In *De humana physiognomonia* ('On Human Physiognomy', 1586), Giovanni Battista della Porta provides a selection of perceptive and frequently amusing comparisons.

Giuseppe Arcimboldo, *The Four Elements*, 1566

This series was painted for the Holy Roman Emperor Maximilian II and reflects his keen interest in science. The personification of Earth is created from animals, Water from sea creatures, Air from birds, and Fire from inanimate objects such as wood and artillery.

element: earthy stones, watery metals, airy plants and fiery animals; touching on elemental beings, each element inhabited by a different elemental spirit (fiery salamanders, watery undines, earthy gnomes and airy sylphs) and also on orders of angels related to particular elements (the fiery seraphim, earthy cherubim, watery archangels and airy principalities). Drawing from Plato and Neoplatonic writings, Agrippa conceives of the cosmos as a living being, possessing a body, spirit and soul. The 'Anima Mundi' or 'World Soul', sometimes identified as 'Nature', was believed to contain as many seed-forms of things as there were ideas in the mind of God. The occult virtues of the World Soul are diffused by the World Spirit or Quintessence, which is taken in by the rays of the planets and stars, and through them occult properties are then conveyed into everything existing in the sublunary word. Such magic is natural, indeed the ancient Egyptians called Nature itself a magician, who works by attracting like to like, in a long continuous series of connections, like a string stretching from the heavens above to the earth below. Like a well-tuned lute, when such a string is played below, it resonates above.

Agrippa makes it clear that it is the task of a magician to learn from the observation of nature and search for things that contain an excess of any particular quality. In order to procure a long life, one should seek out creatures that have the power to renew or regenerate themselves, such as snakes that shed their skins or stags that renew their old age by eating snakes; hence some physicians use remedies made of snakes to restore youth. One needs, he says, to understand the sympathies and antipathies of all things. A drum made of a wolf skin will silence one made of lambskin. Agrippa provides lengthy lists of stones, plants and animals connected with each planet, including creatures he describes as 'solary' or solar (lion, crocodile, phoenix, eagle), and more mischievous, 'mercurial' animals that are under the power of Mercury (the talkative parrot, the thieving magpie, the tricky fox, but also the faithful dog). On the subject of herbs, solar plants include sweet cinnamon, yellow saffron and

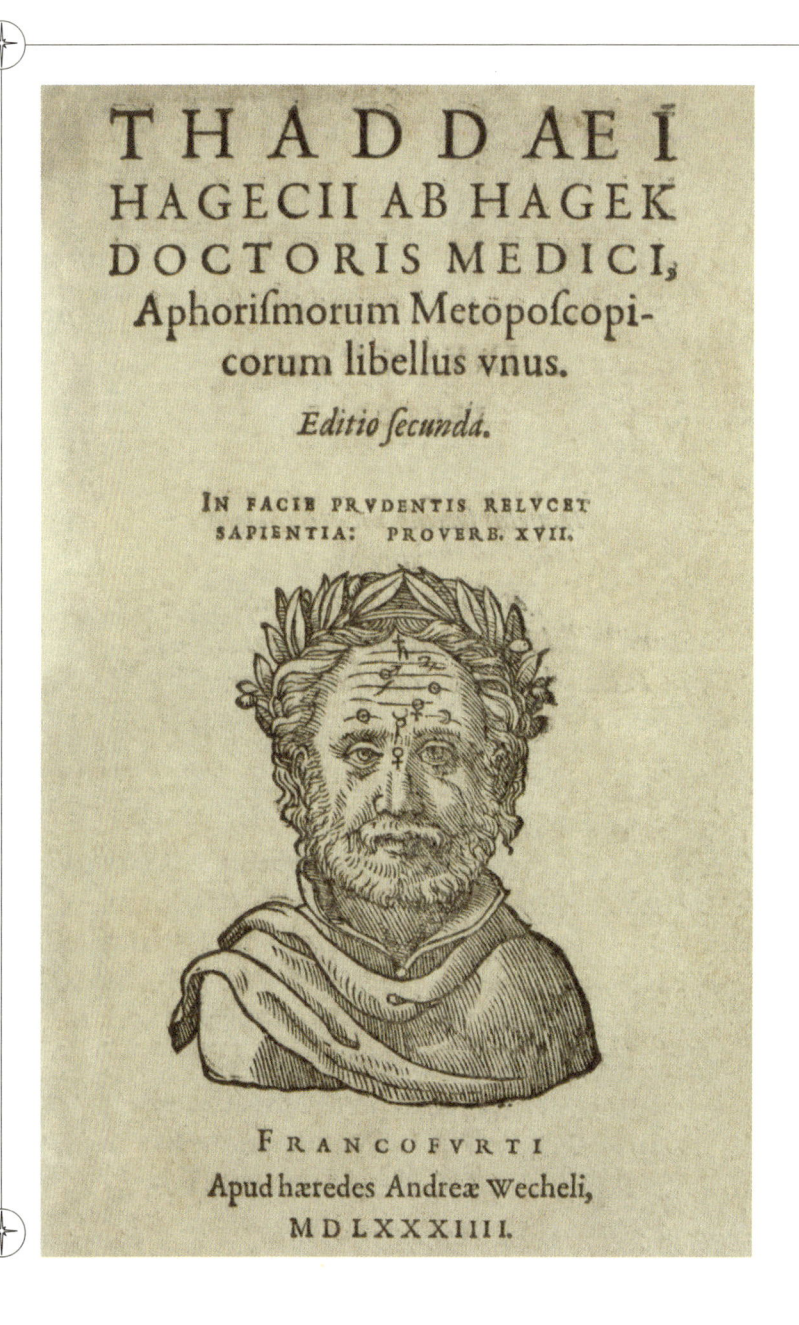

> # THADDAEI
> ## HAGECII AB HAGEK
> ### DOCTORIS MEDICI,
> Aphorismorum Metoposcopi-
> corum libellus vnus.
>
> *Editio secunda.*
>
> IN FACIE PRVDENTIS RELVCET
> SAPIENTIA: PROVERB. XVII.
>
> FRANCOFVRTI
> Apud hæredes Andreæ Wecheli,
> MDLXXXIIII.

PROFILE
METOPOSCOPY

Metoposcopy is the ability to predict someone's destiny by reading the lines on their forehead. Everyone, in theory, could have up to seven principal lines on their forehead. Each line was related to a different planet in astrology. The moon ruled the lowest line, just above the eyebrows, while Saturn, the planet furthest from earth, ruled the highest line, close to the hairline.

Anyone lucky enough to have these lines will have wealth and wives!

And here are the lines of someone both lucky and prosperous.

The sun and moon lines joined like this symbolize good fortune.

Such a line of Jupiter indicates wealth and prudence.

A circle in the line of Jupiter, however, marks losses in wealth.

A line bent to the nose in this way denotes the worst character.

These features denote a good-natured, honest character, without fraud or pretence.

These lines are imaginatively explained to warn of a fall from a high place

The unlucky lines on this forehead predict dangers in waters.

Few foreheads bear all lines, and so those visible were calculated as falling within the zones of particular planets, thereby revealing useful information about the individual. The Czech scholar Thaddaeus Hagecius ab Hagek (1525–1600) was the author of a popular *Aphorismorum metoposcopicorum libellus* ('Booklet of Metoposcopical Aphorisms', 1562).

Magical ingredients
This selection of natural substances represents some of those discussed, for example, by Marsilio Ficino in his Three Books on Life *(1489) or Heinrich Cornelius Agrippa in* Three Books of Occult Philosophy *(1533). On the left is an anthropomorphic mandrake root, looking like a figure at prayer. Mandrake, with its narcotic powers, was categorized as a plant governed by Saturn. The other three substances are saffron, frankincense and cinnamon, all of which were believed to contain the vital, energizing qualities of the sun.*

fragrant frankincense. Martial plants include garlic, onions and leeks, radish and mustardseed, as well as any trees with thorns. Plants related to Venus, on the other hand, are fragrant and sweet-tasting, including coriander, pomegranates, violet, vervain, sandalwood and rose. Jovial plants include trees that bear fruits, like the hazel, fig, apple, plum and pear, as well as barley, wheat, and corn; while Saturnine ones (meaning under the power of Saturn) include mandrake, opium and anything that stupefies the mind. In fact, anything that bears fruit is from Jupiter, everything that bears flowers is from Venus; all seeds are from Mercury; all wood from Mars, leaves from the Moon, and all roots from Saturn. We learn that no single thing naturally contains all the powers of the planets, but that it is necessary, like bees collecting pollen from innumerable flowers, to gather these occult qualities from many sources and bring them together in one form. Agrippa proceeds to instruct the would-be magician concerning practical matters of unguents, potions, perfumes and suffumigations. He writes that the fumes from burning a mixture of linseed, fleabane seed, and roots of violets and parsley help in foreseeing the future, while anyone wishing to see spirits should suffumigate coriander, wild celery, henbane, black poppy and hemlock.

In his widely read *Natural Magick* (*Magia Naturalis*, 1558), the Italian scholar Giovanni Battista della Porta,

Coloured ink drawings by C. Etheridge (1906), after Giovanni Battista della Porta

Here comparisons are made between plants and the antlers and horns of animals, implying that they have similar curative properties. These ink drawings are 20th-century reproductions based on Giovanni Battista della Porta's work on the healing properties of plants, Phytognomonica (1588).

the most famous natural magician of his day, drawing from Pico della Mirandola and Agrippa, states that 'magick is nothing else but the survey of the whole course of nature', 'the very highest point, and the perfection of natural sciences', indeed the 'dutiful handmaid' of nature. In 1560 he established the first scientific society, the Academia Secretorum Naturae (Academy of the Secrets of Nature) in Naples, for experimental research into natural magic. Much of the expanded 1589 edition of *Natural Magick* reveals the fruits of years of investigation and testing of medieval material, with the introduction to the first book (of twenty) setting the tone: 'Wherein are searched out the Causes of things which produce wonderful Effects'. The book covers all sorts of weird and wonderful topics, including theories about how certain creatures were formed, how new plants are produced, the wonders of the lodestone, strange cures, instructions on how to create cosmetics to make women beautiful, cooking tips, catoptrics (including experiments with distorting mirrors), and invisible writing using the juice of onions, lemons or even dormice!

In other works, for example *De humana physiognomonia* ('On Human Physiognomy', 1586), Della Porta is highly instructive about another influential aspect of natural magic, the doctrine of the signatures of natural things, the notion that God fashioned all things in such a way that their external appearance reveals their inner medicinal and related magical qualities. On a human level, this relates to the arts of physiognomy, metoposcopy and chiromancy, respectively, the discerning of a person's character from their face, forehead and hands. Two years later, he published a work on divining the virtues of plants from the appearance of their seeds, roots, flowers and fruits (*Phytognomonica*, 1588).

To return to the encyclopedic 17th-century publications of Robert Fludd and Athanasius Kircher, natural magic was discussed in the former's *Utriusque Cosmi Historia* and the latter's *Oedipus Aegpytiacus*. Kircher had already devoted part of his *Musurgia Universalis* ('The Universal Musical Art', 1650) to consideration of music's natural but occult powers of affecting the human mind and body, as well as to the discussion of the principles of cosmic harmony in relation to the celestial bodies and the animal, vegetable and mineral kingdoms of nature; he even provided a list of 'The Practical Rules of Natural Magic'. As a final example of natural magic, one particularly curious form gave rise to acrimonious disputes involving Robert Fludd: the first between Fludd and the French polymath Marin Mersenne (1588–1648), the second between Fludd and an English Protestant minister William Foster (1591–1643). It concerned Fludd's defence of a practice often promoted by followers of Paracelsus, the creation of a magnetic cure said to take place by action at a distance, instead of through physical contact, which was the traditional Aristotelian explanation favoured by Fludd's opponents: rather than apply remedies to a knife wound, one should anoint the knife with a weapon salve, concocted out of a particularly horrendous list of ingredients (moss grown on the skull of a man who has been strangled or hanged, mummified flesh, warm human blood, and so forth). All going well, the ointment transmits its curative powers by sympathy, the magical, magnetic connection, for example, between the blood on the weapon and the blood in the patient, and the wound magically heals.

Neo-Attic relief of Achilles treating King Telephus' wound, House of the Telephus Relief, Herculaneum, *c.* 27 BCE–14 CE

When the Greeks mistakenly attacked the city of King Telephus thinking that it was Troy, Achilles inflicted a wound on the king that refused to heal. After consulting the oracle of Apollo, Telephus went to Argos where he was healed by Achilles. Ancient authorities claim that Achilles used rust scraped from his spear as the healing agent.

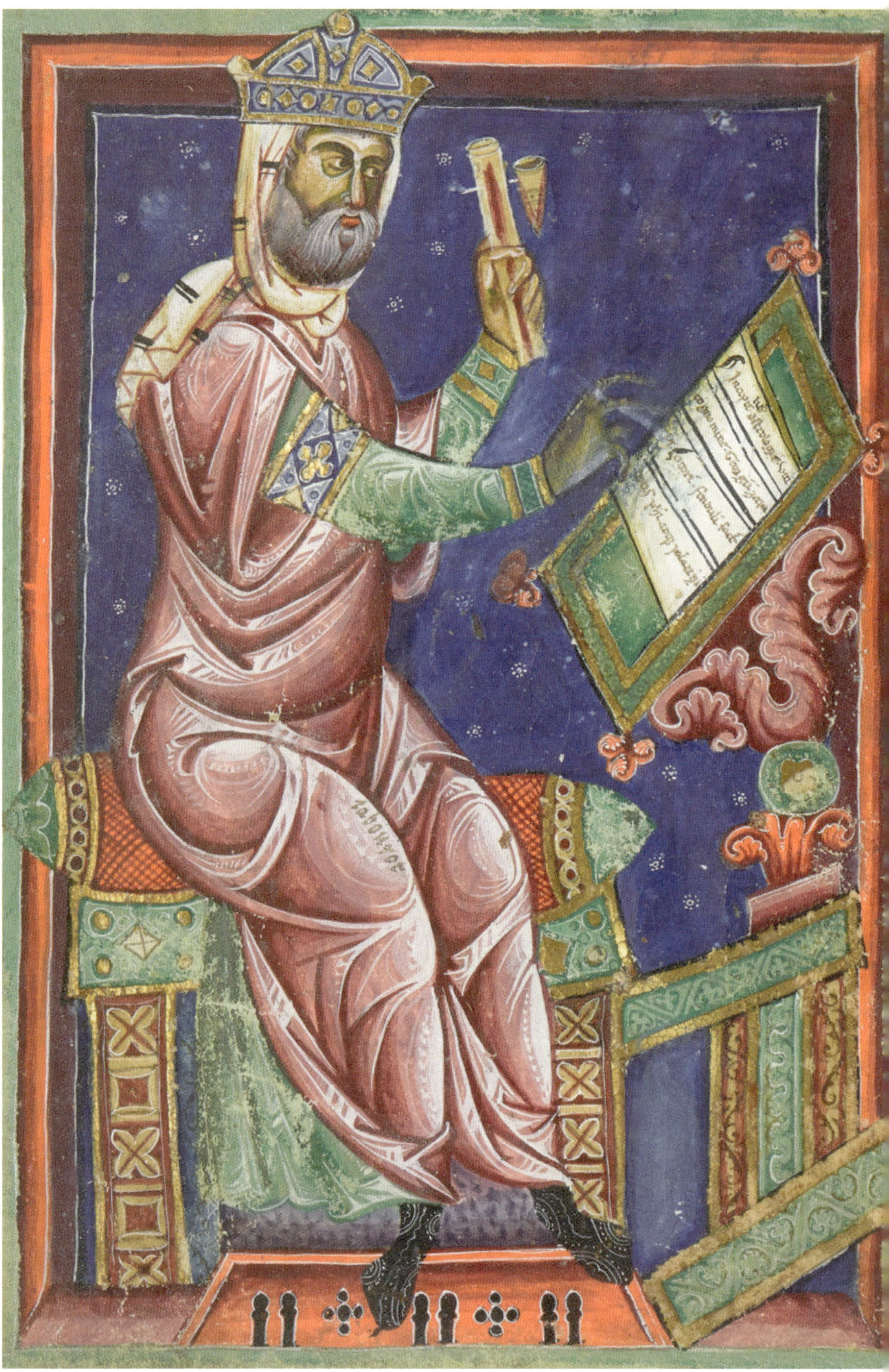

'Why do we think love is a magician? Because the whole power of magic consists in love. The work of magic is the attraction of one thing by another because of a certain affinity of nature.... From this common relationship is born a common love; from love a common attraction. And this is the true magic.'

MARSILIO FICINO, COMMENTARY ON PLATO'S SYMPOSIUM (1484)

ASTRAL MAGIC

Astral magic is the belief that astrological influences from the heavens can be harnessed and manipulated through the creation of physical objects, such as rings or talismans, that became containers of celestial energies. The material used to make the item influenced its purpose, with each item being fashioned under correct astrological conditions, when the planets were in favourable places in the heavens.

Moving from the terrestrial focus of natural magic, let us now turn to a slightly more abstract concept – what is broadly called mathematical magic by magicians like Heinrich Cornelius Agrippa and Giordano Bruno. For them, this included the mathematical disciplines taught in the four arts of the quadrivium (arithmetic, geometry, music and astronomy), which together with the linguistic trivium (grammar, logic and rhetoric) made up the seven liberal arts, considered the foundation for the study of philosophy, theology and medicine. In the occult sciences, this included the study of astrology (number in relation to space and time), the occult properties of music (number in time), as well as a Pythagorean understanding of symbolic numbers, to which could be added symbolic geometry (number in space), and kabbalistic numerical calculations of the values of words.

In his *Three Books of Occult Philosophy*, Agrippa gives a sense of how the abstract mathematical concepts of astronomy and particular figures or square numbers have an even higher force than the stars themselves, such that mathematical magic becomes a kind of celestial magic. This magic teaches us to know the quantity of all bodies in the natural world, as extended into three dimensions, in order to understand the motion and course of celestial bodies. In Book 2, Agrippa expands on this to discuss the power of numbers in natural and supernatural things, the relationship between numbers and letters, geometric and geomantic figures (divinatory patterns made in sand or soil), the proportions of the human body, musical harmony, the harmony of the human soul and material concerned with the planets and zodiac. In his *De Magia* ('On Magic', *c.* 1590) the famous Italian Hermetic philosopher Giordano Bruno, who was burned at the stake in 1600 for heretical beliefs, including the idea of the existence of a plurality of worlds, explains that mathematical magic or 'occult philosophy' is 'intermediate between the natural and the preternatural or the supernatural' and encompasses the use of 'words, chants, calculations of numbers and times, images, figures, symbols, characters or letters'. It is 'similar to geometry in that it uses figures and symbols,

< *page 138*
Abū Ma'shar at work, from a 14th-century manuscript of Georgius Fendulus's *Liber astrologiae*
The opening illustration in this manuscript of Georgius Fendulus's 12th-century Liber astrologiae *shows Abū Ma'shar at a desk. Fendulus's 'Book of Astrology' combines a translation of the 9th-century Persian astrologer's treatises with richly decorated representations of the zodiac signs and their decans.*

Page from the *Libro de astromagia* (c. 1280) of Alfonso X, King of Castile and León

The miniature on the left shows a magician standing in a magic square; he summons a mercurial spirit riding an elephant with multicolour wings to help create a ring of Mercury. In the scene on the right, the magician imbues a magical ring with the virtues of the stars and planets desired at a suitable astrological day and hour.

PROFILE
PLANETARY SEALS OR TALISMANS

A main practice in astral magic is the creation of magical seals. These are usually related to one particular planet in order to gain its benefits. If possible, the seals are constructed in the metal or precious stone related to that planet. The seal usually includes relevant planetary symbolism, such as the symbols of the planets, the related signs of the zodiac, divine names, usually from Hebrew, the names of planetary angels, spirits and demons, and their sigils, the image of the pagan god related to the planet, and the correct magic square. These were meant to be fashioned at a propitious astrological time, when the relevant planet was in a strong position in the heavens.

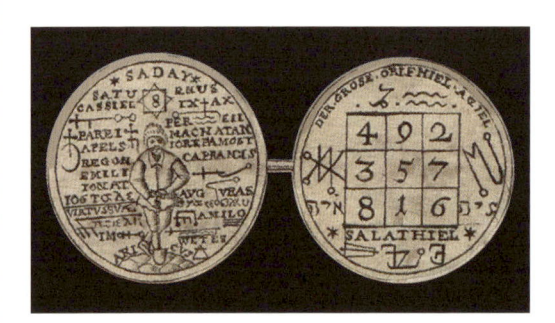

SEAL OF SATURN
The Seal of Saturn, spade in hand, industriously digging into the ground. It includes the divine name Saday, the sigil for the angel Cassiel, the magic square of Saturn, the characters for Agiel the intelligence of Saturn and Zazel the demon of Saturn, the symbol of the planet Saturn, and the zodiac signs of Capricorn and Aquarius.

SEAL OF JUPITER
The Seal of Jupiter, with his eagle at his feet. This includes ten divine names (including Ehieh, Emanuel, Ely, Elohim, Zebaoth), the sigil for the angel Sachiel/Satquiel, the magic square of Jupiter, the characters for Iophiel the intelligence of Jupiter and Hismael the demon of Jupiter, the symbol for the planet Jupiter, and zodiac signs of Sagittarius and Pisces.

SEAL OF MARS
The Seal of Mars, who is clad in armour, sword in one hand, fire grenade in the other. We can see the sigil for the angel Samael, the magic square of Mars, the characters for the intelligence of Mars Graphiel, and Bartzabel, the demon of Mars, the astrological symbol for the planet Mars, and the zodiac signs of Aries and Scorpio.

These seals are from the manuscript *Absonderliche Zubereitung der 7 Siegel der sieben Planeten* ('Strange Preparation of the 7 Seals of the Seven Planets'), Universitätsbibliothek Leipzig, Cod.mag.94.

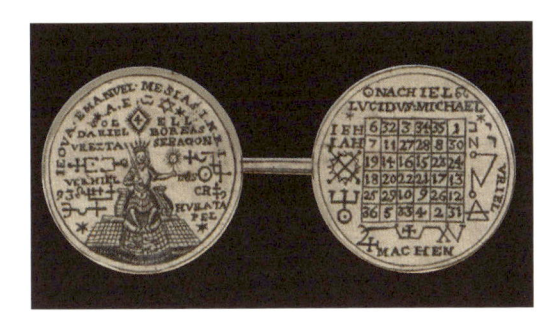

SEAL OF THE SUN
The Seal of the Sun, seated on his regal throne, sceptre in one hand, solar orb above the other. The seal includes the divine names Jehovah, Emanuel and Messiah, the sigil for the angel of healing Raphael, the magic square of the Sun (its total numbers = 666), the characters for Nachiel, the intelligence of the Sun, and the solar demon Sorath, and the seal of Och, Olympic spirit of the Sun.

SEAL OF VENUS
The Seal of Venus, who is playing a lute, accompanied by Cupid with his bow and arrow. Above is the name of the intelligence of Venus, Hagiel. Also depicted are the seal of the angel Anael, the magic square of Venus, the characters for the intelligence and demon of Venus, the symbol for the planet Venus, and the zodiac signs Taurus and Libra.

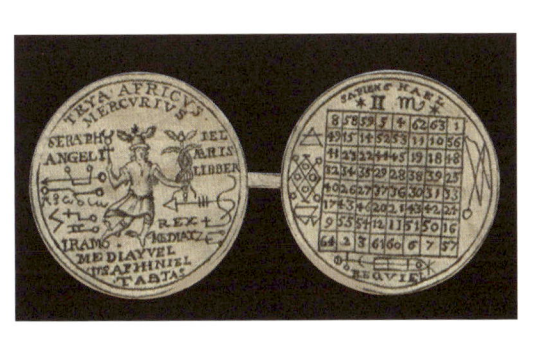

SEAL OF MERCURY
The Seal of Mercury, the messenger god with his caduceus wand in one hand and the symbol for the planet Mercury in the other. We see the name of the angel Seraphiel, the sigil for the angel Michael, the magic square of Mercury, together with the characters for the intelligence and demon of Mercury, plus the zodiac signs ruled by Mercury: Gemini and Virgo.

SEAL OF THE MOON
Encircling the Moon we see the letters of her name Luna, the name and magic character of the lunar angel Gabriel, the seal of the intelligence of the Moon and the zodiac sign of Cancer. On the other side of the seal stands the divine name Jehovah, above the square of the Moon, with the characters for Hasmodai, spirit or demon of the Moon, and the seal of the Olympic spirit Phul (here Boel).

Two illustrations from *Talismans, Cabalistiques, Magiques, grands secretes des Planettes* (1704)
This French manuscript rearranges chapters from Heinrich Cornelius Agrippa's Three Books of Occult Philosophy *(1533), from which both of the illustrations below are taken. They show man in relation to a horoscope and to the planets.*

to music in its chants, to arithmetic in its numbers and manipulations, to astronomy in its concerns for times and motions, and to optics in making observations'.

In a 1503 letter 'on the three principles of natural magic', Agrippa's mentor, the abbot Johannes Trithemius, emphasizes the importance of an understanding of the source of all numbers: 'Every performance of wonders consistent with the limits of nature descends from unity through a binary to the ternary, not before however it rises from the quaternary through the order of grades to simplicity.' Elsewhere Trithemius explains that what he means by unity is not a number, but the thing from which all number arises, all things flowing from this one thing; the 'binary' is composite, for example, the combination of two things in 'composed bodies' (like mercury and sulphur to make the philosophers' stone); the ternary symbolizes the body, spirit and soul of all sublunary things; by the quaternary he means the 'simple bodies' of the four elements (earth, water, air and fire). This numerical progression from unity to quaternary is the very foundation of magic. Agrippa provides tables for each of these numbers, and more, with detailed lists of concordances. For example, for the number 3, he includes the Holy Trinity in the Archetypal World, the world of ideas that contains the blueprint, as it were, of the world in which we live, the name of God with three letters (שדי Shaddai),

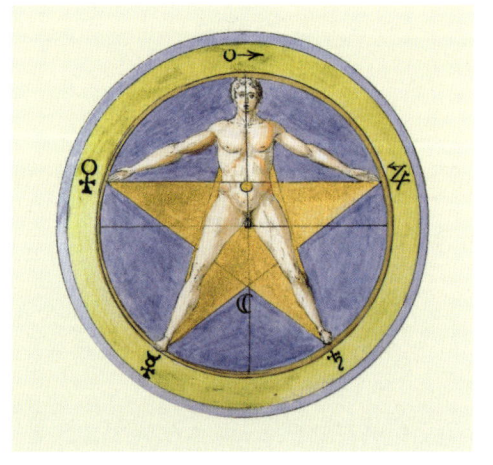

Illustrations from a Latin translation (1458–59) of the *Ghāyat al-Hakīm*, also known as the *Picatrix* *The illustration of the male nude with a naked, long-haired woman, representing Venus, relates to the planet Mars. The woman with flames above her head, standing in a chariot drawn by four horses, holds a mirror in her right hand and a rod in her left, and is said to represent the sun.*

the three astrological modalities (cardinal, fixed, mutable), three types of bodies in the macrocosm (simple, composed, decomposed), and three main parts of the human body, the microcosm (head, chest, stomach), in the Infernal World, the three ranks of the damned (cursed, apostates, infidels). Such lists were not random collections of associations, but were intended to assist magicians in attuning themselves to the different levels of reality. In *Propaedeumata aphoristica* ('An Aphoristic Introduction', 1558) the English mathematician and magus John Dee (1527–1608) expresses this relation between the microcosm and the macrocosm in a particularly evocative way: 'The entire universe is like a lyre tuned by some excellent artificer, whose strings are separate species of the universal whole. Anyone who knew how to touch these dextrously and make them vibrate would draw forth marvellous harmonies. In himself, man is wholly analogous to the universal lyre.'

This brings us to another 'mathematical' way of working with astral virtues, of literally attuning oneself to them through the use of music. There was a long

DECODING A TALISMAN

This is a particularly interesting, complex magical talisman in the British Museum, which combines the powers of several planets. At its centre is a magic square with four cells to each side – 16 cells in total. This immediately identifies it as a square of Jupiter. Each cell contains Hebrew letters, each line adding

146 OCCULT PHILOSOPHY — 2 — *Astral Magic*

up to the value of 34 – the total value of the square being 136. It is surrounded by the seals for the planets Jupiter and Venus on the left; Mercury and the moon on the right. The figure seated above the square, holding a sceptre, may be either Jupiter as the lord of the gods, or Apollo, the sun, whose presence would also be beneficial.

MAGIC SQUARE OF JUPITER

The magic square of Jupiter appears in Arabic and Hebrew numbers in Heinrich Cornelius Agrippa's *Three Books of Occult Philosophy* (1533), Book 2, page CL.

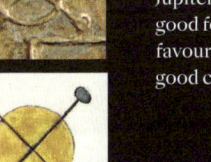

4	14	15	1
9	7	6	12
5	11	10	8
16	2	3	13

THE SEAL OF THE PLANET JUPITER

Jupiter represents good fortune, riches, favour, honours and good counsel.

THE SEAL OF THE PLANET VENUS

Venus brings love, affection, harmony, in matters of the heart, beauty, as well as fertility and fruitfulness.

THE SEAL OF THE PLANET MERCURY

Mercury brings eloquence, ingenuity, quick thinking, wit and good memory; in general, the ability to communicate well.

THE SEAL OF THE MOON

Anyone bearing the seal of the moon will be made amiable, pleasant, safe in travel, in good health.

Marcello Provenzale, *Orpheus*, 1618
In this mosaic, which was commissioned for Cardinal Scipione Borghese and forms part of the collection of the Galleria Borghese in Rome, Orpheus is seen with his lyre, enchanting the animals with his music. A dragon and an eagle, the heraldic symbols of the Borghese family, are among those drawn by the sound of his lyre.

tradition of belief in the powers of music to accomplish marvels. Pythagoras was said to have composed his mind each morning and night with the sounds of the lyre. Al-Kindi wrote of music as a therapy enlisting stellar forces, while Ficino reported successfully exorcising a Saturnian demon by means of Orphic music, and Bruno suggested that all illnesses were due to evil demons, which had to be expelled and replaced with their opposites by means of chants and prayers. Suitable music appropriate to each planet was performed, sometimes with a particular incense, and, following the rules of electional astrology, at a beneficial time.

Just as music has a performative element to it, being a mixture of theory and practice, such is the case with the best-known example of mathematical magic, the practice of what is called either astral magic or image magic. This tradition takes the knowledge of astrology a step further, moving beyond a theoretical understanding of the influence of the heavens on the sublunary world, to an active attempt at harnessing the powers of the planets and stars by directing celestial

Talismanic shirt, 15th–early 16th century
The shirt may have been worn under armour in battle as a form of protection. It is decorated with verses from the Qur'an and the ninety-nine names of God, written in gold on an orange background.

virtues into material objects, into magical images or talismans. This term came from the Arabic *ṭilasm*, which itself came from the Greek *telesma* (religious rite/initiation). Talismans could be in two dimensions (for example, simple painted figures), three dimensions (such as statuettes and figurines) or in between the two (seals). Indeed, in Arabic traditions talismans could include rings, tablets, scrolls and even inscribed shirts. This 'image' magic could encompass abstract geometrical shapes or figurative images, as well as signs, characters, numbers and letters.

Such creations were believed to be a union of *vis rerum* (the 'power of things' – that is, the natural magical virtue of a metal or stone) and *vis imaginum* (the 'power of images', related to planets, planetary angels or daemons). With Al-Kindi, there is no suggestion of rituals directed to planetary spirits, but instead an emphasis on the creator of talismans drawing down celestial virtue. This was not always the case, however, with others writing down instructions for rituals to induce a spirit to imbue a talisman with

Illustrations from a manuscript copy of Francis Barrett's *The Magus, or Celestial Intelligencer: Being a Complete System of Occult Philosophy* (1801)
The writing at the centre of the illustration on the left reads: Talismans & Magical Images made from the 28 Mansions of the Moon. The illustration on the right features the third-century pyramidical figure of the Abracadabra formula of Serenus.

power – instructions that raised anxieties in some quarters. The *Speculum Astronomiae* ('The Mirror of Astronomy', c. 1255–60) – one of the most important medieval works on astrology – speaks of the 'science of images' and distinguishes between three kinds of practice: 'abominable' Hermetic images, requiring suffumigations and invocations to planetary spirits; 'detestable' Solomonic images, with prayers to angels and instructions for compelling inferior spirits through demonic seals and sacrifices; and acceptable astrological images, such as those found in *De Imaginibus Astrologicis* ('On Astrological Images') by the Sabian scholar and philosopher Thābit Ibn Qurra (826–901), which restrict themselves to absorbing stellar influxes.

A few years later, in *De occultis operibus naturae* ('On the Occult Works of Nature'), the theologian and philosopher Thomas Aquinas argued that some bodies, such as magnets, have powers that cannot be caused by the qualities of the elements and so their actions must result from higher principles, such as the heavenly bodies. In his treatise *Summa contra gentiles* ('Summa against the Gentiles', 1259–65), however, he drew a distinction between amulets as natural, unfashioned

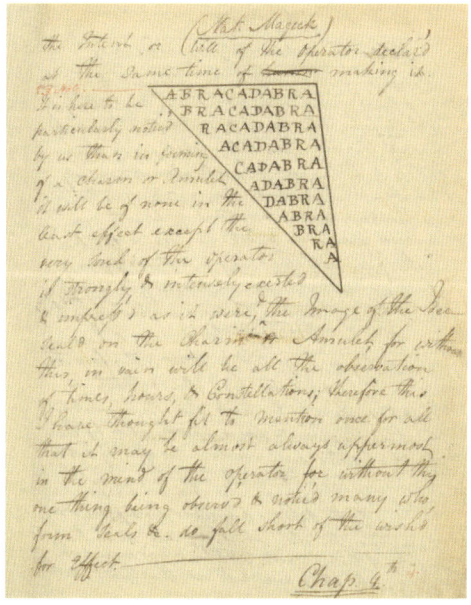

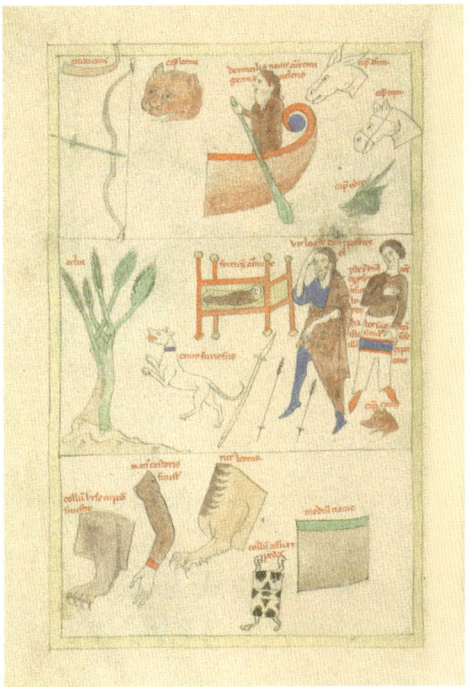

Pages from a 14th-century manuscript of Georgius Fendulus's *Liber astrologiae*
The illustration on the left celebrates the zodiac sign of Leo, while the one on the right depicts the three decans of Leo.

objects, such as a stone or a shell, worn on the body, and talismans as manmade objects engraved with images of the planets, signs of the zodiac, symbols of the constellations, and other powerful signs and characters. He believed that such inscriptions implied communication with sentient beings, possibly demonic, who may well imbue the objects with power, but at great risk to the user.

Despite his familiarity with Aquinas's reservations, Marsilio Ficino is a famous exponent of a combination of natural and talismanic magic in the cure of melancholy. In his *Three Books on Life* of 1489, he declares that 'the rays of the stars...quickly penetrate metal and precious stone when they are engraved with images, and imprint in them wonderful gifts'. In making a talisman, it was necessary to select a material sympathetic to a particular planet, such as a piece of lead to attract Saturn to assist in intellectual work or metaphysical thinking. As someone born with Saturn having a strong placement in his horoscope (conjunct his Ascendant in Aquarius) and deeply immersed in the

Magical bell of Holy Roman Emperor Rudolf II, *c.* 1600

Rudolf II was a keen supporter of the arts and the sciences, including astrology and alchemy. This alchemical table bell, crafted by the Czech artist Hans Bulla, is possibly made of electrum magicum, an alloy of the seven planetary metals, following a recipe by Paracelsus.

translation of Platonic and Neoplatonic philosophy, Ficino was extremely familiar with ways of dealing with Saturn's potentially baleful influence in his life. Although Ficino promotes himself as someone practising a safe and acceptable form of astral magic, we know that he was influenced by a rather notorious Arabic compendium, the *Ghāyat al-Ḥakīm* or *Goal of the Wise*, known in the Christian West as the *Picatrix*. The book is thought to have been composed in Spain in the 10th century by Maslama al-Qurṭubī (d. 964) and translated into Castilian *c.* 1256–58 in the scriptorium of King Alfonso X, who also sponsored the *Libro de astromagia* ('Book of Astral Magic', *c.* 1280). Essentially a manual for constructing talismans, the *Picatrix* introduces itself as a book of necromancy and includes far more dangerous practices, including animal sacrifices directed at spirits and rituals using human blood.

Material from Ficino and the *Picatrix* reappears in Agrippa's *Occult Philosophy*, combined with Hebrew divine names and an awareness of kabbalistic gematria. In Book 2, Agrippa provides a list of Hebrew names that relate to the planets: for example, the Hebrew word *Ab* (father) has the numerical value 3; *Hod* (the eighth *sefira* on the kabbalistic Tree of Life, meaning 'majesty') has the value 9; the divine name *Yah* (a short form of YHVH) has the value 15; *Agiel*, the Intelligence (beneficial spirit) of Saturn, has the value 45, as does *Zazel*, the Demon of Saturn. The significance of these numbers becomes clear when we look at the magic squares connected with the planets (each planet is associated with a series of numbers in a particular arrangement within a magic square), a practice inherited from Arabic astral magic. The square for Saturn has 3 × 3 cells; the numbers in each of the three rows add up to 15, with the sum of all the numbers in the square being 45. Agrippa provides these squares in both Western Arabic numerals and Hebrew letters. He also provides the *signacula* (seals) or *characters* for the planet Saturn, the Intelligence of Saturn and the Demon of Saturn, each of which can be geometrically extracted from the magic squares. These magic seals, and those for the other planets, can be used for various purposes, such as rings, mirrors and talismans.

Ein Immerwährender Natürli[cher]
Schauung der Allertieffsten und Geheimesten

Der Name Gottes mit einem Buchstaben ausgedruckt.

Eine Einige Höchste Wesenschafft.

Im Anfang u. Ende aller Sachen, Die Seele der Welt, Eine Welt.

Die Einige Gottseligkeit, ein Grund aller Einträchtigkeit u. Drei[nigkeit]

	Der Stunden						
	Stunden der Tages	1	2	3	4	5	6
	Sontags						
	Montags						
	Dienstags						
	Mittwochs						
	Donnerstags						
	Freytags						
	Sambstags						
		1	2	3	4	5	6

Gottes Name mit 2 Buchstaben ausgedruckt. Jah

Ei. Naturen in Christo
Verständnüß: Selbständigkeit
Zwei Lichter
Eleme[nta] der leibl[ich] u. Geistl
Haupttheile der Seelen
Principia, Charakteres des Drachen Haupt u. Schwantzes

Zween Cherubim

Göttliche Engel Göttliche Erde Herz forma Drachenhäupt
ΛΛΔΛΔ

Männlich Würckende

Die Zweyzahl ist die der verbündnüs und der kleinen Stunden nach Mitternacht.

Gottes Name mit 3 Buchstaben ausgedruckt.

Personen der Gottheit
Englische Heerschafften
Arten der Seelen
Zeiten
Theologische Tugenden
Principia der Welt
Intellectualische Kräffte
Reiche der Natur
Elementa
Principia

Vater	Sohn	H. Geist	
Höchste	Mittelste	Unterste	
Sinnliche	Geistes	Wachsende	
der Natur		der Gnaden	
Hoffnung	Glauben	Liebe	
Gott Omnipot.	Gemüth Natura	Geist Anima	
Gedächtnüs	Gemüth	Wille	
Animalisch	Mineralisch	Vegetabilisch	
Reines	Componirtes	Decompositez	
Sulphur	Sal	Mercurius	

Die Heilige u. Mächtigste Dreyzahl, die Vollkommene Zahl

Gottes Name mit 4 Buchstaben Tetragrammaton.

Elementa
Oberste der Elementen Engel
Buchstaben der Hebräer und Griechen und
Dreyfache Winde
Ecken der Welt
Dreyfache Zeichen
Beschaffenheiten der Element.
Elementa des Menschen
Kräffte der Seelen
Schuhlen der Naturlehrer
Ecken des Himmels
Bewegungen der Natur
Termini der Natur
Termini der Mathem.
Termini der Physic.
Termini der Metaphys.
Tugend in der Sittenlehre
Spirit. Theophr.
Mit ihren Characteren.

Feuer △	Lufft	Wasser ▽	Erde
Seraph שרף	Cherub כרוב	Tharsis תרשיש	Aziel אריאל
Raphael	Michael	Gabriel	Uriel
			Stella fixa
Ostwind	Westwind	Nordwind	Südwind
Aufgang	Untergang	Mitternacht	Mittag
♈ ♌ ♐	♉ ♍ ♑	♊ ♎ ♒	♋ ♏ ♓
Liecht	Durchscheinend	Geschwindigkeit	Gesellschafft
Gemüth	Geist	Seel	Leib
Verstand	Vernunfft	Fantasie	Sinne
Thun	Leben	Wissen	Versehen
Aufgang	Untergang	Mitte	Letzter
Aufgehende	Niedergehende	Fortgehende	Umbgehende
Verständigkeit	Beschaffenheit	Grösse	Bewegung
Punct	Linea	Fläche	Tiefe
Samende Tugend	Dinge frucht dr Nat	Leben sindes	Zusammen gesetzter
Leben	Wesen	Tugend	Verrichtung
Klugheit	Gerechtigkeit	Mässigkeit	Stärke
Menealop	Amadich	Emachel	Damalch

Die Vierzahl ist eine Würtzel und Grund der Zahlen, ein Gr[...]

Gottes Nahmen mit 5 Buchstaben Jhesuh

Sinn
Verdorbene Arten
Kräffte in der leb. Dingen
Ruhe
Irrende Sterne
Vermischte Arten
Getöne der Thiere

		Chyromantia der Lincken Hand, Die 7 Planeten zeigend.		Einbild der Menschen, wel. die 12 Zeichen in sich fas.
	Rinden		Jesam	
	Wasser		Licht	
	Wachsende		Fühlende	
	Leben		Hören	
	Saturnus		Jupiter	
	Steine		Metalle	
	Menschen		Vierfüsige	

Die gefünffte Zahl ist die Helffte von Zehen, aus gleich und un[...]

...scher Calender, Welcher die Be=
...n die Erkäntnuß der gantzen Philosophiæ in sich fasset

GOTT. Der doch ohne Anfang u. Ende ist.
Der Stein der Weisen.
Ein Hertz.

IN ARCHETYPO.
IN MUNDO INTELLIGIBILI.
IN MUNDO MINORE.

Ursprung, vor welcher Er gewesen, u. nach welcher auch Er werde wird.

Nahmen			Zwey Gesetz Tafeln.	**IN ARCHETYPO.**
7 8 9 10 11 12		Menschliche		In der Intellectualischen
♄ ♃ ♂ ☉ ♀ ☿ Gut.		Seele		
		Mond		Himlischen
		Wasser		
		Gehirn		Kleinen
		Materia		Elementalischen
		præcedens		Welt.
7 8 9 10 11 12 Stunden.		Weibliches Leidendes		

Stunden vor Mitternacht. Welt, welche die gebährende Materia anzeiget.

				Gottes Name mit 3 Buchstaben.
Beweglicher	Unbeweglicher		Gemeine	Vierfache Windzeichen
Anfangender	Folgender		Fallende	Vierfache Haupt Zeichen
Tägliche	Nächtliche		Theilhaffte	Dreyfache Personen
Anfang	Mittel		Ende	In Ewigkeit und Zeit
Vergangenes	Gegenwärtiges		Zukünftiges	Maas der Zeit
Linea	Umbschweiff		Corpus	Gemeine Theile
Länge	Breite		Dicke	Unterscheide der Leiber
Seele	Geist		Leib	Theile des Menschen. Princip.
Haupt	Brust		Bauch	Theile des Menschen an sich.
Feuer	Luft		Wasser	Haupt Elemente

durch Dreyfache Vermehrung denen Göttlichen Formen zugeeignet.

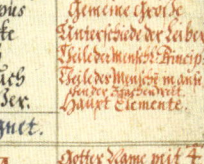

I O V A

Galle △	Blut ⊕	Schleim ▽	Schwartzgeblüt ⊖	Gottes Name mit 4 Buchstaben.
Ungestümigkeit	Hurtigkeit	Trägheit	Langsamkeit	Feuchtigkeiten
Sommer	Frühling	Winter	Herbst	Zeiten des Jahrs
Casmaran	Talvi	Farlass	Amabael	der Zeit und
Gargatel	Caracasa	Amabael	Tarquam	Engel
Tariel	Amatiel	Ctazari	Gualbarel	Nahmen
Jubiel	Amadai			
Gariel	Spugiel	Altarib	Torquaret	Hauptstück der 4 guten
Sestatui	Amadai	Gerenia	Rabianira	Nahme der Erde
Marcus	Johannes	Matthæus	Lucas	Evangelisten
Löwe	Adler	Mensch	Kalb	4 Thiere
Thiere	Pflantzen	Metalla	Steine	
Gehende	Fliegende	Schwimmende	Kriechende	Arten der Thiere
Saame	Blume	Blätter	Wurtzel	leibl. Elementa de Kräuter
Warm	Feucht	Kalt	Trocken	und derer Eigenschafft.
☉	☿	☽	♄	Metalle so mit den Elementen
Gold	Eisen	Queksilber	Bley und Silber	übereinkommen
Leuchtende	Feste	Helle	des Meer	Stimme somit die Elementa überlegen
Thoar ♈	Censor ♊	Basan ♎	Pantheon ♑	der 4
Coron ♌	Error ♍	Zarneth ♏	Erim ♒	Himlischen
Heremon ♐	Jassor ♓	Elysan	Naim ♉	Zeichen.
Bael	Moymon	Poymon	Egin	Principia der 4 Geister aus aller 4 Theile der Welt
Silphani	Aerei	Nymphæ	Pigmæi	Geister der Elemente.

die vollkommene Zahl in sich hält.

Menschen figur, die	Die Rechte Handt Got=		**IN ARCHETYPO.**
5 Planeten in sich haltend	tes die Welt Seiten in sich		
Unserer		Heylander	In der Kleinen
Erde		Vermißter	Welt.
Zürnende		Vernünftige	
Schmecken		Füssen	
Venus		Mercurius	In der Elementali=
Gewürme		Thiere	schen Welt.
Schwimmende		Fliegende	

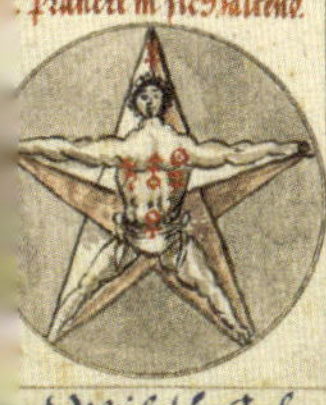

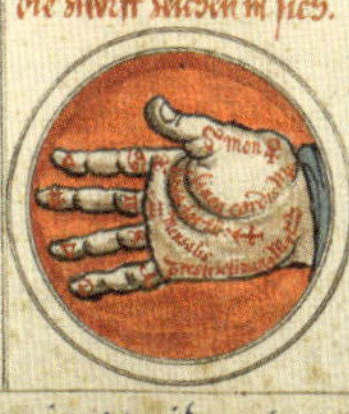

...nd Weib/ bestehende/ dem Mercurio gewidmet.

The influential *Archidoxis Magicae* ('Chief Teachings of Magic', 1590), purportedly by Paracelsus, includes a recipe for the creation of magical electrum, an alloy of all seven planetary metals, praised for its utility in the fashioning of magic mirrors and necromantic bells. This astral magical amalgam was created over a long period of time, by paying attention to conjunctions of the planets (e.g. a conjunction of Mars and Venus as the best time for combining iron and copper; Saturn and Jupiter, for combining lead and tin), in order to make mirrors that were astrologically attuned to the horoscopes of their users. Such mirrors could be used for evocations of spirits of the dead, or invocations of angels and demons, usually with the goal of divination. Heinrich Khunrath followed these instructions in order to fashion magical armour, advising the reader of his manuscript to strike Agrippa's seal of Mars into the armour at the same time as fiercely shouting a martial incantation.

One final exponent of astral magic will have to suffice: the Italian philosopher Tommaso Campanella. Pope Urban VIII (1568–1644), who had a reputation for commissioning horoscopes of cardinals and openly predicting the dates of their deaths, grew extremely concerned about predictions of his own death in connection with a sequence of solar and lunar eclipses. He released Campanella, who had spent many years languishing in papal prisons for heresy and insurrection, and asked him to help. In 1628 at the papal palace in the town of Castel Gandolfo they sealed the doors and windows of their safe room and purified the air within by sprinkling perfumes and scents. They lit two lamps and five torches to represent the planets, together with lights for the constellations of the zodiac. Music evoking the benefic virtues of Jupiter and Venus was played, and they surrounded themselves with stones, plants and colours sympathetic to these benign energies; they even drank astrologically distilled liquors. The operation was a success and the Pope dodged the astrological bullets. Unfortunately, the Pope's enemies published Campanella's private record of the ritual without his consent. Urban was enraged and Campanella left Rome, finding refuge in Paris at the Court of Louis XIII.

⟨ *pages 154–55*
An everlasting natural-magical calendar, 1582
This example includes Hebrew divine names, sacred geometry, astrology, palmistry, seals and characters of angels, magic squares, personifications and sigils of the seven classical planets.

Albrecht Dürer,
Melencolia I, 1514

Probably the most famous example of the magic square of Jupiter appears in this engraving by the German artist Albrecht Dürer. Dürer's horoscope shows that he is under the influence of the planet Saturn, which is conjunct his sun in Gemini. This gives him learning, but also inflicts melancholy. Dürer includes the square for the beneficial planet Jupiter as a way of counteracting Saturn. If you look closely at Dürer's magic square, you see that the bottom row has these numbers: 4, 15, 14, 1. The middle two numbers provide the date of the production of the engraving: 1514. The numbers 1 and 4 allude to Dürer's initials A and D, the first and fourth letters of the alphabet.

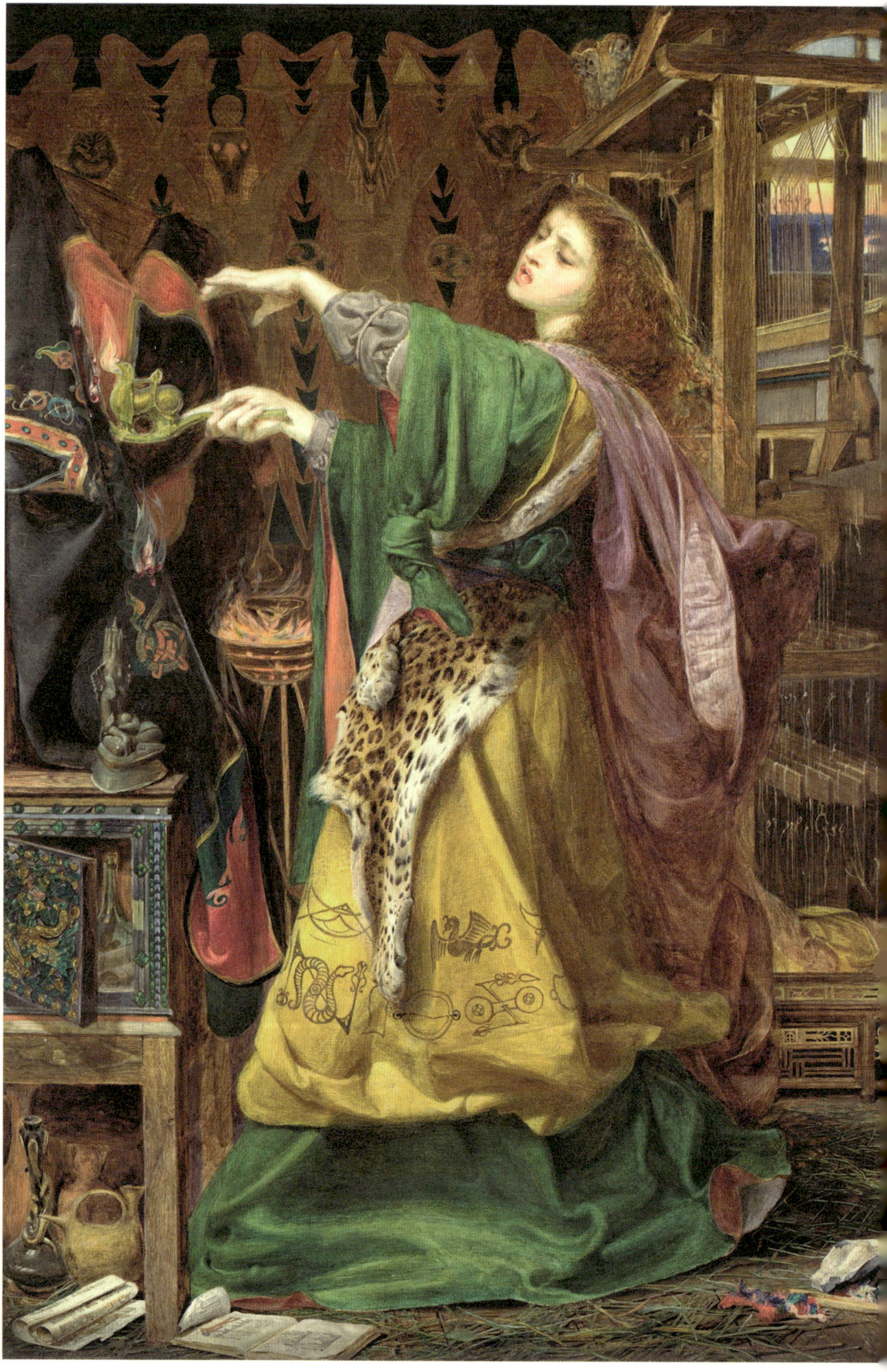

'These metaphysics of magicians,
And necromantic books are heavenly;
Lines, circles, scenes, letters, and characters;
Ay, these are those that Faustus most desires.
O, what a world of profit and delight,
Of power, of honour, of omnipotence,
Is promis'd to the studious artizan!'

CHRISTOPHER MARLOWE,
THE TRAGICAL HISTORY OF DOCTOR FAUSTUS (1604)

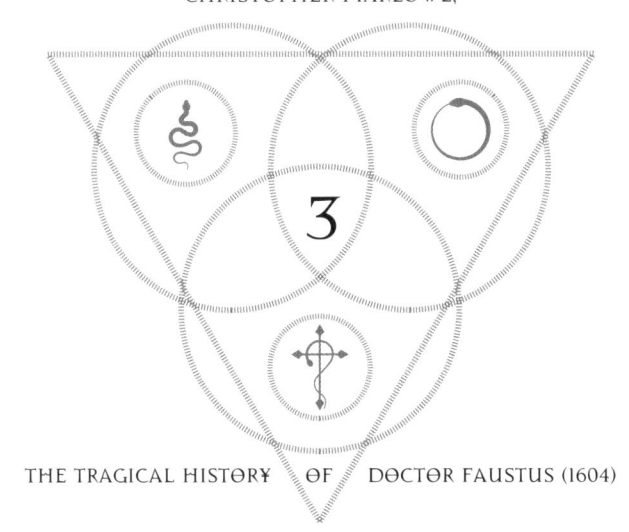

RITUAL MAGIC

Ritual magic is the most contentious form of magical practice, dealing with the supernatural world, the invocation of angels and the summoning of demons. It often involved complex sequences of action, such as the creation of magic circles for the protection of the magus and confinement of the spirits, the use of words of power to coerce evil spirits, and long preparatory rites of purification and prayer.

Here let us turn to a third, far more contentious and potentially more perilous kind of magical practice, ritual or ceremonial magic, which has existed in various forms since antiquity and continues to the present day. While natural magic and even astral magic were to a certain extent tolerated by the church, ritual magic existed in close proximity to religion, especially in the Middle Ages when those capable of reading the manuscripts had usually been trained as monks or priests. Members of the medieval clergy without a stable income might well become members of what has been termed the clerical underworld, willing to attempt or assist in magical rituals and to compile or author new magical works. Needless to say, at the very least they risked being accused of usurping the power of the church, not to mention blasphemy, liturgical idolatry and heresy.

Of particular note in antiquity is the Graeco-Egyptian collection of spells and rituals from Egyptian, Babylonian, Greek, Jewish and Christian texts known as the *Greek Magical Papyri*, dating from the 2nd century BCE to the 5th century CE. The *Sefer ha-Razim* ('Book of Secrets', late 3rd or early 4th century CE) shows the influence of the *Greek Magical Papyri*, but also provides around 700 names of angels. This prominent Jewish grimoire was said to have been given to Noah by the angel Raziel and to have been passed down to King Solomon, famed not only for his great wisdom, but also for his magical power over demons. The oldest work of Solomonic magic, the *Testament of Solomon*, has been described as an encyclopedia of demonology. It emerged in late antiquity, with its earliest manuscript remnant dating from the 5th or 6th century CE, and, together with the Byzantine Greek *Hygromanteia* or 'Magical Treatise of Solomon', was the source for what is arguably the best known grimoire in the Latin West, the late 14th- or early 15th-century *Clavicula Salomonis* (*The Key of Solomon The King*).

These manuals of ritual magic incorporated practices of natural and astral magic but added something new: an interest in conjuring spirits, whether that meant the summoning of infernal demons to perform their wishes

⟨ *page 158*
Frederick Sandys,
***Morgan-le-Fay*, 1864**
In this Pre-Raphaelite depiction of the enchantress and sister of the legendary King Arthur, Morgan le Fay is presented as a dangerous femme fatale. She stands in front of a loom on which she has created an enchanted robe that is designed to set alight when Arthur puts it on, consuming his body in flames.

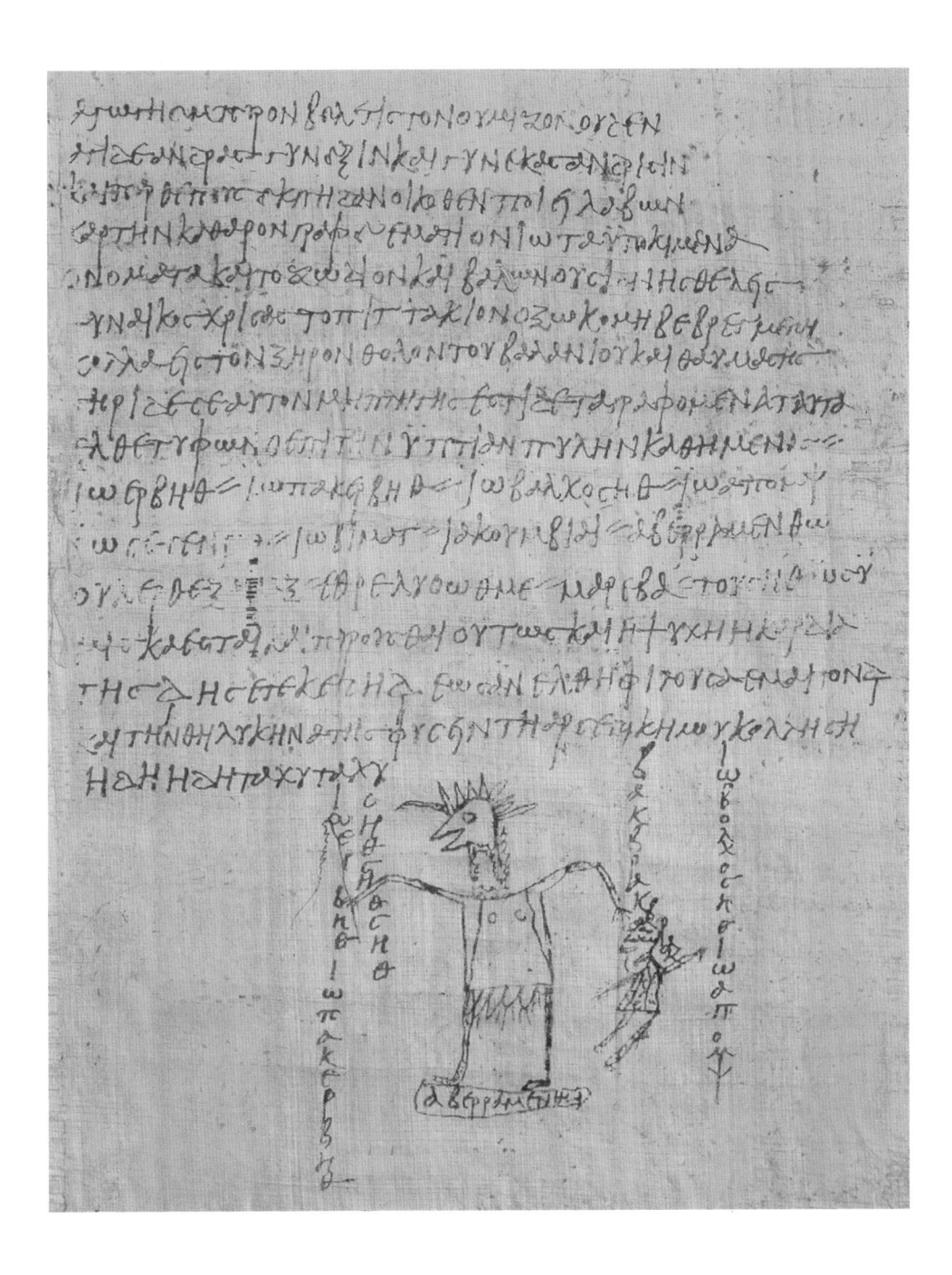

Conjuration 36 from the *Greek Magical Papyri*, 2nd century BCE–5th century CE

The text explains that this is 'A love spell of attraction, excellent divination by fire, than which none is greater. It attracts men to women and women to men, and makes virgins rush out of their homes.' One should write the names and figures provided, which include an invocation to the serpentine monster Typhon, on pure papyrus with the blood of an ass, incorporate magical material from the person desired, and glue the spell in the dry vapour room of a bath.

***Clavicula Salomonis*,**
18th–19th century
This is an Italian-produced copy of a manuscript that includes elements from both the Key of Solomon and the Heptameron. The illustration on the left depicts King Sarabotes, the aerial spirit ruling Friday and the planet Venus; his angels are connected with the west wind. The illustration on the right shows King Arcan, the spirit ruling Monday and the moon, whose angels are also associated with the west wind. Beneath Arcan are the opening verses of Psalm 32: 'Blessed is he whose transgression is forgiven....'

or the invocation of heavenly angels. The appeal for supernatural assistance, involving the magicians' use of prayers and conjurations for communicating with these powerful beings, dramatically distinguishes this magic from its more licit natural and astral forms. While these texts of ritual magic, like those of other forms, clearly show the influence of earlier Greek, Arabic Neoplatonic and Jewish traditions, the surviving Western manuscripts draw for the most part on Christian biblical and liturgical texts and practices, most notably exorcism, for their structure and justification. Moreover, in contrast to natural and astral magic, ritual magic practices were often long and complex, sometimes taking months to complete. Ritual magic exists in two basic forms, following classical distinctions between *theurgia* (god-work) and *goētia* (sorcery): the former concerned with angelic powers, the latter involving both angelic and demonic forces but often with negative connotations.

There are various definitions of theurgy, but generally there is the sense of magic with an

Scenes from *Cantiga 125*, illustrated in a manuscript of *Cantigas de Santa Maria*, 13th century
Translated as the 'Canticles of Holy Mary', the Cantigas *are poems set to music, traditionally attributed to Alfonso X, King of Castile and León.* Cantiga 125 *is about a priest who performs magic to compel a woman to sleep with him. Surrounded by demons, he is seated inside a magic circle that not only has magic symbols around the circumference, but also a protective pentagram inside. The woman is saved by the intercession of the Virgin Mary.*

underlying religious purpose, a sacerdotal art intent on associating with pure spirits and unification with the gods. Theurgy's most popular sources were the Neoplatonists: *On the Mysteries of the Egyptians, Chaldeans and Assyrians* by the 4th-century Syrian Iamblichus, the Greek philosopher Proclus's 5th-century *On Sacrifice and Magic* (also known as *On the Hieratic Art*), and the early 6th-century Christian writings of Pseudo-Dionysius the Areopagite (possibly a Syrian monk, known only by his pseudonym). The pagan Proclus writes of the theurgic use of symbols for exaltation to heaven and self-deification, leading to unification with the One. Ultimately, the theurgist becomes simultaneously man and god, aligning his particular microcosmic soul with the powers of the World Soul and thereby participating in the 'whole' to become a *theios anēr*, a 'divine man'. In a theurgical rite, the divinity could be seen when the theurgist was in a trance, either when the practitioner's soul ascends to heaven or when the divinity descends to earth to appear either in a dream or a waking state. The Christian Pseudo-Dionysius presents theurgy

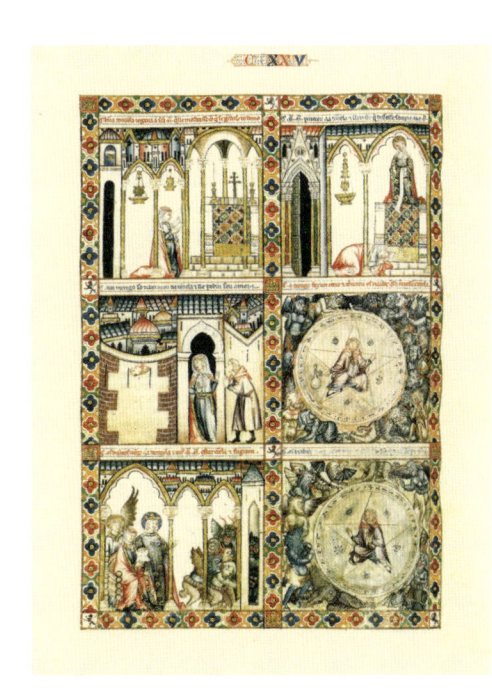

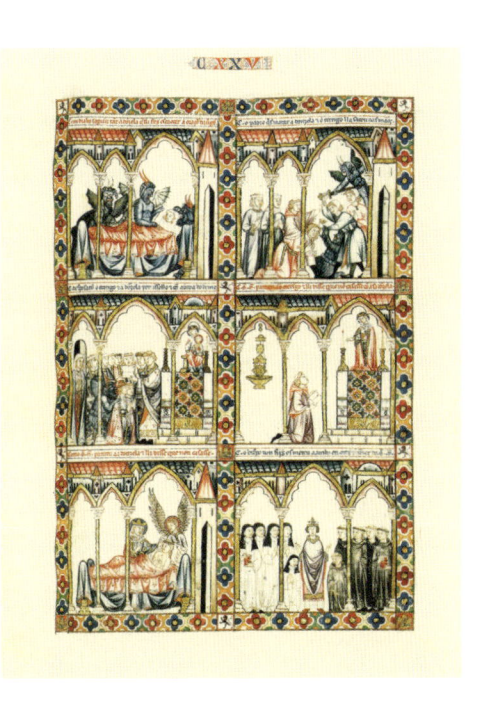

OCCULT PHILOSOPHY — 3 — *Ritual Magic*

PROFILE
MAGIC CIRCLES

Inside the magic circle is the place of conjuration; its boundary is a barrier against dangerous spirits that may appear. In some manuscripts it is a simple circle, the most perfect geometrical shape, in itself able to ward off beings that flinch from perfection. Sometimes there are concentric circles, between which are inscribed magical symbols and divine names, as in the example on the left from *The Astrologer of the Nineteenth Century* (1825). Occasionally there is a space to contain any spirits.

DEMON WITH TREASURE
In *The Pilgrimage of the Life of Man* (1425–50), a necromancer stands in a magic circle with a sword for additional protection. A demon brings him treasure, which is presumably added to the piles already inside the circle.

MERCURY
This illustration from the *Songs of the Holy Mary* (13th century), attributed to Alfonso X, shows a priest using magic to gratify his sexual desires. Surrounded by demons, he sits inside a magic circle and pentagram.

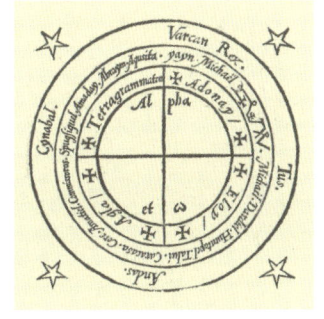

TIME-RELATED CIRCLE
In the *Heptameron*, attributed to Pietro d'Abano (1250–1316), the circle's inner band has divine Hebrew names; the outer bands list demon kings, zodiac signs and angels, all related to the hour, day and season of its construction.

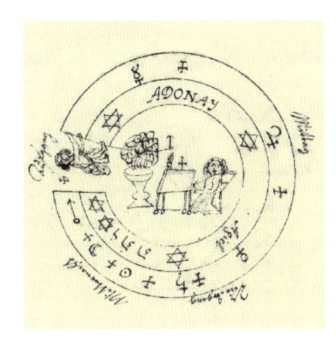

CIRCLE WITH OPENING
This circle, from *Necromancy or Black and White Cabala of Doctor Johann Faust* (c. 1750), has an entrance, opened or closed by an assistant, a ritual table and an incense burner. We see the names of Adonai and Agiel.

DOCTOR FAUSTUS
The 1628 title page of Christopher Marlowe's tragedy shows Faustus holding a grimoire and staff inside a circle with the signs of the planets and zodiac, conjuring the demon Mephistopheles.

TREASURE SEEKERS
A necromancer holding a grimoire invokes, or perhaps tries to banish, a demon, while an assistant brandishes a sword, and another digs in the hope of finding treasure, in a 1532 edition of a work by Francesco Petrarch.

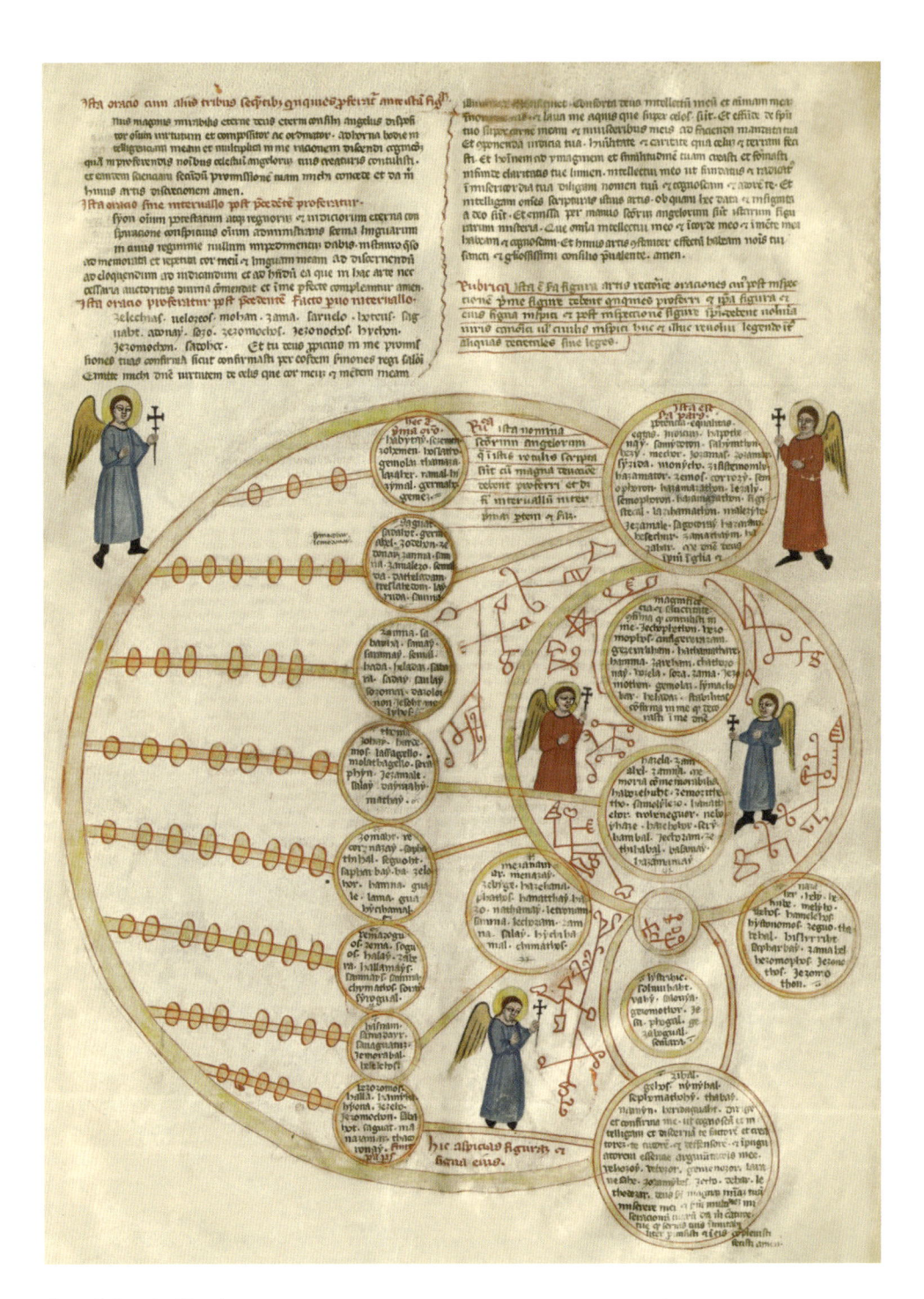

***Sacratissima Ars Notoria*,**
14th century

This diagram, which appears in a 14th-century copy of a 12th-century manuscript, includes illustrations of angels and descriptions of their qualities, and their notae *- magical notes or marks - together with lists of angelic names. Prayers are also featured, intended to be said by the practitioner to gain knowledge.*

as the 'consummation of theology', with Christ as the ultimate elevating symbol: Christ becoming *theánthrōpos* (God-man) was itself a theurgic act that resulted in negating the boundary between mankind and divinity. The goal of Dionysian theurgy was not simply self-elevation, but the salvation and divinization of every being endowed with reason and intelligence. In a Christian context theurgic activity often translates into 'angel magic', which includes rituals concerned with revelation, techniques for inducing dreams and visions, for speaking to spirits, or for a direct infusion of knowledge and experience of the celestial realm, but also steps to develop the practitioner's memory, eloquence and understanding, with the ultimate aim of improving their chances of salvation. This normally involved intensive and extensive, time-consuming rituals for the purification of the practitioner's body and soul, preparations in the form of fasting, confession, periods of silence and meditation, and lengthy prayers to the Holy Trinity and accompanying angels.

One of the most important representative works of learned angel magic is the 12th-century Solomonic *Ars Notoria* ('Notory Art'), which claims to enable the solitary practitioner – the student aiming to improve himself in his studies or the monk earnestly hoping for visionary experience – to acquire spiritual and intellectual gifts from the Holy Spirit by means of angelic intermediaries. The account of God's appearance to Solomon in a dream in 1 Kings 3:5–15 was evidently a source of inspiration, for the *Ars Notoria* is presented as a set of holy prayers revealed to Solomon by an angel in order for the successful practitioner to become the beneficiary of a divine infusion of the liberal arts, philosophy, theology, and medical and divinatory knowledge. This involves a high degree of asceticism, the recitation of prayers (some recognizably orthodox, others containing mysterious *verba ignota*, or unknown words), purificatory rituals, contemplative exercises involving the inspection of *notae* (complex figures composed of words, shapes and magical characters), and even drinking special decoctions, the whole ritual

DECODING THE SON OF MAN

The *Clavis Inferni sive Magia Alba et Nigra* ('Key of Hell or Black and White Magic') is a grimoire of ritual magic dating from the 18th century, attributed to Saint Cyprian, who was reputedly a magician before becoming a Christian. The manuscript contains prayers, conjurations, bindings and banishings of demons, with images including four demon kings. This image depicts the Son of Man from Revelation 1:12–18, who says that he has the keys of death and Hell. He is described in Revelation 1:13–16 as follows:

REVELATION 1:13–16

¹³ And in the midst of the seven golden candlesticks, one like to the Son of man, clothed with a garment down to the feet...with a golden girdle.

¹⁴ And his head and his hairs were white, as white wool, and as snow, and his eyes were as a flame of fire,

¹⁵ And his feet like unto fine brass, as in a burning furnace....

¹⁶ And he had in his right hand seven stars. And from his mouth came out a sharp two edged sword: and his face was as the sun shineth in his power.

1. SON OF MAN
This depiction of the Son of Man reflects the description in Revelation 1:12–18.

2. TETRAKTYS
The Pythagorean *Tetraktys* contains the divine name YHVH, written in the magical alphabet Scriptura Caelestis ('Heavenly Writing').

3. HEBREW ARCHANGELS I
To the left of the *Tetraktys* are the Hebrew names of the archangels Gabriel and Uriel.

4. HEBREW ARCHANGELS II
To the right of the *Tetraktys* the names of the archangels Michael and Raphael are written in Hebrew.

5. ARCHANGELS RAPHAEL, CAMAEL AND ZADKIEL
The names of three of the seven archangels are written in the Scriptura Malachim or 'Angelic Writing'. From top to bottom: Raphael, Camael and Zadkiel. According to Agrippa, these angels relate to the Sun, Mars and Jupiter.

6. ARCHANGELS GABRIEL, MICHAEL AND HANIEL
On the right are the names of three more of the seven archangels: Gabriel, Michael and Haniel. In Agrippa's *Three Books of Occult Philosophy*, he associates these angels with the Moon, Mercury and Venus.

7. ARCHANGEL ZAPHKIEL
Beneath the illustration is the name of the seventh archangel, Zaphkiel, whom Agrippa relates to Saturn.

8. ALPHA
Beneath the illustration, on the left, is the Greek letter Alpha, which symbolizes Christ as the beginning (Revelation 1:11).

9. OMEGA
Beneath the illustration, on the right, is the Greek letter Omega, which symbolizes Christ as the end (Revelation 1:11).

Illustrations from an English manuscript copy of *The Sworn Book of Honorius*, 16th century
These pages show angels connected with Mars, the sun and Venus, including their names and seals.

extending over a four-month period. The influence of this treatise can be seen in the 14th-century *Liber visionum* ('Book of Visions') of John of Morigny, as well as in other forms of Christianized magic, such as the *Ars Crucifixi* ('Art of the Crucifix'), attributed to the Majorcan hermit Pelagius (d. 1480), which provides a ritual of dream incubation in order to grant the earnest practitioner a vision of Christ during sleep.

Another influential treatise of angel magic is the *Liber iuratus Honorii* (*The Sworn Book of Honorius*), or *Liber sacer* ('Holy Book'), which probably originated in southern France in the 14th century. This work claims to provide a twenty-eight day ritual that will result in no less than the beatific vision, a vision of God in all His glory, as enjoyed by the blessed in heaven, although the complete Honorius ritual, which enables the operator to conjure spirits, requires seventy-two days! The prologue speaks of a general council of eighty-nine masters of magic from Naples, Athens and Toledo, who defend the magical art, and argues that the spirits invoked (good and bad) can be constrained by

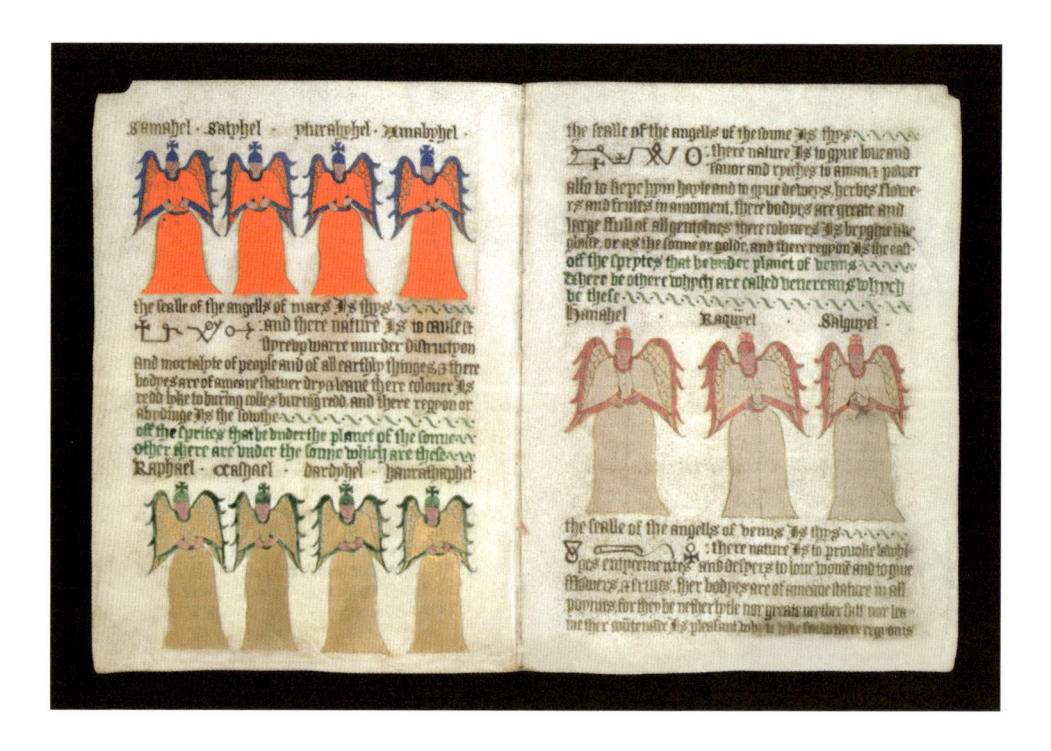

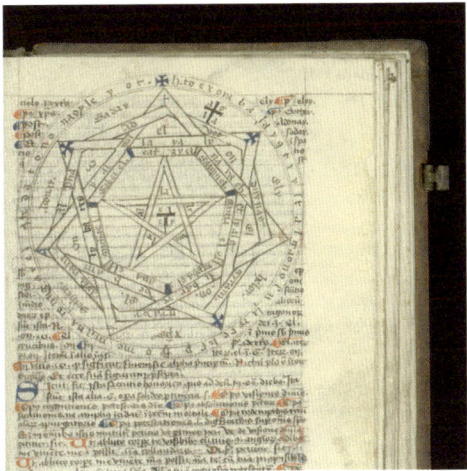

A pentagram (left) and a *Sigillum Dei* (right), from Berengarius Ganellus's *Summa sacre magice* (1346) *This copy of Ganellus's compendium of magic, now part of the University of Kassel's collection, was once owned by the 16th-century English magus John Dee.*

pure men. Then follows a detailed set of instructions for fashioning a *Sigillum Dei* (Seal of God) – vital for both the protection of the magus and the control of spirits – directions for the rituals of consecration, and the requisite prayers and invocation of a set of around one hundred divine names, so that the operator can conjure angels and demons for various purposes. The highest activity is the *opus visionis divine* (work of divine vision), an operation leading to the radical transformation of the practitioner through a vision of God while still in mortal frame. Other parts of the manual include rituals for conjuring planetary, aerial and terrestrial spirits, the construction of a magic circle, and the use of magical equipment (such as a hazel wand, swords or a whistle) and *voces magicae* (magical words or names). Significant parts of this material are also found in the impressive 14th-century compendium of magic, the *Summa sacre magice* ('Compendium of Sacred Magic'), by the Catalan scholar Berengarius Ganellus, which similarly assures the operator that the use of the Seal of God will grant a vision of God, knowledge of God's power, the absolution of sins, sanctification and dignification over all spirits.

The other, potentially far more subversive form of ritual magic, *goētia*, frequently accused of idolatry, is described by Agrippa and Della Porta as dealing with foul, unclean spirits, wicked curiosities and unlawful

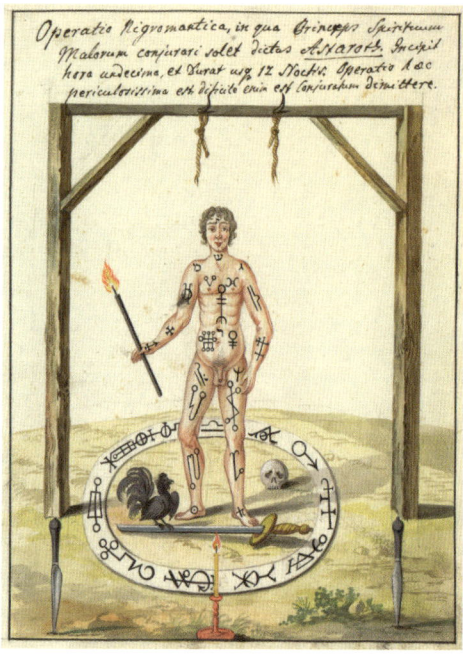

Necromancers in magic circles, from the *Compendium rarissimum totius Artis Magicae* (c. 1775)
Both circles have been constructed near gallows. The figure on the right, himself covered with magic symbols, is conjuring the demon Astaroth.

charms, detested by all good and learned men. It is most often associated with necromancy, a word adapted from the Latin *necromantia*, translated as 'divination by the dead'. The earliest description of such a ceremony dates back to the 7th century BCE, in Homer's *Odyssey*, where the enchantress Circe advises Odysseus, king of Ithaca, to consult the ghost of the seer Tiresias in Hades concerning the best way home following the fall of Troy. *Pharsalia* (61 CE), by the Roman poet Lucan, introduces the notion of reanimation when the witch Erichtho pumps blood and magical herbs into the corpse of a soldier, and the biblical 1 Samuel 28:3–25 has the account of the Witch of Endor who summons the spirit of the prophet Samuel at the request of King Saul. Gradually, however, necromancy came to be understood as the conjuring of demonic beings (*nigromantia*), through practices inspired by religious rites of exorcism, with the intention of forcing them to do the operator's will. The aims of necromantic practitioners might range from locating hidden treasure and stolen goods (or identifying the thief), discovering secret information, gaining invisibility and creating illusions, to the more malign goals of manipulating human emotions, causing physical or mental harm, and dominating others to gratify sexual desires.

As with angel magic, necromantic rituals are derived from liturgy, with multiple invocations of God, the Virgin Mary, the saints and angels. The operations, loosely based on exorcism, conjure and bind demons through the power of the Christian operator, who has ritualistically prepared himself through a strict regimen of abstinence, prayer, confession, communion and penance. The 15th-century *Liber Consecrationum* ('Book of Consecrations') advises fasting and prayer, providing many examples of prayers filled with divine names and words of power, followed by conjurations of Satan, details of how to obtain knowledge from a magical mirror, lists of demons and extensive instructions for summoning spirits. What is far more visible in these goetic rites is the use of suffumigations, magic circles with pentagrams (used to protect the magician by restraining the spirits), astrological characters, demonic seals and the inclusion of an impressive array of *instrumenta magica*: the rings, mirrors, wands, swords, knives, lances and so forth that are found in such works as *The Key of Solomon*. In Trithemius's *Antipalus Maleficiorum* ('Adversary of Black Magic', published in 1605, nearly a century after

Magical equipment said to have belonged to John Dee
The collection of objects includes a crystal ball and obsidian mirror, for scrying, as well as a gold disc and three Seals of God for invoking spirits and angels.

his death), the German abbot included a list of 'all the prescribed books of the necromancers', beginning with *The Key of Solomon* and ending with Al-Kindi's *De radiis: A Theory of the Magical Art*. Perhaps contrary to Trithemius's intentions, the list was to become a valuable resource for anyone seeking to learn about the rich traditions of astral and ritual magic.

In the 17th century there appeared a compilation of magical works in a grimoire called the *Lemegeton* or *The Lesser Key of Solomon*, containing five books that cover the spectrum of ritual magic, from angelic to demonic: *Ars Goetia*, *Ars Theurgia-Goetia*, *Ars Paulina*, *Ars Almadel* and *Ars Notoria*. Some of this material could already be found in published sources, including Trithemius's *Steganographia* (c. 1499), Agrippa's *Three Books of Occult Philosophy*, Johann Weyer's *Pseudomonarchia Daemonum* (*The False Monarchy of Demons*, 1563 which is essentially a catalogue of demons and devils) and Johann Baptist Großschedel's *Calendarium Naturale Magicum Perpetuum* ('Perpetual Natural Magical Calendar', c. 1619). The *Ars Goetia* contains a famous list of seventy-two demons, each with their own sigil; while the *Ars Paulina*, attributed to the apostle Paul, contains prayers and magical figures to the Holy Trinity, to the Virgin Mary and angels, with names of angels and their respective seals, piously requesting (rather than arrogantly invoking) spirits, most notably the Holy Guardian Angel, to appear in a crystal stone. The *Ars Almadel* also involves crystallomancy (divination using crystals or a crystal ball) and represents an exceptionally unusual magical ritual with the promise of salvation, in which the magician is blessed with grace and saved from damnation after speaking to an angel conjured by means of an altar made of brass or wax (the *figura Almandal* or table of Solomon), a different colour of altar and candles being made depending on the zodiacal sign or season (white for spring; red for summer; green for autumn; black for winter).

Much of this material influenced later magical belief during the occult revivals of the 19th century and continues to be used by practitioners today.

Dr Johann Faust's *Magia naturalis et innaturalis* (1612)

This multi-volume manuscript contains many colour illustrations of demons and spirits, including Mephistopheles (row 2, far right), Anael (row 3, centre), Ariel (row 2, left and also row 4, left), together with lesser-known ones like Psohdon (with his bugs and reptiles), Laoobis (with the stag and hunting dogs) and Apadiel (in the leopard skin).

LA PLUS FORTE POUSSÉE DE L'INFLATION DEPUIS 54 ANS
L'UMP EN COLÈRE CONTRE LA SUSPENSION DES OGM
LA FRANCE VA INSTALLER PLUSIEURS CENTAINES D'HOMMES DES TROIS ARMES À ABU DHABI AU COEUR DU PROCHE ORIENT
MERCREDI 16 JANVIER 2008
LE FIGARO
L'ARMÉE FRANÇAISE OUVRE UNE BASE DANS LE GOLFE
IRAN
Golfe Persique
Détroit d'Ormuz
Abu Dhabi
EMIRATS ARABES UNIS
ARABIE SAOUDITE
SURVIVRE AVEC LES LOUPS
UN FILM ÉMOUVANT
UNE HISTOIRE VRAI
RECENSEMENT: NOUS SOMMES 63,7 MILLIONS DE FRANÇAIS
DÉLINQUANCE: COUP D'ARRÊT AUX
DE DÉGRADATION
ANGELA MERKEL A PRIS SES DISTANCES
DE MERKEL ET SARKOZY
NUCLÉAIRE CIVIL POUR LES PAYS ARABES
AU NOM DE QUOI LES PAYS ARABES DEVRAIENT-ILS ÊTRE PRIVÉS DE L'ÉNERGIE DU FUTUR ?
TÉLÉVISION: LES RÉVÉLATIONS
L'IDENTITÉ DE LA JOCONDE ENFIN PROUVÉE

CHAPTER THREE

OCCULT REVIVAL

OCCULTISM — 1

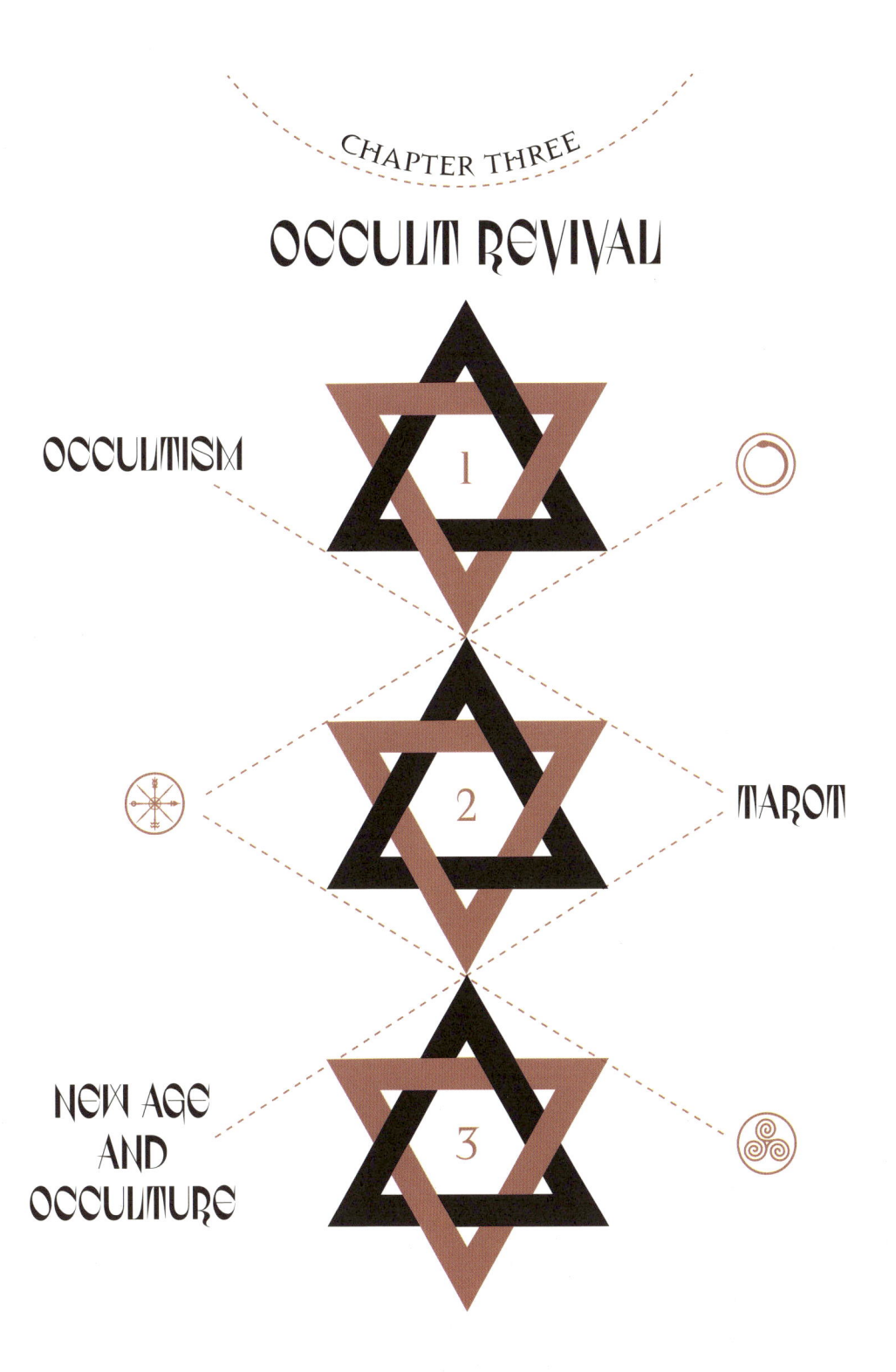

2 — **TAROT**

NEW AGE AND OCCULTURE — 3

/rɪˈvaɪvəl/noun
An instance of something becoming popular, active or important again.

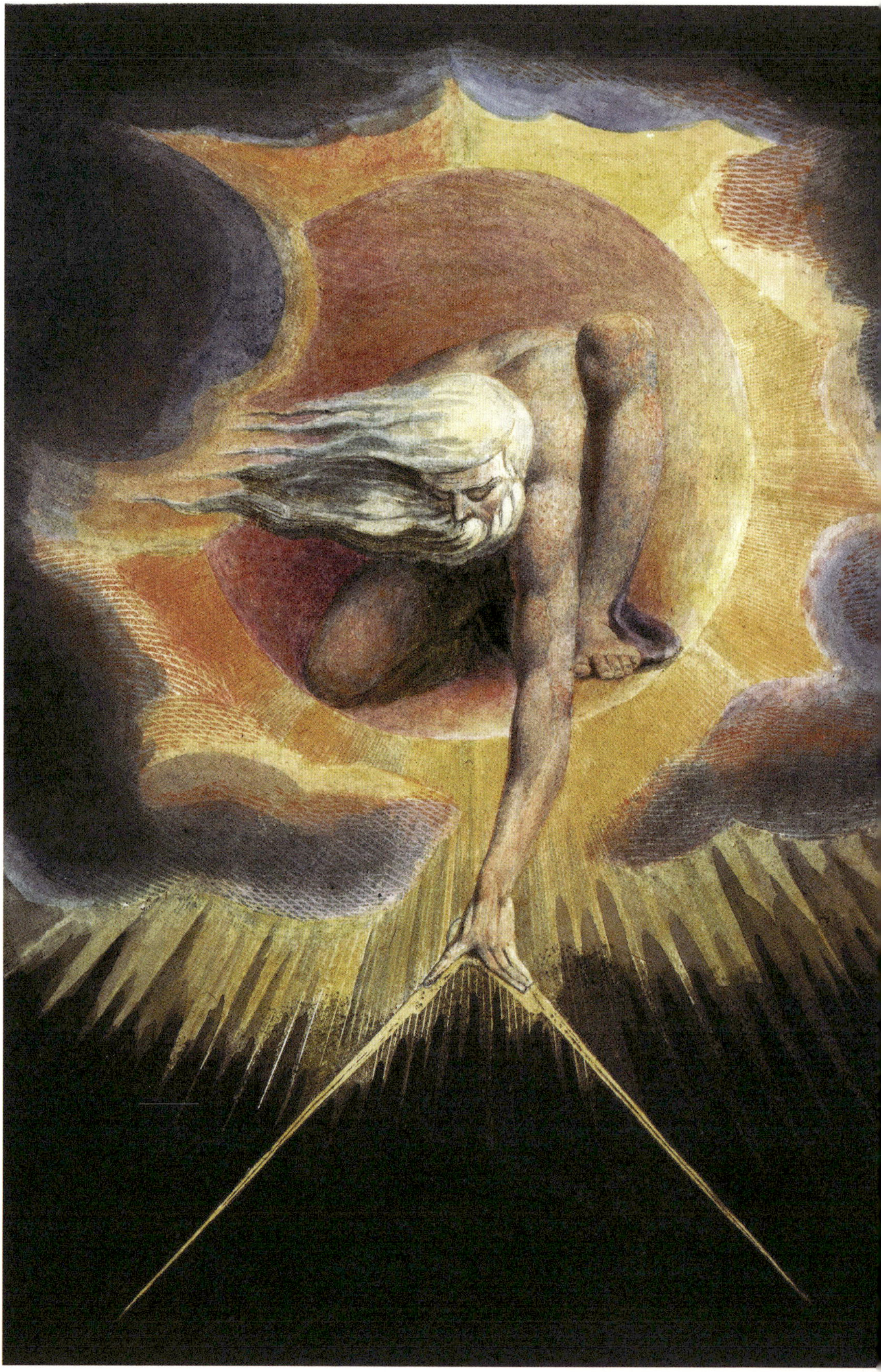

'There are two Paths to the Innermost: the Way of the Mystic, which is the way of devotion and meditation, a solitary and subjective path; and the way of the occultist, which is the way of the intellect, of concentration, and of the trained will.'

DION FORTUNE, ESOTERIC ORDERS AND THEIR WORK (1928)

OCCULTISM

Although public interest in occult philosophy declined during the Enlightenment, it survived in Masonic lodges and experienced a revival in the 19th century, initially in France, but later in the United States and England, with the foundation of organizations like the Theosophical Society. Occultism drew on earlier material, but added new dimensions, such as an enthusiasm for spiritualism.

Occultism emerged during the mid-19th century French occult revival, popularized through the writings of Alphonse Louis Constant, better known by his pseudonym Éliphas Lévi, and was then adopted and promoted by two major organizations, the Theosophical Society and the Hermetic Order of the Golden Dawn.

Expressions of renewed interest in the occult were already visible in the 18th century. One important innovator was the Swedish scientist and mystic Emanuel Swedenborg, who with a background in science and technology, and having conducted many studies of metallurgy, anatomy and physiology, was in many ways a paragon of the Enlightenment. Then in the 1740s he began to experience waking visions and dream conversations with angelic beings, giving him new insights into the relationships between the physical and spiritual worlds, and culminating with an episode in 1745 during which he claimed to have been admitted into the kingdom of God 'by the Messiah Himself'. He abandoned his worldly pursuits, devoted himself to uncovering the inner meaning of scripture, and recorded his experiences of this spiritual dimension for the rest of his life, publishing several influential works. *De Coelo et ejus Mirabilibus et de Inferno* (*Heaven and Hell*, 1758) is arguably his best-known work, but one of the most controversial must surely be *De Telluribus in Mundo Nostro Solari, quæ vocantur Planetæ* (*Earths in our Solar System, which Are Called Planets*, 1758), in which he claimed to have spoken with spirits from the other planets, including worlds beyond our solar system. Three 'extraordinary occurrences' of clairvoyance have been recorded about Swedenborg. The first and most famous is his vision while in Gothenburg in 1759 of a fire 300 miles away in Stockholm; the second, his knowledge of the contents of a secret letter to the Queen of Sweden from her younger brother; and the third, the assistance he provided to the widow of the Dutch ambassador in finding a lost receipt, when its location was known only by her deceased husband. Swedenborg's ideas were to have an influence on many, including the development of Freemasonry.

⟨ *page 176*
Suzanne Treister,
Le Figaro (16 January 2008), from the series
Alchemy (2007–8)
This series of eighty-two works transcribes front pages of international daily newspapers into early modern alchemical engravings to explore the notion of man's power to transform.

⟨ *page 178*
William Blake,
The Ancient of Days, 1794
Ancient of Days is one of God's names in the Book of Daniel, found also in the Zohar and Kabbala denudata, although Blake related the name to the character Urizen in his mythological prophetic Book of Urizen (1794), the oppressive embodiment of conventional reason and religious dogma. This etching is the frontispiece of Blake's Europe: A Prophecy.

English occultist Aleister Crowley in ceremonial garb, early 1920s

The closed hands at Crowley's temples, with thumbs facing outwards, are meant to resemble the horns of the god Pan. They are said to create the ritual sign of the letter 'O' in the word N.O.X. (the Night of Pan), a concept of Crowley's Thelema: the state of ego-death in spiritual attainment. The symbol on his hat is the Eye of Providence or all-seeing eye of God, although here it may represent the eye of the Egyptian god Horus.

Anonymous (possibly Claude-Louis Desrais), *Untitled*, c. 1778–84
This oil painting captures a scene of mesmeric therapy. On the left a figure perched on a tabletop winds a magnetized rope around his head in order to transmit magnetic energies to those seated around the table. On the right Franz Anton Mesmer seems to be touching a friar with a magnetic wand.

The second pioneer was the German physician Franz Anton Mesmer, who is most famous for his theory of animal magnetism, a universal invisible fluid or force that he believed could be found in all living things. Mesmer, who had investigated the influence of the planets on the human body in the 1780s, argued that illnesses, especially nervous disorders, were due to a disturbance or blockage of the fluid's movement. He developed a new style of healing known as mesmerism, which involved making magnetic passes over a patient's body in order to restore the correct flow of energy. This provoked a healing 'crisis', with convulsions and fainting often taken as visible symptoms, after which the patient's natural bodily order was believed to be recovered. One of Mesmer's followers, the Marquis de Puységur (1751–1825), in refining these techniques by paying more attention to his patients' mental and emotional states, discovered that one of the effects of this mesmeric treatment was a deep sleeping trance. In this state, one particular patient, a young field worker, Victor Race, was even able to read the thoughts of the magnetizer and describe other

Swiss psychiatrist Carl Gustav Jung, the founder of depth psychology, 1960
Jung's fascination with occult themes, in particular alchemy, was instrumental in the revival of interest in these subjects in the mid-20th century.

people's medical problems and prescribe treatment. Puységur called this effect 'artificial somnambulism' or 'magnetic sleep'. Other responses in patients included suggestibility, lack of recollection about experiences in the sleeping state upon waking, and an elevation of alertness and self-confidence, phenomena now associated with hypnotism (which first appeared as the term *neurohypnotism* in 1842). His procedure was used in hospital to heal the sick, and even to perform surgery and amputations on soldiers on the battlefield. In some cases, it was said to have provoked second sight and the gift of prophecy. This phenomenon lies at the origin of the new disciplines of psychology and psychiatry, its influence evident in the work of the Swiss psychologists Théodore Flournoy (1854–1920) and Carl Jung (1875–1961), whose research into the psychology of the occult appeared in *From India to the Planet Mars* (1900) and *On the Psychology and Pathology of So-called Occult Phenomena* (1902), respectively.

Other forerunners of occultism include Ebenezer Sibly (1751–99), an English mesmerist, physician, Freemason and astrologer who contributed to the

Catherine and Margaretta Fox, New York, c. 1852
These two sisters from Hydesville, New York, became famous for their role in the birth of spiritualism. In March 1848, they claimed to have heard strange 'rapping' sounds in their cottage, which was reputed to be haunted, and word soon spread. Their accounts of communications with spirits helped to spark a spiritualism craze in the USA and Europe.

renewed fascination with the occult in his *New and Complete Illustration of the Celestial Science of Astrology* (1784–92) and *A Key to Physic, and the Occult Sciences* (1794). One form of astrology, 'mundane' or 'political' astrology, deals not with individuals but with the government of nations, states, or cities. Sibly is perhaps best known for his horoscope commemorating the Declaration of Independence of the United States of America on 4 July 1776, in which he promotes the relevance of occult insight into political matters. Following in Sibly's footsteps, Francis Barrett (c. 1770–c. 1802) rekindled an interest in Hermetic–Cabalist magic with his compilation of material, mostly from Agrippa's *Three Books of Occult Philosophy*, published as *The Magus, or Celestial Intelligencer* (1801).

One of the major new occult developments in the 19th century, spiritualism, was influenced by the somnambulist trance states of mesmerism. Spiritualism first appeared in Hydesville, New York, in 1848, when two sisters, 10-year-old Catherine Fox (1837–1892) and 14-year-old Margaretta Fox (1833–93), claimed to hear 'rapping' sounds in their house, supposedly from a poltergeist, the spirit of a man buried in their basement, and very rapidly a new movement developed around them. By 1852 it had already spread to France. Spiritualists sought

Séance scene from
Dr Mabuse, der Spieler,
1922
Fritz Lang directed this epic silent movie, known in English as Dr Mabuse, The Gambler. *The film follows the antics of the eponymous villain, a gambler, hypnotist, master of disguise and all-round criminal mastermind.*

connections between the living and the dead, and looked for concrete evidence of an afterlife; in search of consolation and to connect with deceased loved ones. Related to this is spiritism, codified and presented as a religious and philosophical doctrine independent of spiritualism in 1857 by the French educator Hippolyte Léon Denizard Rivail (1804–69), better known by his pen name Allan Kardec. He was the author of *Le Livre des Esprits* (*The Spirits' Book*), a work that he claimed was dictated to him by the 'Spirit of Truth', which introduced the doctrine of spiritual evolution and perfection through successive incarnations. Both spiritualism and spiritism have a strong Christian perspective, although Kardec considered spiritism a practice that originated in antiquity, with Pythagoras as a precursor. Kardec's spiritism continues to be practised in Brazil, alongside related Afro-Brazilian practices of spirit possession in African diasporic religions like Umbanda and Candomblé, as well as Afro-Caribbean Santería, each of which is a syncretic mixture of traditional West African religions and Roman Catholicism.

Over the following decades, the mesmeric seers in their French salons were to give way to spiritualist

DECODING LEVI'S BAPHOMET

The Baphomet was originally connected with the Knights Templar in the Middle Ages, but reappears in the 19th-century French occult revival in Éliphas Lévi's *Dogme et rituel de la haute magie* (*The Dogma and Ritual of High Magic*, 1854–56, volume 2). Lévi introduces it as the 'Sabbatic Goat' Baphomet and describes it as the 'sphinx of the occult sciences'. Baphomet represents the absolute, the equilibrium of opposites: it is half-human, half-goat, both male and female, darkness and light, good and evil. The Baphomet was an important figure for Aleister Crowley, who writes in *Magick: Liber ABA, Book 4* (1912–13) that it is the divine androgyne, the hieroglyph of arcane perfection, an embodiment of the principle of 'As Above, So Below'. In the Creed of the Gnostic Mass, the central rite of Crowley's Ordo Templi Orientis, he included the words 'And I believe in the Serpent and the Lion, Mystery of Mysteries, in His name BAPHOMET'. Lévi's image alludes to Heinrich Khunrath's Alchemical Hermaphrodite in the *Amphitheatre of Eternal Wisdom* (1595/1609).

1.

HEAD
The upward-pointing pentagram on Baphomet's forehead is a symbol of the light. Between his horns shines the flame of intelligence, magical light of universal balance, the image of the soul elevated above matter.

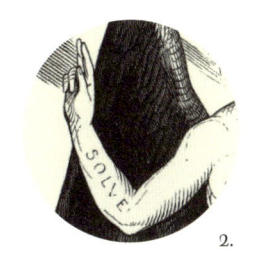

2.

ARMS
The arms – one masculine, the other feminine – bear the words 'Solve' and 'Coagula', alluding to the alchemical maxim *Solve et Coagula* ('Dissolve and Coagulate'). This is taken from Heinrich Khunrath's image of the Alchemical Hermaphrodite in the *Amphitheatre of Eternal Wisdom*.

3.

HANDS
The Baphomet's hands make the 'sign of occultism'. One hand points upwards to the white moon of the kabbalistic *sefira* of Chesed (Mercy), and the other downwards to the black moon of Geburah (Strength), expressing the perfect harmony of mercy with justice.

4.

SEAT
The cube on which Baphomet is seated is a symbol of earth, while the sphere on which Baphomet's hooves rest presumably represents the terrestrial globe, as it does in Khunrath's engraving.

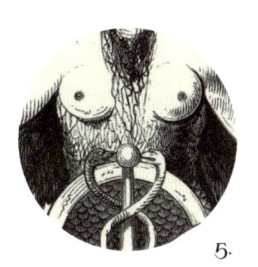

5.

BREASTS AND CADUCEUS
Baphomet has two breasts, which represent the feminine and humanity, but a phallic caduceus, the staff of Hermes with its two snakes, which symbolizes eternal life, as well as the union of opposites.

6.

SCALES AND WINGS
The scales on Baphomet's lower torso symbolize the element of water, the semi-circle above represents the atmosphere, and the large feathery wings signify volatile spirit and the element of air.

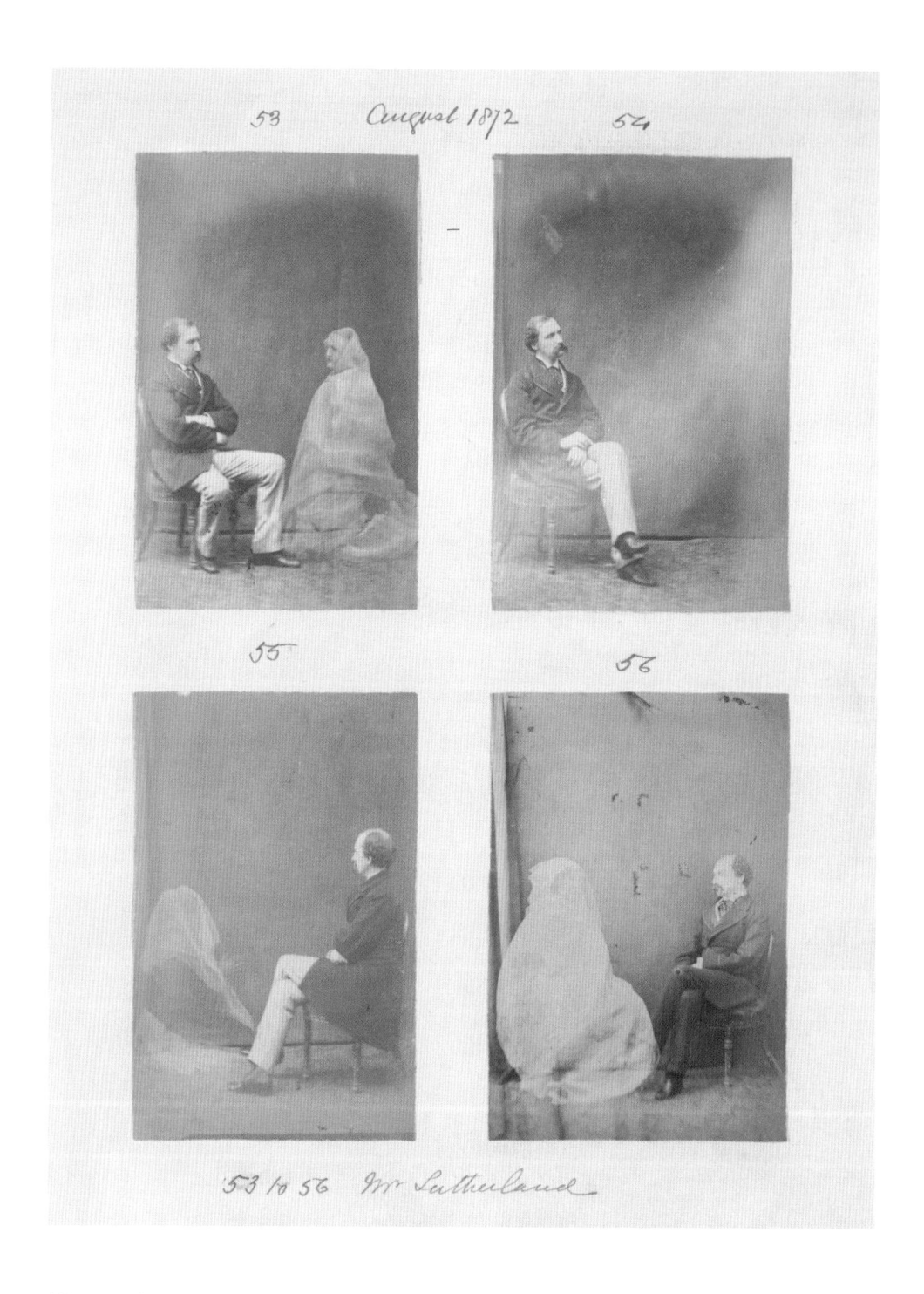

Album of spirit photographs by Frederick Augustus Hudson, 1872

Hudson is considered to be the first spirit photographer in Britain. He worked with the early abstract artist and medium Georgiana Houghton, who published his photographs in Chronicles of the Photographs of Spiritual Beings and Phenomena Invisible to the Material Eye *(1882).*

mediums, sensitives and psychics in séance rooms. These intermediaries between the living and the dead, or discarnate entities, provided a platform for communication that centred on manifestations of paranormal phenomena. This might involve the clairvoyant ability to gain information by extrasensory perception, telepathy, precognition and retrocognition (respectively, knowledge of a future or a past event that could not have been learnt by conventional means) and the out-of-body experience of astral travel, as well as automatic writing, telekinesis, ectoplasmic materializations, the production of sounds without any apparent physical cause, such as the ringing of bells, as well as table-tapping or table-turning in order for the dead to communicate with the living. Spiritualist séances became a popular activity in America and Europe, enabling people to contact the invisible world and explore the possibility of survival after death outside the authority of the church.

In France, the occult revival – especially the rebirth of magic – was spearheaded by Éliphas Lévi, who was inspired by the German Cabalist Knorr von Rosenroth's *Kabbala denudata*, as well as the works of writers such as Agrippa, Boehme and Swedenborg. On a visit to England in 1854, Lévi allegedly invoked the spirit of the ancient magus, religious leader and famous wonder-worker Apollonius of Tyana (fl. 1st century CE). He is the author of several influential modern books on magic, including *Dogme et Rituel de la Haute Magie* (*The Dogma and Ritual of High Magic*, 1854–56), *Histoire de la Magie* (*The History of Magic*, 1860) and *La Clef des Grands Mystères* (*The Key of the Mysteries*, 1861), as well as posthumously published works such as *Le Grand Arcane, ou l'Occultisme Dévoilé* (*The Great Secret, or Occultism Unveiled*, 1898). Lévi integrated new elements into the occult philosophy of previous centuries, most notably perhaps the divinatory system of the tarot and awareness of Eastern forms of wisdom. Occultists had a tendency to distinguish their practices from their spiritualist contemporaries, displaying far more interest in, for example, elemental beings and angels, or discarnate masters, than the spirits of the dead.

Pages from Éliphas Lévi's *Clavicules de Salomon* (1860)

This is Éliphas Lévi's personal copy, in French, of the Clavicula Salomonis, *a grimoire attributed to the biblical King Solomon, who had a reputation for being able to control demons. It is illustrated by Lévi and written in his own hand. The drawing on the left is labelled 'Pantheistic Figure of Baphomet', while the one on the right is described as a 'Hermetic Pentacle of Extraordinary Experiments'.*

Madame Blavatsky, one of the leading lights of the 19th-century occult revival, had been involved in spiritualism but had grown disillusioned, finding inspiration instead in medieval and early modern occult philosophy and the growing interest in Eastern thought, especially Hinduism and Buddhism. The Theosophical Society that she co-founded in New York in 1875 was to become the most influential occultist organization for the next fifty years. Blavatsky promoted her synthesis of Eastern and Western traditions as an alternative to conventional Christianity and positivist science in two major works, *Isis Unveiled* of 1877 and *The Secret Doctrine* of 1888, as well as countless articles, two of which are of particular note in this context, 'Practical Occultism' and 'Occultism versus the Occult Arts', both published in 1888. In the first of these articles, she identifies theosophy and occult sciences, respectively, as theoretical and practical occultism, emphasizing that occultism is focused on the inner man, freed from the dominion of the physical body and its surroundings. In the second article she rejects the occult sciences – especially magic – as sorcery, because they concern themselves with the material world and ego-orientated

Madame Blavatsky, 1889
Born into a Russian aristocratic family, Blavatsky travelled widely in her younger years, and it was her accounts of spiritual enlightenment during her travels that initially brought her to public attention. She was one of the founders of the Theosophical Society in New York in 1875.

Rudolf Steiner, *c.* **1905**
Austrian occultist and self-professed clairvoyant Rudolf Steiner became General Secretary of the German branch of the Theosophical Society in 1902 and went on to establish the spiritual movement anthroposophy, founding the Anthroposophical Society in 1912.

goals, the desire for possession and power, as opposed to true occultism (or theosophy), which is about the inner world and renunciation of self. One must choose, she says, between 'the life of the world and the life of Occultism'. Blavatsky became a central figure in the promotion of occultism and her Theosophical Society influenced the development of other organizations, including the Hermetic Brotherhood of Luxor (1894) and the Hermetic Order of the Golden Dawn (1888), both founded in Britain. The Austrian occultist Rudolf Steiner (1861–1925), who was appointed as General Secretary of the German section of the Theosophical Society in 1902, broke away from the theosophists to found the Anthroposophical Society in 1912, which focused far more on Christian esoteric traditions. Steiner was a prolific author, numbering *Geheimwissenschaft im Umriss* ('An Outline of Occult Science', 1910) among his many works. In this book, he expounds an approach to knowledge that seeks to free the scientific method and spirit of research so that it

Januarius (January),
Calendrier magique
(for the year 1896), 1895

This magical calendar features lithographs by Italian art nouveau illustrator Manuel Orazi and text by French journalist and folklorist Austin de Croze. Note the presence of Lévi's Baphomet presiding over a sabbath of witches, as well as references to astrology and Solomonic magic.

becomes open and receptive to the non-sensible world. On the basis of his own clairvoyant experiences he argues that, behind the visible world that we readily perceive, there is an invisible, hidden world where unexplained phenomena occur; he encourages his readers to bridge the gap between these two realms by developing spiritual forces within themselves.

While the French occult revival had its origins in the writings of Lévi, it did not become a fully fledged social force until the 1880s. The principal character in this was a young medical student Gérard Encausse, better known by his nom de plume, Papus (meaning 'physician'). Papus was originally a member of Madame Blavatsky's Theosophical Society, but left in 1890 to establish his own Groupe Indépendant d'Études Ésotériques in Paris, becoming one of the leaders of a new French occult movement, based on the Judeo-Christian traditions and the wisdom of ancient Egypt, rather than on the Eastern traditions of Hinduism and Buddhism. He was a prolific author of many works on the occult, including *Traité élémentaire de magie pratique* ('Elementary Treatise on Practical Magic', 1893) and what was to become a classic of late 19th-century occultism, his encyclopedic *Traité méthodique de science occulte* ('Methodical Treatise on Occult Science', 1891), both of which helped generate popular interest. Another influential figure, Marquis Marie Victor Stanislas de Guaita, wrote a series of works informed by his knowledge of the occult traditions, beginning with *Au seuil du mystère* (*At the Threshold of Mystery*, 1886), which made esoteric knowledge more widely available to the general public. In 1888 he founded the Kabbalistic Order of the Rose-Cross, the first occult society in France.

Around the same time, on the other side of the Channel, the Hermetic Order of the Golden Dawn was formed. Its initiates, both men and women, were responsible for creating the groundwork of much of what constitutes modern ritual magic, with a particular emphasis on theurgy and spiritual development. The group's teachings made a huge impact, and although the Order dissolved in 1903 due

Louis Le Breton, *Astaroth* (left) and *Flauros* (right), two demons from the *Dictionnaire Infernal* (1863)

First published in 1818, the Dictionnaire Infernal was written by the French occultist and demonologist Jacques Collin de Plancy and had several editions. The most famous is that of 1863, which features sixty-nine illustrations by Louis Le Breton.

to internal conflicts, it was immensely influential on 20th-century Western occultism. One of the founding members, the Master Mason Samuel Liddell MacGregor Mathers, was the author of almost all of the important Golden Dawn teachings, rituals and documents, and translated and made accessible such significant works as *The Kabbalah Unveiled*, *The Key of Solomon* and *The Lesser Key of Solomon: Goetia*, which are still of great relevance today. Another influential figure, Arthur Edward Waite, Grand Master of the Golden Dawn and later founder of the Fellowship of the Rosy Cross (formed in 1915), wrote many works on Rosicrucianism, Kabbalah, alchemy and magic, as well as publishing translations of related material. One of Waite's first publications was a digest of the writings of Éliphas Lévi, *The Mysteries of Magic* (1886), followed a decade later by an edited translation of Lévi's *Dogme et Rituel de la Haute Magie* under the title *Transcendental Magic: Its Doctrine and Ritual*.

Aleister Crowley was also a prominent member of the Golden Dawn, but was expelled in 1900 for trying to take over the Isis-Urania temple in London. In 1907 he formed the magical order of the A∴A∴ or *Argenteum Astrum* ('Silver Star'), which combined Golden Dawn ceremonial magic with Eastern

Stele (*c*. 680–670 BCE) of the Egyptian priest Ankh-ef-en-Khonsu, discovered in Cairo in 1858
It includes material from the Egyptian Book of the Dead. *In 1904 Aleister Crowley, who commissioned a facsimile, named it the 'Stele of Revealing' and identified the figures as the three chief deities of Thelema: Nuit, Hadit and Ra-Hoor-Khuit.*

Aleister Crowley poses with the facsimile 'Stele of Revealing' and magical weapons, 1912

practices, before eventually joining the Ordo Templi Orientis (Order of the Temple of the East) in the early 1910s. At the O.T.O. he revised the Golden Dawn's ritual system by incorporating sexual magic, styling himself as the 'Great Beast 666' of the Apocalypse, and prophet of a new religious movement, Thelema, whose foundational text, *The Book of the Law*, had been dictated to him in Egypt in 1909 by the non-corporeal entity Aiwass. The classical Greek word *thelēma* translates as 'will' or 'desire' and the essence of Crowley's doctrine is found in three declarations appearing in *The Book of the Law*. The first of these, the 'Law of Thelema' – 'Do what thou wilt shall be the whole of the Law' – urges the Thelemite to seek their own true path. The other two declarations, 'Every man and every woman is a star' and 'Love is the law, love under will', reinforce this sense of self-power and self-determination. Among Crowley's other principal works are the *Holy Books of Thelema* (1909), which includes the foundational text for Thelema, and his later *Magick in Theory and Practice* (1929), a fusion of Golden Dawn material and yogic practice, in which Crowley defines the object of all ritual magic as the unity of the microcosm and the macrocosm, the highest and most complete example of this being the invocation of one's Holy Guardian Angel, leading to union with God. His last book, *Magick Without Tears*, which was written in the 1940s but published posthumously in 1954, seven years after his death, takes the form of eighty letters to students of 'magick' (his preferred spelling for his own system of occult practice), which Crowley defines as 'the Science and Art of causing Change to occur in conformity with Will'. Thelema was (and continues to be) a powerful influence on occultism, inspiring modern Wicca and aspects of Satanism, as well as the postmodern practices of chaos magick (which seeks to remove, for example, the Judeo-Christian religious elements of magical practice and even challenges the notion of a single, unified system).

Other well-known Golden Dawn members were the Irish poet and dramatist W. B. Yeats (1865–1939) and Sir Arthur Conan Doyle (1859–1930), creator of the fictional detective Sherlock Holmes. In the 1930s, the British-American occultist Israel Regardie (1907–85), who for a time worked as personal secretary to Crowley, added psychologized interpretations to ritual practice, influenced by the ideas of the Austrian psychoanalyst Wilhelm Reich (1897–1957), famous for coining the phrase 'the sexual revolution', and the depth psychologist Carl Jung, who developed influential theories of the collective unconscious, the four archetypes (The Persona, The Shadow, The Anima/Animus, The Self) and synchronicity. Regardie published works inspired by Qabalah, magic and alchemy, including *The Tree of Life: A Study in Magic* (1932) and *The Middle Pillar: The Balance Between Mind and Magic* (1938), and controversially made public the secret teachings of the Golden Dawn in four volumes (1937–40), collectively titled *The Golden Dawn: The Original Account of the Teachings, Rites, and Ceremonies of the Hermetic Order*.

Double cube altar, based on a design by Aleister Crowley and developed by Steffi Grant, c. late 1940s

Steffi Grant was co-founder of the Typhonian Order with her husband Kenneth, a ceremonial magician and writer, and the personal secretary of Aleister Crowley. The top of the altar has a human figure in concentric coloured circles, resembling an engraving from Fludd's Utriusque Cosmi Historia (1617-21), the upper sections of the four sides relate to the elements, while the lower sections contain the Enochian tablets.

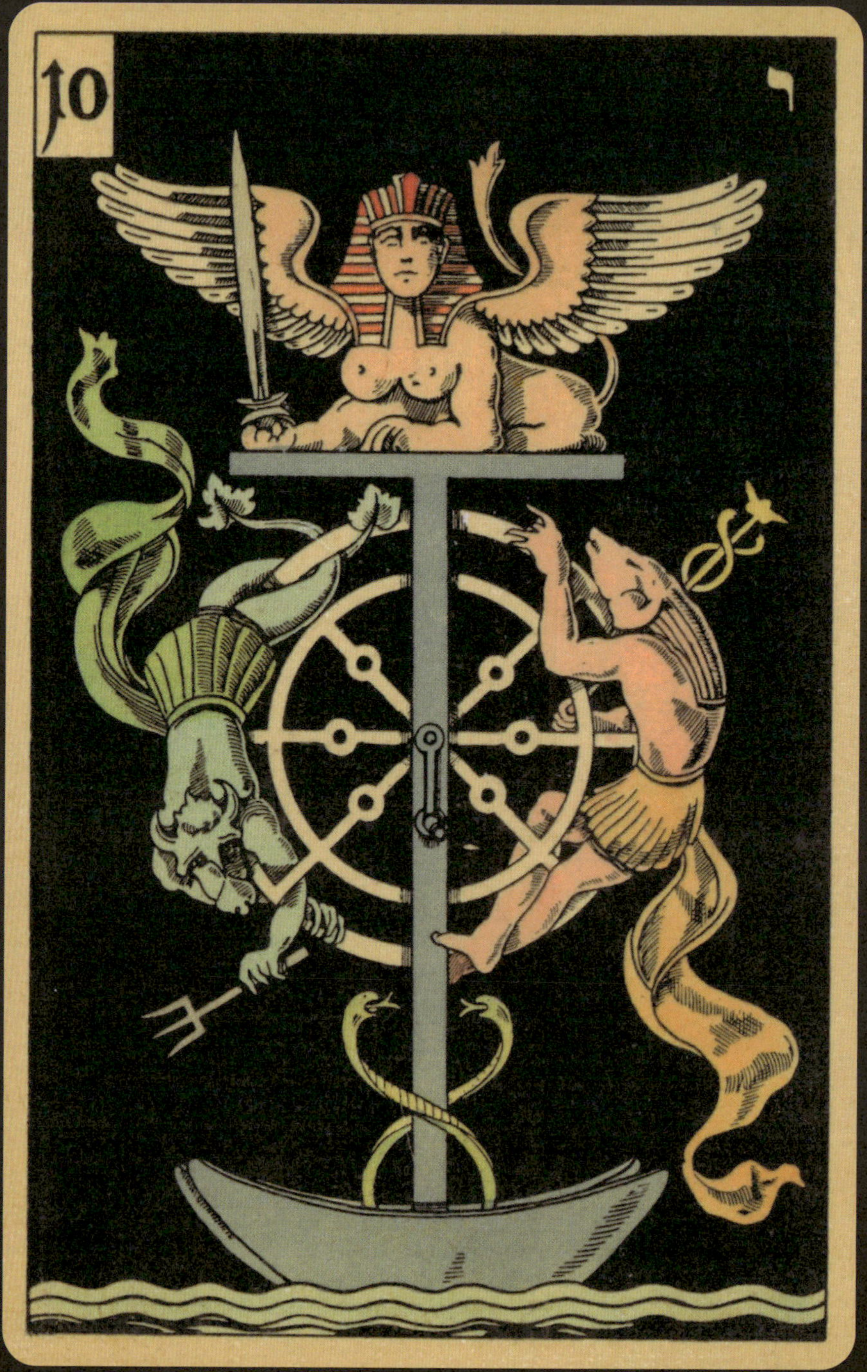
10
י

'An imprisoned person with no other book than the Tarot, if he knew how to use it, could in a few years acquire universal knowledge, and would be able to speak on all subjects with unequalled learning and inexhaustible eloquence.'

ÉLIPHAS LÉVI, *TRANSCENDENTAL MAGIC: ITS DOCTRINE AND RITUAL* (1854–56)

TAROT

One of the new developments of the occult revival was the transformation of the tarot from the game that had been played since its origins in 15th-century Italy into an occult practice. The 19th century introduced romantic theories of tarot's origins in ancient Egypt and gave rise to the creation of new occult decks, rich in esoteric symbolism and used for both self-discovery, the cultivation of the powers of the imagination, and as a tool for divination.

We have already touched on various divinatory or 'mantic' arts in the context of the medieval and early modern periods, from the natural magical practice of chiromancy (palm-reading, see pp. 238–39) to supernatural forms of magic, such as necromancy (divination through the spirits of the dead), and scrying with crystal balls (crystallomancy) or mirrors (catoptromancy) in order to communicate with spirits, be that angels or demons. Here we shall focus on a form of divination closely connected with occultism: the tarot.

The earliest known hand-painted tarot cards were produced for the Italian nobility. There is no consensus on their dates, although most scholars agree that they date from around the middle of the 15th century. No one deck survives complete, but the three most intact are linked with the Dukes of Milan: the Visconti de Modrone (67 cards) and Brambilla (48 cards) decks, created for Duke Filippo Maria Visconti (1392–1447), and the Visconti–Sforza Tarocchi (74 cards), which may have been commissioned by Duke Filippo as a commemorative gift for the marriage in 1441 of his daughter Bianca Maria Visconti (1425–68) to Francesco Sforza (1401–66), who was to be his successor as Duke of Milan. All three decks are believed to have been created by the Milanese court painter Bonifacio Bembo (1420–*c.* 1480). Tarot decks generally have seventy-eight cards: twenty-two trumps or major arcana and fifty-six minor arcana. The minor arcana are divided into four suits, in a similar way to standard playing cards, which are commonly called Wands, Swords, Cups and Pentacles. Each suit has ten numbered cards, from Ace to 10, indicated by the number of swords, for example, on the card, plus four court cards (king, queen, knight and page). The twenty-two *trionfi*, or trumps, of the major arcana are unique to tarot and represent archetypal characters or situations. The cards' titles and even their sequence can vary, but one of the most common sequences is: 0 Fool, 1 Magician, 2 High Priestess, 3 Empress, 4 Emperor, 5 Hierophant, 6 Lovers, 7 Chariot, 8 Justice, 9 Hermit, 10 Wheel of Fortune, 11 Strength, 12 Hanged Man, 13 Death, 14 Temperance, 15 Devil, 16 Tower, 17 Star, 18 Moon,

< *page 198*
Pierre de Lasenic (Petr Pavel Kohout) and Vladislav Kužel, The Wheel of Fortune, Lasenikuv Tarot, 1938
This tarot deck, inspired by Oswald Wirth's 1889 major arcana deck Les 22 Arcanes du Tarot Kabbalistique, was designed by the Czech occultist Pierre de Lasenic (from drawings by Vladislav Kužel) for members of the Czech Hermetic society Horev-Club, to be used with Lasenic's book, Tarot: The Key to Initiation *(1939).*

Bonifacio Bembo, cards from the Visconti–Sforza Tarocchi, 15th century

Although a full deck of the Visconti-Sforza Tarocchi has not survived, enough cards remain to give a sense of the beauty of the designs, some of which are quite different from current popular decks. Shown on the top row, from left to right, are The Fool, The Hermit and Death, and on the bottom row Temperance, The Knight of Swords and The Magician. Note how The Hermit, for example, is holding an hour-glass instead of a lantern.

Tarot engravings of The Magician and The Fool, from Antoine Court de Gébelin's *Monde primitif* (1781) *These sketches of two of the major arcana cards are included in plates at the very end of the eighth volume of* Monde primitif. *They represent Card 1,* Le Joueur de Gobelets *(Player of Cups), or* Bateleur *(Sleight-of-hand Street-Magician), on the left, and Card 0, The Fool, on the right.*

19 Sun, 20 Judgment, 21 World. Tarot readers generally make use of the full 78-card deck in divinatory readings, but some focus on the major arcana; nowadays many tarot artists produce 'majors only' decks.

While examples of cartomancy, or fortune-telling, with packs of cards date back to at least the 16th century as a form of oracular casting of lots, and tarot cards have been produced and used as a card game since the 15th century, it was not until the 18th century that the tarot deck began to be used for divination. The driving force behind this is generally considered to be the Swiss-born Freemason Antoine Court de Gébelin (1725–84), who included an essay 'Du Jeu des Tarots' ('On the Game of Tarots', 1781) in his multi-volume *Monde primitif, analysé et comparé avec le monde moderne* ('The Primitive World, Analysed and Compared with the Modern World', 1773–84). There he made influential (albeit inaccurate) claims as to the antiquity of the tarot, dating it back to ancient Egypt: ancient Egyptian priests, he argued, had preserved their wisdom in the images on the cards, disguising

The Devil (here The Black Magician) and The Empress, from Frank Glahn's Deutsches Original-Tarot, 1924
This small-size deck is interesting for its highly Egyptian style of imagery together with its use of a letter of the Hebrew alphabet (in the top left corner of each major arcana card) and a Germanic rune (in the top right corner), with divinatory meanings included.

it as a game, which was kept safe over the centuries and spread throughout Europe by the travelling community. Although Jean-François Champollion (1790–1832) was not to publish his first breakthrough in deciphering the hieroglyphs in the Rosetta Stone until 1822, this did not prevent predecessors from speculating. Court de Gébelin considered the word 'tarot' to be derived from the Egyptian words 'Tar' ('road' or 'way') and 'Ro' ('king' or 'royal'), giving the meaning 'royal road of life', and described the 'atouts' (French for trump cards), beginning with The Fool. He then proceeded to explain how to use the cards as a game, with a section on the tarot as a game of political geography (for example, with each suit associated with a different part of the world: Swords–Asia; Wands–Egypt; Cups–North; Pentacles–Europe or the West), before finally concluding with a discussion of the application of the tarot to divination, relating it to the interpretation of dreams. This essay was followed by one specifically devoted to tarot as divination, by Louis-Raphaël-Lucrèce de Fayolle (1727–1804), Comte de Mellet,

Chaos, The Querent, and Folly or the Alchemist, from Jean-Baptiste Alliette's Etteilla II Tarot, Livre de Thot (Book of Thoth), *c.* 1890

Alliette did not divide his deck into separate major and minor arcana, but provided them in a very different arrangement, with each card numbered from 1 to 78. Some cards resemble standard tarot, such as Card 78, The Fool, while others, such as Card 1, Chaos, are radically different.

who provides a different etymology, suggesting that the cards were invented by the Egyptian god of writing and knowledge Thoth, whose book was called 'A-Rosh', in which 'A' meant 'doctrine' or 'science', and 'Rosh' was the Egyptian name of the god Thoth/Mercury. These words, joined with the article 'T', signified 'Tableaus of the Doctrine of Mercury'. Mellet was the first person to link the twenty-two trumps with the twenty-two letters of the Hebrew alphabet; he was also the first to call the suit of coins (pentacles) 'talismans'. At the end of the volume, Court de Gébelin provided etchings of the trumps.

Around the same time, the print-seller and teacher of numerology Jean-Baptiste Alliette (1738–91), better known by his professional name of Etteilla (his surname in reverse), published a book on fortune-telling, *Etteilla, ou manière de se récréer avec un jeu de cartes* ('Etteilla, or How to Entertain Yourself with a Deck of Cards', 1770). Here, although his focus is on divination with regular playing cards, Etteilla makes the earliest known reference to the use of tarot for fortune-telling. As the French word for playing card was *carton*, he called this form of divination 'cartonomancie', which later evolved into 'cartomancy'. Following Court de Gébelin's *Monde primitif*, Etteilla published the first manual of tarot in a

Two engravings from books by Éliphas Lévi, mid-19th century
The one on the left is The Chariot of Hermes, from Dogme et Rituel de la Haute Magie *(1854–56). The one on the right shows The Wheel of Fortune, from Lévi's* La Clef des Grands Mystères *(1861).*

series of four volumes, *Manière de se récréer avec le jeu de cartes nommées tarots* ('How to Entertain Yourself with the Deck of Cards Called Tarot', 1783–85). In 1789 he published a divinatory deck of seventy-eight cards, now known as the Grand Etteilla, ou Tarots égyptiens, which has a completely different sequence to what has become the standard set of cards; it begins with a depiction of Chaos and ends with 'La Folie ou l'Alchimiste' (Folly or the Alchemist).

The next major promoter of tarot was Éliphas Lévi, who gave tarot a significant place in *Dogme et Rituel*. Rather than using Etteilla's cards, however, he promoted a more traditional version of the tarot, similar to those provided by Court de Gébelin at the end of Volume 8 of *Monde primitif*. Inspired by Mellet's association of the major arcana with the Hebrew alphabet, Lévi innovatively connected the tarot with Kabbalah by linking the twenty-two major arcana cards with the twenty-two letters of the Hebrew alphabet,

PROFILE
MAJOR ARCANA

Les 22 Arcanes du Tarot Kabbalistique ('The 22 Arcana of the Kabbalistic Tarot') are considered by some to be the first occult tarot. They were painted by the Swiss occultist and Freemason Oswald Wirth, following the instructions of Stanislas de Guaita, and were published in Paris in 1889 as hand-coloured lithographs in a limited edition of 350 decks, for the use of initiates in De Guaita's Kabbalistic Order of the Rose-Cross.

Wirth follows the traditional sequence of the major arcana as found in the Tarot de Marseille, but includes additional, esoteric details, including the attribution of each card to a letter of the Hebrew alphabet. Only the Fool lacks a number, but its place in the sequence is indicated by the Hebrew *shin* (ש), the penultimate letter of the Hebrew alphabet; so it appears before the World, which has the final letter *tav* (ת).

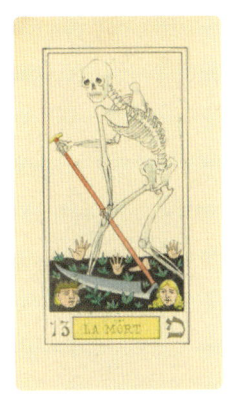

1. Magician
2. The Popess
3. Empress
4. Emperor
5. The Pope
6. Lovers
7. Chariot
8. Justice
9. Hermit
10. Wheel of Fortune
11. Strength
12. Hanged Man
13. Death
14. Temperance
15. The Devil
16. The Fire of Heaven
17. The Star
18. The Moon
19. The Sun
20. Judgment
— The Fool
21. The World

Tarot Égyptien: Grand Jeu de l'Oracle des Dames, 1890

This richly coloured 19th-century Egyptian tarot, inspired by Alliette's designs, is also known as the Grand Etteilla III. It provides divinatory meanings for when the cards are placed upright or reversed. On the top row, from left to right: Man and the Quadrupeds (a variant of The World), The Querent and Strength; on the bottom row, The Devil, The Magician or the Mountebank, and The Wheel of Fortune.

and the twenty-two paths connecting the ten *sefirot* on the Tree of Life. Lévi includes illustrations of a couple of the cards, including the 'Chariot of Hermes', in Volume 2 of *Dogma and Ritual*, and an extremely original Egyptianized version of The Wheel of Fortune, which features the alchemical terms *Hyle*, *Archeus*, and *Azoth* in *The Key of the Mysteries* of 1861, but he did not produce a full set of the major arcana, let alone a complete deck of seventy-eight cards.

What some consider to be the first standard occult tarot was produced by the Swiss Freemason Oswald Wirth (1860–1943), who worked as personal secretary to Stanislas de Guaita and at his suggestion created a major arcana deck influenced by Lévi's writings and closely following the traditional designs found in the Tarot de Marseille, a new design of the cards first printed by Philippe Vachier of Marseilles in 1639. The Marseille cards were far more affordable and were (with some variations in design) to be the most popular versions of the tarot until the advent of occult tarot in the 19th century. Wirth's deck was published in 1889 as Les 22 Arcanes du Tarot Kabbalistique ('The 22 Arcana of the Kabbalistic Tarot'). Wirth follows Lévi, however, in modifying elements in the Marseille deck. The Magician, for example, is presented behind a table that holds the implements of the four tarot suits: the cup, pentacle and sword on the table, the wand in his hand. While the Marseille Chariot is pulled by horses, here, as in Lévi's version, there are Egyptian sphinxes (though markedly more feminine than Lévi's rather androgynous pair). Wirth's Devil has the same alchemical terms 'solve' ('dissolve') and 'coagula' ('coagulate') found on Lévi's image of the Baphomet. Each card has an Arabic numeral on the left and a Hebrew letter on the right of the card's name.

Wirth had worked on this project in collaboration with the physician and occultist Papus. In the same year as the publication of Les 22 Arcanes, the cards appeared, in black and white, in Papus's *Clef absolue de la Science Occulte. Le Tarot des Bohémiens. Le plus ancien Livre du Monde, à l'usage exclusif des initiés* ('Absolute Key to Occult Science: The Tarot of the

Justice and The Moon, from Gérard Encausse's (aka Papus) *Le Tarot Divinatoire*, 1909
These large-format cards were probably cut from the back of Papus's book, hand-coloured and then mounted on card. They are a clear example of the syncretic nature of occultism with their inclusion of Hebrew, Sanskrit and Egyptian letters, and signs of the zodiac.

Bohemians, the Most Ancient Book in the World, for the Exclusive Use of Initiates'), which codified Lévi's teachings on the tarot and included an essay by Wirth on the 'Astronomical Tarot', together with others on 'The Initiatic Tarot' (François-Charles Barlet) and 'The Kabbalistic Tarot' (Stanlisas de Guaita). In 1909 Papus published *Le Tarot Divinatoire* (*The Divinatory Tarot*), a work containing seventy-eight large plates of Egyptian-style cards, their borders containing 'French', Hebrew, Sanskrit and Egyptian letters relevant to each, as well as planetary or zodiac signs. He also included five plates, said to be copies by Lévi of an Indian tarot. De Guaita's three-volume *Le Serpent de la Genèse* (*The Serpent of Genesis*), which formed the second part of his *Essais de sciences maudites* ('Essays on the Accursed Sciences', 1891–1949), was structured around meditations on the tarot major arcana. All three books are concerned with tarot, with each volume covering seven of the major arcana; the twenty-second is dealt with in the conclusion. Their titles are *Le Temple de*

Mosaics in the chapel of the Château des Avenières, Cruseilles, France, *c.* **1917**
The chapel was constructed by engineer and occult enthusiast Assan Farid Dina in 1917, just a few years after the castle, which was built by his wife, the American heiress Mary Shillito. The mosaics are inspired by Oswald Wirth's major arcana, but with a pronounced Egyptian style. Shown here are (top) Strength and (bottom, from left to right) The Lovers, The Wheel of Fortune, The Emperor and The Hanged Man.

Satan ('The Temple of Satan', 1891), *La Clef de la Magie Noire* ('The Key to Black Magic', 1897) and *Le Problème du Mal* ('The Problem of Evil', 1949), the last volume completed and published by Wirth long after De Guaita's death in 1897. In 1926 Wirth redesigned the twenty-two arcana, adding new elements, such as the yin-yang disc on the book held by the High Priestess. He also corrected the Devil card, having placed Baphomet's 'solve' and 'coagula' on the wrong arms in the 1889 deck. The following year Wirth published *Le Tarot des imagiers du Moyen Âge* ('The Tarot of the Medieval Artists', translated into English in 1985 as *Tarot of the Magicians*), in which he revised some of the statements he had made in his 1889 tarot essay and included a discussion of Masonic concordances of the tarot; it also featured an appendix in which Wirth elaborated on related topics such as Hermetism and alchemy.

Meanwhile, in England, the tarot was to occupy an important place in the teachings of the Golden

The Juggler (or Magician), from the Austin Osman Spare hand-painted tarot deck, c. 1906
An associate of Aleister Crowley, Spare took his occult practice in new directions, writing his own grimoires, experimenting with automatic writing and drawing, and developing his own method of creating sigils.

Dawn. The mysterious *Cypher Manuscript*, a collection of loose papers on which the magical initiation rituals of the Golden Dawn were based, also include Lévi's innovative correlation of the twenty-two tarot trumps with the twenty-two pathways on the kabbalistic Tree of Life, apparently due to the manuscripts' author Kenneth Mackenzie (1833–86) having visited Lévi in Paris in 1861. The first English-language references to the occult tarot appeared in Waite's 1886 translation of selected writings by Lévi, *The Mysteries of Magic*, which included material from *Dogme et Rituel de la Haute Magie* in the fifth chapter on divination: 'Of all oracles the Tarot is the most astonishing in its results, because every possible combination of this universal key of the Kabbalah gives as solutions the oracles of science and truth, on account of the analogical precision of its numbers and figures. This miraculous and unique book of the ancient Magi is an instrument of divination which may be employed with complete confidence.' In 1888, a year before Wirth brought out his deck, Samuel Liddell MacGregor Mathers published *The Tarot: Its Occult Significance, Use in Fortune-Telling, and Method of Play*, which was the first home-grown work to introduce tarot divination to the

The World and The Querent, from Charles Watilliaux's Le Jeu de la Princesse, 1876

Another 19th-century French cartomancy deck inspired by Alliette, The Game of the Princess uses a particularly powerful woman standing in a magic circle to represent the person asking for a tarot reading.

British public. Mathers makes clear the book's debt to its French predecessors, although he proposes a new etymology, tracing the term tarot back to the 'Egyptian' word 'táru', which allegedly meant 'to consult'. Initially the Golden Dawn's members probably used imported tarot decks, but eventually Mathers designed a version that was illustrated by his wife Moina, for private use by members, each of whom was expected to make their own copy. The decks were utilized not only in divination, but also in meditation and visualization, with the major arcana figures in particular conceived as beings to be encountered during trance-induced astral projection.

The Order's secrets were not to remain concealed for long, when in 1909 Crowley published his *Liber 777*, in which he revealed the attributions of Hebrew letters to the major arcana, and then proceeded to publish some of the Golden Dawn's rituals and instructions in his journal *The Equinox*. This was a watershed

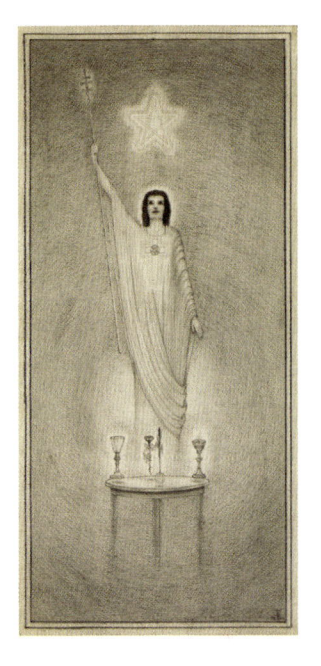

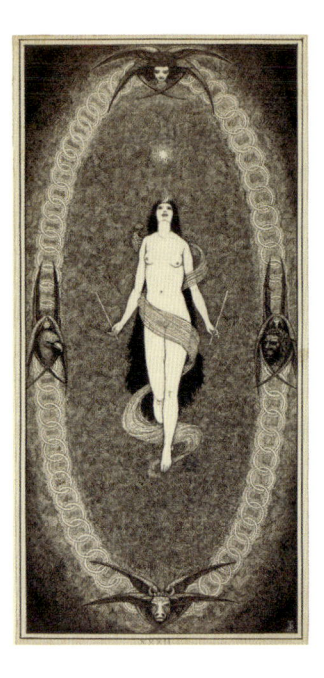

John B. Trinick and
Wilfrid Pippet,
Great Symbols of the Paths,
1917–22
These drawings, created as designs for a tarot set, were commissioned by Arthur Edward Waite for his Fellowship of the Rosy Cross. The cards on the left and in the centre are by John B. Trinick and the card to the right is likely by Wilfrid Pippet.

moment in the history of occultism – the cat being let out of the bag. By the end of the same year, Waite had published what is now arguably the best-known set of tarot cards, the Rider–Waite deck (Rider was the name of the publisher). Painted by a fellow member of the Golden Dawn, the British artist Pamela Colman Smith (1878–1951), under Waite's instructions, the deck was accompanied by a guide entitled *The Key to the Tarot*, which in later editions was revised and published as *The Pictorial Key to the Tarot*. The Waite–Smith designs for the minor arcana were a radical departure from previous decks, replacing the typically simple representations of the Swords, Wands, Cups and Pentacles of the four suits with richly illustrated scenes, full of occult symbolism. Far less known is a second collection of tarot-related images, known as the *Great Symbols of the Paths*, which were commissioned by Waite from Wilfrid Pippet (c. 1873–1946) and John Brahms Trinick (1890–1974) in 1921–22, for his Fellowship of the Rosy Cross.

Two decades later, Crowley produced his own tarot deck, the closest to compete with the Waite–Smith design for popularity. Although some tarot artworks

Pamela Colman Smith, painter of the Waite–Smith Tarot (1909), *c.* 1912
Colman Smith made a name as a book illustrator and writer of books on Jamaican folklore. She supported women's suffrage, and established the Green Sheaf Press to publish primarily women authors. She was introduced to the Golden Dawn by the famous Irish writer W. B. Yeats.

Arthur Edward Waite, designer of the Waite–Smith Tarot, 1911
Waite, co-creator of the Waite–Smith tarot deck, was a prolific author of many aspects of esoteric thought, with translations and original works on alchemy, magic, Kabbalah, Rosicrucianism and Freemasonry.

by Crowley exist, the seventy-eight cards of his deck were painted by Lady Frieda Harris (1877–1962), who combined his designs with her studies of projective synthetic geometry to create a special effect: rays emanating from one card can be seen projecting into another card. The original oil paintings were publicly exhibited in London on 1 July 1942. The images subsequently appeared in *The Book of Thoth* (1944), written by Crowley under the pseudonym The Master Therion, where he explained the complex and sophisticated symbolism of the cards, many of which included Egyptian motifs. Crowley renamed four of the major arcana, referring to the trump cards as either 'keys' or the 'Atu of Tahuti' ('Trumps of Thoth'): Justice becomes 'Adjustment'; Fortitude is 'Lust'; Temperance becomes 'Art'; and Judgment is 'Aeon'. The 'Art' card is a notable instance of tarot adopting explicit alchemical imagery. Unlike the Waite–Smith deck, which went on sale shortly after its creation, the Crowley–Harris deck was not commercially available until 1969–70.

PROFILE
WAITE-SMITH
MINOR ARCANA (PART 1)

The minor arcana supplement the twenty-two archetypal cards of the major arcana. They each have four court cards (King, Queen, Knight, Page), plus number cards, Ace to 10.

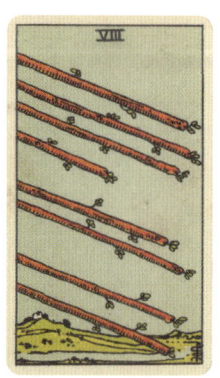

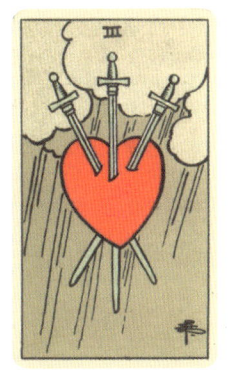

WANDS (OPPOSITE)
The suit of Wands corresponds to the catalysing, transformative element of fire, the world of the imagination, inspiration, intuition, creativity and the will.

SWORDS (THIS PAGE)
The suit of Swords represents the element of air, the realm of the mind, of thought, intellect, abstraction, the powers of reason and understanding.

PROFILE
WAITE-SMITH MINOR ARCANA (PART 2)

The number cards represent everyday life experiences and lessons. The Court cards symbolize character types, qualities we encounter in others and possibly need to develop in ourselves.

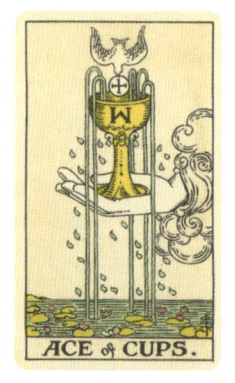

CUPS (OPPOSITE)
The suit of Cups symbolizes the fluid and changeable element of water, the realm of the heart, of emotions, the experience of love – passionate, spiritual or platonic – and relationships in general.

PENTACLES (THIS PAGE)
The suit of Pentacles represents the grounding element of earth, the requirements of our body, our possessions, matters of practicality and accomplishments in the material world.

The first German tarot book was *Der Tarot: die kabbalistische Methode der Zukunftserforschung als Schlüssel zum Okkultismus* ('The Tarot: The Kabbalistic Method of Enquiry into the Future as the Key to Occultism'), published in 1920 by Ernst Kurtzahn (1879–1939), which traces the origins of tarot back to Atlantis, making it 21,000 years old! Kurtzahn's small-format, monochromatic tarot deck appeared in the same year under his magical name Daïtyanus, as the Tarut-Spiel Daityanus. While its images mostly copied Etteilla's deck, its sequence did not, with the major arcana beginning, instead, with The Fool (*Der Narr*) as 0 and ending with The World (*Die Welt*) as XXII. Another deck with claims to being the first German tarot is the Deutsches Original Tarot of August Frank Glahn (1865–1941), author of *Das deutsche Tarotbuch: Wahrsagung/Astrologie/Weisheit, drei Stufen der Einweihung* ('The German Tarot-Book: Prediction/Astrology/Wisdom, three Levels of Initiation', 1924). Mostly likely published the same year as the book, the seventy-eight small cards, designed by Hans Schubert of Reinfeld, belong to the Egyptianized style of tarot. Each card has its own astrological symbol; each of the major arcana has both a Hebrew letter and one of the Germanic runes.

Other notable early 20th-century occult tarots include the Revised New Art Tarot (1929), fruit of the collaboration between the American artist John Augustus Knapp (1853–1938) and the Canadian Masonic author Manly Palmer Hall (1901–90), founder of the Philosophical Research Society in Los Angeles; the Wirth-inspired Lasenic Tarot (1938) of the prominent Czech Hermetist Pierre de Lasenic (born Petr Pavel Kohout, 1900–44), founding member of the Czech occult organization Universalia and founder of the Hermetic Horev-Club; and Le Tarot Traditionnel (1948) of the French Martinist Jean Chaboseau (1903–78), who introduces alchemical symbols into the minor arcana. Many more decks could be discussed, and there has been a veritable florescence of tarot deck production since the 1970s – some occult or esoteric, others less so – with the number of decks from all over the world now reaching the thousands.

Maestro dei Giochi Borromeo, *The Tarocchi Players,* **Palazzo Borromeo, Milan,** *c.* **1445**

This 15th-century fresco is considered the earliest known representation of tarot players. Three aristocratic-looking women and two men can be seen absorbed in a card game, although no major arcana cards are visibly in play.

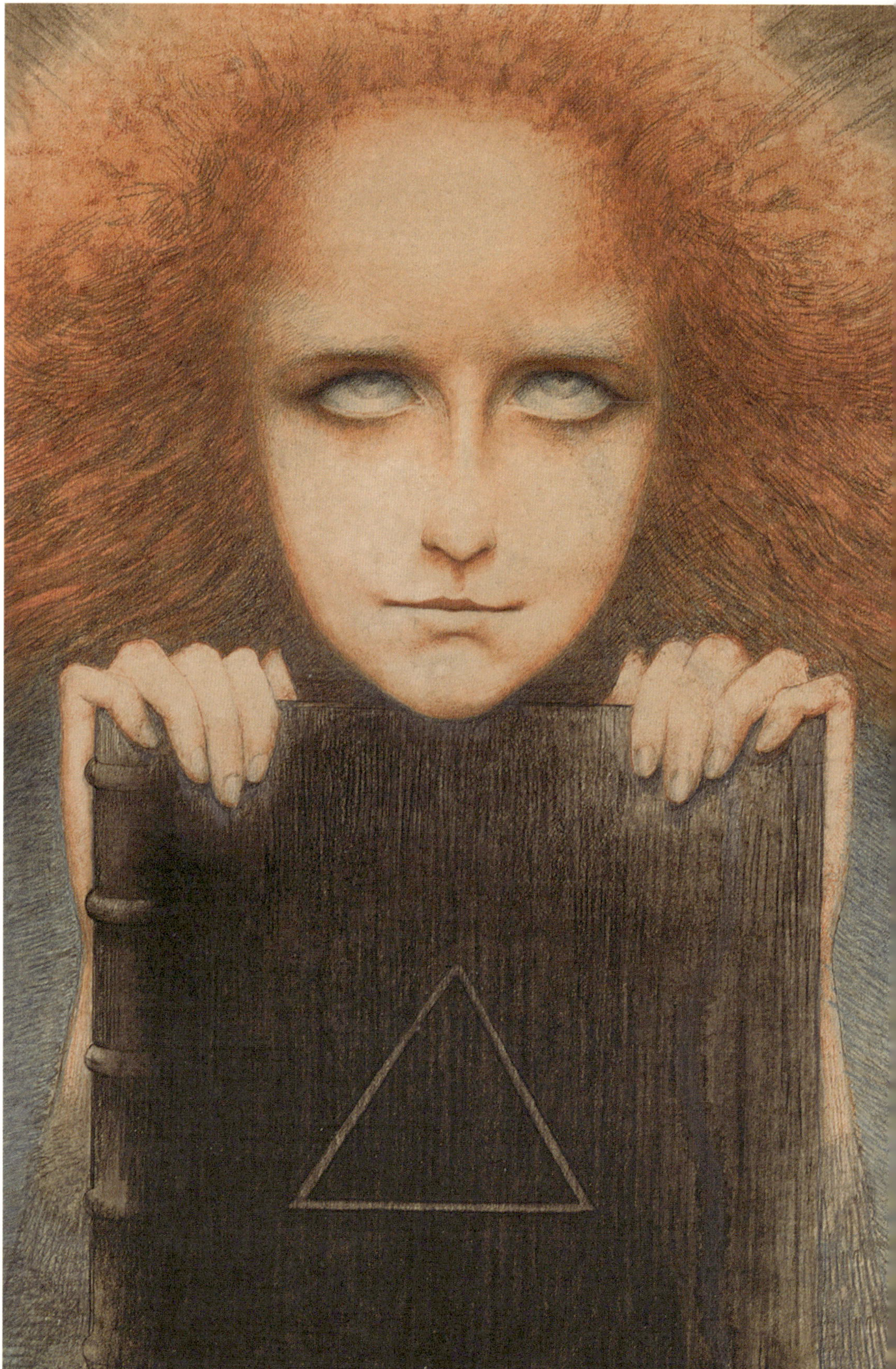

> 'Books are ports of entry to perceiving the experience of life differently, and that's as powerful as it gets — that's alchemy.'
>
> GENESIS P-ORRIDGE, NONBINARY: A MEMOIR (2022)

NEW AGE AND OCCULTURE

Nowadays much of what was secret and hidden in previous centuries is available in bookshops, its influence visible in art and music, film and television, novels and comics, even computer games. Much of this is due to the explosion of interest in alternative thought and lifestyles in the New Age movement during the 1970s and the development of occulture, the presence of the occult in popular culture since the 1980s.

Finally we arrive at the relatively modern concept of the 'New Age', a term extensively used by the theosophist Alice Bailey (1880–1949). In the same generation, Aleister Crowley heralded the 'New Aeon of Horus' (the religious system he created, Thelema, divided the history of humanity into three aeons, each named after an Egyptian god), and Carl Jung – who was interested in the idea of astrological ages, each ruled by a zodiac sign for 2,160 years, in which the change from one zodiac sign to the next influences human culture and the rise and fall of civilizations – wrote of the 'New Aion', the 'Way of What is to Come', with reference to the imminent transition from the Age of Pisces, which began around the birth of Christ, to the Age of Aquarius. This, in theory, represents a move away from adherence to tradition to one of freethinking and innovation, a gravitation from top-down to bottom-up approaches to social issues, the growth of humanitarianism. The New Age covers a wide range of spiritual practices: eclectic and syncretic, with no central authority and draws from many different currents of Western occultism and Eastern spiritual traditions. Although some speak of a New Age movement, it is highly subjective, a personalized form of practice, with people synthesizing elements from varied sources that particularly resonate with their view of the world and their sense of being spiritual individuals seeking transformation of self and society, independent of (and in reaction to) traditional religious authority. Some focus on social change, on environmental issues, on humanity's holistic relationship with the natural world; others on self-development, on spiritual healing and alternative medicine; others still on occult practices, performance of rituals, or channelling messages from guardian angels, spirit guides and even extraterrestrials. The New Age individual stands at the cross-roads of many paths.

Early signs of this phenomenon can be found in the counterculture of the 1960s. Centres began to be established to encourage alternative lifestyles and ways of developing human potential. The early beginnings of the Findhorn Foundation in Scotland

< *page 222*
Jean Delville, *Mysteriosa* or *The Portrait of Mrs Stuart Merrill*, 1892
This chalk drawing is one of Delville's best-known works. It shows a red-headed young woman, apparently in a trance with her eyes gazing upwards, while her chin rests on an old black leatherbound book bearing a triangle on its cover. Delville considered Kabbalah, magic and Hermeticism to be the 'perfect triangle of human knowledge' and perhaps that is the implication here.

Victor Brauner,
The Surrealist, 1947

This painting, a portrait of the artist as a young man, is infused with tarot motifs. The Hebrew letter aleph on the figure's hat denotes that this is Card 1 of the major arcana, with the traditional lemniscate below symbolizing the infinite possibilities of The Magician.

Ernst Fuchs, *Moses and the Burning Bush*, 1957
Fuchs, one of the founders of the Vienna School of Fantastic Realism, dramatically captures the moment of the encounter when Moses learned the first divine name, Ehieh.

can be traced back to 1962, the same year that the Esalen Institute was founded in California. It was in the 1970s, though, that the New Age flourished, promoted by many who had been part of the hippie subculture of the previous decade. Increasing numbers of people sought alternatives to the mainstream. New Age shops began to appear, selling books, tarot cards, crystals and incense. New kinds of events were staged, such as the first Mind Body Spirit Festival in London in 1977, bringing together workshops, stalls and demonstrations by a wide range of spiritual practitioners, alternative healers, astrologers, tarot readers, experts in yoga and tai chi, advocates of psychic development, aromatherapists and homeopathists, among others – even offering Kirlian photography, the art of capturing the impression of a person's aura. What was evident was the New Age desire to connect science and spirituality, be that in the form of relating Eastern mysticism to quantum theories of the new physics in such popular works as Fritjof Capra's *The Tao of Physics* (1975) and Gary Zukav's *The Dancing Wu*

Stonehenge Free Festival, Salisbury Plain, England, June 1984
This distinctly alternative and countercultural event took place at Stonehenge annually between 1974 and 1984, around the summer solstice, with performances by psychedelic rock bands such as Hawkwind, Here & Now and Ozric Tentacles, as well as Jimmy Page and Roy Harper.

Li Masters (1979) or Rupert Sheldrake's hypothesis of morphic resonance in *A New Science of Life* (1981).

New Age beliefs and practices have percolated into the mainstream, evolving into what is now called occulture. The original concepts that took shape in occult organizations like the Golden Dawn and the Theosophical Society in the 19th and early 20th centuries, and were then absorbed by 1960s counterculture and gradually broadened in scope in New Age subcultures, have now expanded into a vast system of beliefs and practices in contemporary culture. Occulture is polymorphic, potentially mixing and matching Eastern spirituality, paganism, spiritualism, theosophy, alternative science and medicine, Jungian psychology and the paranormal, and ranges across the religious and political spectrums. Occulture consists of groups and individuals who are dissatisfied with conventional reality and display a readiness to adopt and adapt a wide variety of alternative occult and esoteric material as inspiration and support for their way of life.

The notion of occulture seems to have originated in 1980s Britain, in an increasingly secular environment, among circles disenchanted with orthodox religion but with an interest in occult knowledge and the paranormal. The term was allegedly coined by the

PROFILE
CRYSTALS & GEMSTONES

A New Age alternative therapy that connects with earlier practices found in medieval lapidaries is crystal healing that uses crystals and semiprecious stones. Many practitioners combine the occult powers of stones with an interest in the Indian system of the chakras in Kundalini yoga and believe that by placing crystals and stones on specific parts of the body, or around the body, they can rebalance the flow of subtle energy, release stress and blocked energy, and retune its aura. In New Age practice the seven chakras each came to be paired with the colours of the rainbow, the lowest being red and the highest being violet. Different stones, shown on the right, are often recommended for each of the chakras.

SAHASRARA,
THE CROWN CHAKRA
The crown chakra, at the top of the head, is believed to resonate with ultraviolet, as well as the combination of wavelengths in white light.

AJÑA,
THE THIRD EYE CHAKRA
The brow chakra, related to imagination and decision-making, is held to relate to the colours purple or indigo.

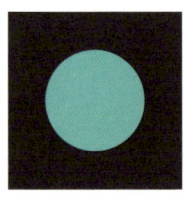

VISHUDDHA,
THE THROAT CHAKRA
The colour blue is associated with the expressive and communicative qualities of the throat chakra.

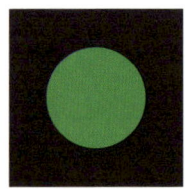

ANAHATA,
THE HEART CHAKRA
Gentle pink and green connect well with the qualities (love, joy, peace) associated with this chakra.

MANIPURA,
THE SOLAR PLEXUS CHAKRA
Radiant, sunny yellow energizes the personal power of our core self at the solar plexus chakra.

SVADHISTHANA,
THE SACRAL CHAKRA
Sexuality, confidence and self-worth are symbolized by a vibrant orange at the location of this chakra.

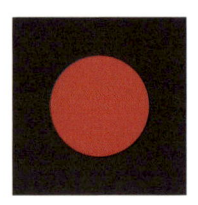

MULADHARA,
THE ROOT CHAKRA
The longest wavelength of the spectrum, red represents the physical and spiritual grounding of energy at the root chakra.

Rock Crystal	Diamond	Selenite
Amethyst	Purple Fluorite	Lapis Lazuli
Aquamarine	Turquoise	Chrysocolla
Peridot	Malachite	Rose Quartz
Topaz	Chrysoberyl	Golden Rutilated Quartz
Citrine	Carnelian	Tiger's Eye
Red Jasper	Ruby	Bloodstone

Johfra Bosschart, *Unio Mystica*, 1973
The surreal fuses with the occult in this central painting of a triptych that features Hermes on the left and Aphrodite on the right - by implication a union of opposites. The central vision of the pentagram is multicultural, with an Egyptian Eye of Horus, a Taoist yin-yang, a Buddhist dharma wheel and the four creatures from the vision of Ezekiel. The chthonic dragon adds a possible alchemical element of transformation, while the cobra curling around the Tree of Life mingles Abrahamic notions of Eden with allusions to the Hindu god Shiva. The two women seem strikingly different, the introspective priestess below, gazing down into the chalice; the dynamic huntress aiming upwards.

English punk/electronica musician and occult practitioner Genesis Breyer P-Orridge (1950–2020), founder of industrial band Throbbing Gristle and experimental pop-rock band Psychic TV, whose foremost mentors in magic were the American author William S. Burroughs (1914–1997) and British-Canadian artist and writer Brion Gysin (1916–86). Psychic TV performances employed musical beats to alter consciousness in concerts that were collective ritual experiences, raising awareness of chaos magick in the industrial music scene. In 1981 P-Orridge and other members of the group founded a new religion or occult order, Thee Temple ov Psychick Youth (TOPY), which P-Orridge led for a decade, a church without orthodoxy or dogma, a global confederation of magick practitioners, engaged in a form of (popular) cultural engineering, to help encourage and support the development of multi-dimensional individuals.

It could be argued, however, that occulture existed long before the coining of the term. The confluence of the occult, literature and the arts is not a new phenomenon. Mozart's *The Magic Flute* (1791) was inspired by Freemasonry, and he is known to

Jan Toorop, *O Grave, Where Is Thy Victory?*, 1892

The title of this drawing refers to the words of the apostle Paul in 1 Corinthians 15:55, concerning the victory of faith over Death; with Christ's sacrifice and resurrection comes the promise of spiritual rebirth. The dying man seemingly floating towards his grave is defended by two heavenly spirits on the left, while a group of darker, more earthy forces claw at him on the right.

have composed music specially for gatherings at his Masonic lodge. An attentive reader of Mary Shelley's *Frankenstein* (1818) will note that the reading habits of young Victor Frankenstein included 16th-century works by the magus Agrippa and the revolutionary alchemist Paracelsus. We see early evidence of occult influence in fine art, particularly the late 19th-century Symbolist movement and 20th-century Surrealism. The Belgian Symbolist painter and theosophist Jean Delville (1867–1953) had been initiated into the Martinist order by Papus, as well as into De Guaita and Péladan's Kabbalistic Order of the Rose-Cross. In the 1890s, he exhibited his work in Péladan's Salons de la Rose+Croix. One of his best-known works, *Mysteriosa* or *The Portrait of Mrs Stuart Merrill* (1892), shows a young woman seemingly in a trance-like state holding a large black leather book inscribed with a triangle, which symbolizes Delville's belief in perfect human knowledge through occult practices. Dutch-Indonesian artist Jan Toorop (1858–1928) displays Eastern occult influence in the 'spook style' of *O Grave, Where Is Thy*

Paul Ranson, *The Witch in Her Circle*, 1892

A sky-clad witch kneels in a surprisingly small circle, while her black cat familiar sits nonchalantly outside, ignoring the floating blue python and the bird dancing a jig. Does the curling glass apparatus at the side perhaps indicate that distillations contributed to the experience?

Victory?, a drawing of 1892 in which Death appears as the deliverer from earthly suffering. Another piece from the same year, *The Witch in Her Circle* by Paul Ranson (1861–1909), is typical of this French artist, who had a penchant for painting witches and their familiars.

Some of the Surrealists were particularly interested in the tarot. The Chilean artist Roberto Matta (1911–2002) designed four cards (Lovers, Chariot, Stars and Moon) for André Breton's poetic *Arcane 17* (*Arcanum 17*, 1945), which took its title from the seventeenth trump of the major arcana, The Star. The Romanian Victor Brauner (1903–66) painted both the memorable *The Surrealist* (1947), a portrait of himself as a young man borrowing motifs from the tarot, and *The Lovers* (1947), a title that alludes to the sixth trump of the major arcana, although it is the first two trumps, The Magician and The High Priestess, that Brauner depicts. Spanish surrealist Salvador Dalí (1904–89) painted *The Alchemist* (1962), followed by a whole series on the 'Alchemy of the Philosophers' (1976),

Roberto Matta, tarot cards designed for André Breton's *Arcane 17* (*Arcanum 17*, 1945)
Chilean artist Roberto Matta designed four cards for Breton's book Arcane 17, *which takes its name from the Star card in the major arcana:* Lovers *(above left),* Chariot, Stars *(above centre) and* Moon *(above right).*

including representations of the *Emerald Tablet* and *The Ouroboros*. The year 1984 saw the publication of a *Tarot Universal Dalí*, a 78-card deck Dalí started creating in 1970 by painting over and collaging famous masterpieces, presenting himself, needless to say, as The Magician. Inspired by both the Tarot de Marseille and the Waite–Smith deck, English Surrealist Leonora Carrington (1917–2011) produced her own set of major arcana, but also included tarot symbolism in some of her paintings, especially in *La Maja del Tarot* ('The Belle of the Tarot', 1965), where different cards from the major arcana can be seen on her dress.

What is new, today, though, is the current proliferation of occulture in such a wide variety of music genres, popular novels, comics, art, television series and films, even videogames. Popular music has been central to the dissemination of occulture. In 1966 American artist and film director Andy Warhol (1928–1987) made a film, *The Velvet Underground Tarot Cards*, of the American rock band The Velvet Underground having their cards read (using the Waite–Smith deck), as background footage for their debut album, *The Velvet Underground & Nico* (1967),

DECODING LEONORA CARRINGTON'S *LA MAJA DEL TAROT*

This painting is by the English surrealist artist Leonora Carrington (1917–2011). It is a portrait made in 1965 of the Mexican film actress and singer María de los Ángeles Félix (1914–2002). It is called both *La Maja del Tarot* ('The Belle of the Tarot') and *La Maga del Tarot* ('The Tarot Magician'). Carrington was extremely interested in the tarot and painted her own set of major arcana. Looking carefully, one can find here many images from the major arcana, from both the Waite–Smith Tarot and the Tarot de Marseille. The card-numbers she provides are from the Marseille deck.

1. *MAGICIAN*
The lemniscate symbol of eternity above her head is taken from the Magician I.

2. *HIGH PRIESTESS*
The crescent moon below her inverted head probably alludes to the one in the High Priestess II card.

3. *THE SUN*
The Sun XIX copies the Waite–Smith deck but includes two children, like the Marseille Sun.

4. *THE DEVIL*
The Devil XV, without his male and female demons.

5. *THE FOOL*
A dog bites the bottom of the Marseille Fool.

6. *THE EMPEROR*
The Emperor (Card IV) in profile, holding his sceptre.

7. *THE WORLD*
The World, Card XXI, with the wreath, Ox and Lion.

8. *JUDGMENT*
Judgment XX, with the angel blowing the trumpet.

9. *STRENGTH*
Strength XI is represented with a lion.

10. *TEMPERANCE*
Temperance XIV pouring the waters.

11. *THE MOON*
The Moon XVIII, with the dog, wolf and crab.

12. *THE CHARIOT*
The Chariot, Card VII, with charioteer and sphinxes.

13. *JUSTICE*
Just the crowned female head of Justice, Card VIII, can be seen.

14. *TOWER*
The Tower, Card XV, struck by lightning, with two figures falling to earth.

15. *THE HANGED MAN*
A serene-looking Hanged Man, Card XII, suspended upside-down from a tree.

16. *THE WHEEL OF FORTUNE*
Card X, with a sphinx-like creature, a dark canine figure and a cat-like figure.

17. *THE HERMIT*
The Hermit, Card IX, is not present, but he is often depicted carrying a lantern and this may be its light.

18. *DEATH*
Could that diamond-shaped figure, with its serpentine tail draped over her like a feather boa, be Death?

19. *THE STAR*
Could this octopus-like constellation in the night sky be The Star XVII?

20. *THE LOVERS*
Could the trees allude to the Waite–Smith Lovers VI?

235 OCCULT REVIVAL — 3 — *New Age and Occulture*

The Beatles in Rishikesh, India, with the Maharishi Mahesh Yogi, 1968
The group includes Ringo Starr, Maureen Starkey, Jane Asher, Paul McCartney, George Harrison, Patti Boyd, Cynthia Lennon, John Lennon, Beatles roadie Mal Evans, Prudence Farrow, Jenny Boyd and Beach Boy Mike Love.

during their performances in the multimedia events he organized under the name *Exploding Plastic Inevitable* in 1966 and 1967.

In the UK, the Beatles' famous trip to Rishikesh to study Transcendental Meditation with the Maharishi Mahesh Yogi and George Harrison's later initiation into the Hare Krishnas had a profound impact on youth culture, on a generation disillusioned with the status quo and looking for something new. Look closely at the cover of *Sgt. Pepper's Lonely Hearts Club Band* (1967) and, together with Carl Jung, Paramahansa Yogananda and Aldous Huxley, you will find Aleister Crowley included in Peter Blake's collage. In the same year, *Hair: The American Tribal Love-Rock Musical* celebrated this sense of an age of change with its song about the dawning of the Age of Aquarius. Two years later, posters for the definitive countercultural event of the era, the 1969 Woodstock Festival in Bethel, New York, advertised it as 'An Aquarian Exposition: 3 Days of Peace & Music'.

Jimmy Page (b. 1944), guitarist in the rock band Led Zeppelin, is well known for his interest in Crowley

Guitarist Jimmy Page of the English rock group Led Zeppelin performing at the Empire Pool, Wembley, London, 23 November 1971
Page's sweater bears the 'Zoso' symbol that he chose for the artwork of the album Led Zeppelin IV, released the same year. It is based on an astral-magical seal of Saturn, tying in with Page's zodiac sign Capricorn, which is ruled by the planet.

and for a time even owned Crowley's former residence Boleskine House on the shore of Loch Ness in Scotland. Page had Crowley's sayings 'So mote it be' and 'Do what thou wilt' inscribed in the run-off grooves of the first pressings of *Led Zeppelin III* (1970). The artwork for the next album, *Led Zeppelin IV* (1971), includes a personal symbol for each of the four band members. Page's symbol is based on an astral-magical seal of Saturn found in *De Rerum Varietate* ('On the Variety of Things', 1557) by the Italian astrologer Girolamo Cardano (1501–76), which turns up again later in the grimoire *Le Dragon Rouge* ('The Red Dragon', 1850). Page's astrological sun-sign is Capricorn, which is ruled by Saturn, so the choice of the planet as his symbol is appropriate. The album's inner illustration features 'The Hermit', based on the tarot card in the Waite–Smith deck. Having been described as 'the most famous hard-rock album ever recorded', it ranks high as an occultural influencer.

David Bowie (1947–2016) is another leading musician to have expressed an interest in magic, perhaps best reflected in the lyrics 'I'm closer to the Golden Dawn/Immersed in Crowley's uniform of

PROFILE
CHIROMANCY / PALMISTRY

Chiromancy, or palmistry, looks for significance in the lines on the palm and takes note of the length and shape of the fingers and nails, as well as the features of the hand in general. The chiromancer considers all these elements to determine an individual's physical and moral character, as well as to predict what the future holds. Each finger is assigned to a planet, each with its own meaning: the thumb to Venus (willpower), the index finger to Jupiter (ambition, leadership), the middle finger to Saturn (justice, morality), the ring finger to the Sun (creativity), and the little finger to Mercury (communication, self-expression), while Mars rules the centre of the palm and the Moon the side or percussion.

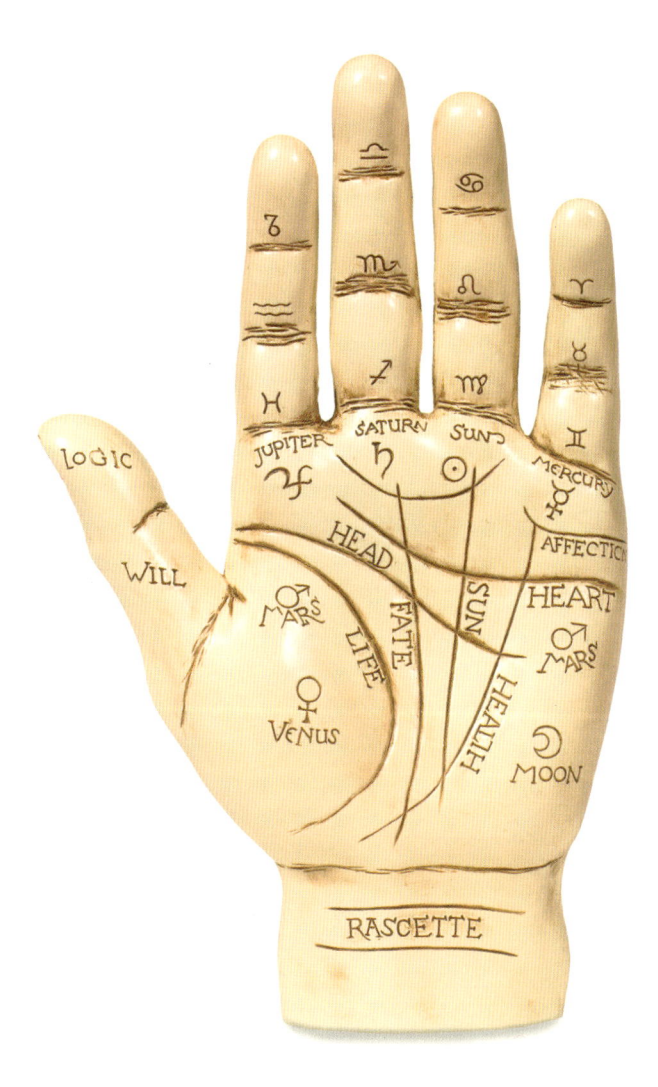

HEART LINE
One of the main lines, the Heart Line, above the Head Line, extends often from the little-finger side of the palm, across the top of the palm. It relates to our feelings, emotions, and how we deal with relationships, commitment, love, friendship and sexuality.

HEAD LINE
The Head Line is another main line, extending from between the thumb and the index finger, across the middle of the palm. It is concerned with the depth or complexity of intellect, our way of thinking, the brain and the tenacity of memory.

LIFE LINE
The Life Line is one of the major lines, visible here on the left of the hand, between the thumb and index finger, and stretching downwards, towards the base of the thumb. It represents one's health and physical vitality, and also, depending on its depth, the richness of life experience.

LINE OF FATE
The Line of Fate, Fortune or Destiny is a vertical line approximately in the centre of the palm. One's fate is determined by where the line ends. If it heads towards the little finger, one may be gifted in business; if to the ring finger, talented in the arts.

LINES OF AFFECTION
The Lines of Affection or Marriage are found on the Mount of Mercury, below the little finger. Vertical lines suggest children. Horizontal lines indicate relationships – the deeper and stronger the line, the more serious the love and relationship.

FINGERS
Fingers with smooth joints indicate someone who is intuitive and perceptive with quick thought processes, possibly carefree, impatient and impulsive. Fingers with knotty joints signify slower, attentive, patient, deliberative and analytical thought processes.

David Bowie drawing the kabbalistic Tree of Life in charcoal, Los Angeles, California, 1974

It is interesting to see which sefirot Bowie has filled in first: 1. Kether (Crown), 2. Chochmah (Wisdom) and 4. Chesed (Mercy), plus a sun in the place of Tifereth (Beauty) and a moon for Yesod (Foundation). A larger, rougher version can be seen on the wall behind him.

imagery' in 'Quicksand' on *Hunky Dory* (1971). An image of Bowie drawing the Tree of Life in charcoal, used on the back cover of the 1976 album *Station to Station*, suggests an exploration of Kabbalah at the time. The same period saw the release of Queen's *A Night at the Opera* (1975) and *A Day at the Races* (1976), both album covers featuring the Queen crest designed by Freddie Mercury (1946–91), which he based on the astrological signs of the band members. The cover of American rock band Blue Öyster Cult's 1976 album *Agents of Fortune* showed a magician flourishing four tarot cards. Early originators of the heavy metal genre, British band Black Sabbath is well known for experimenting with satanic imagery, and in 1980 their lead singer Ozzy Osbourne (b. 1948) released a solo album, *Blizzard of Ozz*, which contained the song 'Mr Crowley'. Frank Zappa (1940–93) is another known reader of Crowley and seems to have been interested in alchemy too, including the solo 'But Who Was Fulcanelli?' on his 1988 live album *Guitar*. Bruce Dickinson (b. 1958) of the British band Iron Maiden recorded the solo album, *The Chemical Wedding* (1998) – a reference to an influential Rosicrucian manifesto of 1616 (originally written in German and translated as *The Chemical Wedding of Christian Rosenkreutz*). In 2008 a science fantasy/horror film of the same name was produced, based on a screenplay by Dickinson, in which the lead character becomes a reincarnation of Crowley.

In Scandinavia, the majority of the lyrics for the symphonic metal band Therion have been written by Thomas Karlsson (b. 1972), founder of the Swedish Left-Hand Path magic order Dragon Rouge in 1989; Therion's lead composer, Christofer Johnsson (b. 1972), has been a member of the order since the early 1990s. Their album *Gothic Kabbalah* (2007) centred around the figure of the Swedish occult philosopher Johannes Bureus (1568–1652). Since the mid-1990s Madonna (b. 1958) has become famous for her embrace of Jewish Kabbalah, assuming the name Esther and studying at the Kabbalah Centre in Los Angeles. On her 2004 'Re-Invention World Tour' she screened kabbalistic images and Hebrew letters from a manuscript of the

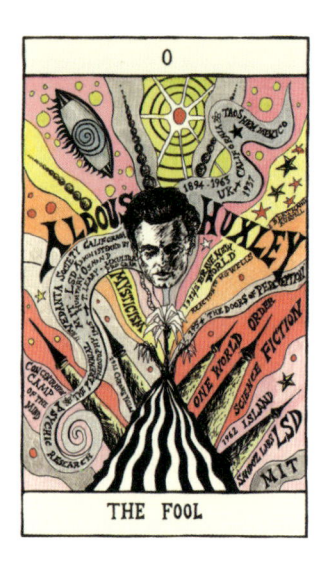

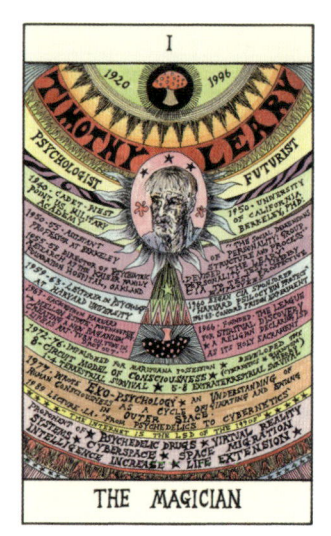

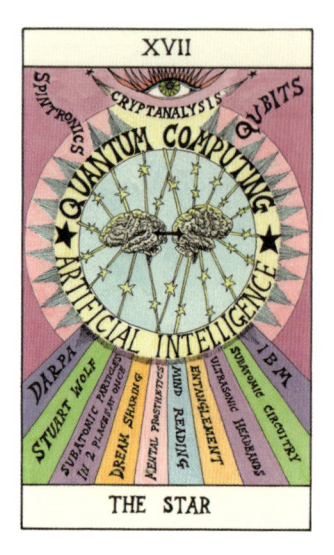

Suzanne Treister, cards from the HEXEN 2.0 tarot, 2009–11

This series, to quote the artist, 'looks into histories of scientific research behind government programmes of mass control, investigating parallel histories of countercultural and grass roots movements'. Here we see Aldous Huxley, author of the psychedelic Doors of Perception *(1954) as The Fool, clinical psychologist and advocate of LSD Timothy Leary as The Magician, and developments in artificial intelligence, quantum computing and cryptanalysis appear as The Star.*

13th-century Kabbalist Abraham Abulafia. Danny Carey (b. 1961), drummer in the American rock band Tool, is another musician fascinated by Crowley, whose influence appears in their work. Carey is an enthusiastic collector of Crowley's works and wrote the foreword to *The Wickedest Books in the World: Confessions of an Aleister Crowley Bibliophile* (2009), which includes many first editions from his personal collection. The year 2011 saw the debut performance of *Dr Dee: An English Opera*, based on the life of Elizabeth I's occult philosopher John Dee, and composed by Blur's frontman Damon Albarn (b. 1968).

Occult themes were introduced to an unprecedentedly wide audience through the cinematization of two highly successful series of popular novels. Dan Brown's (b. 1964) mystery thrillers *Angels & Demons* (2000), *The Da Vinci Code* (2003), *The Lost Symbol* (2009), *Inferno* (2013) and *Origin* (2017), whose protagonist is a professor of symbology, stimulated a huge amount of interest in occultist groups and organizations. But in terms of books (and movie adaptations), no one has done more to bring these themes into the mainstream than J. K. Rowling (b. 1965), whose phenomenally successful seven-volume *Harry Potter* series (1997–2007), as well as the more recent *Fantastic Beasts* trilogy, draw on many of the traditions

Occultural advertising
These two posters advertising TV series – the American supernatural teen drama Buffy the Vampire Slayer and the more recent German science-fiction thriller Dark – reflect the impact of occult themes in popular culture.

that have been explored in this book. A character called Nicolas Flamel is even woven into the story, a nod to the real-life 14th-century French scribe who developed a posthumous reputation for alchemy and was believed to have discovered the philosophers' stone.

Occulture is increasingly present on the small screen, too. While popular series such as *Charmed* (1998–2006) and *Buffy the Vampire Slayer* (1997–2003) engaged with the supernatural in an imaginative way, there was little connection with previous occultism. This was to change, however, with series such as the German-language Netflix thriller *Dark* (2017–2020), in which a tattoo on the back of the villainous time-travelling priest Noah is taken from an engraving in Heinrich Khunrath's *Amphitheatrum Sapientiae Aeternae*, the latter drawing inspiration from the *Emerald Tablet* of Hermes Trismegistus. John Dee's well-known occult glyph from his *Monas Hieroglyphica* (1564) appears in the British supernatural thriller *Requiem* (2018), and the long-running American dark fantasy series *Supernatural* (2005–20) references several magical alphabets, including Enochian,

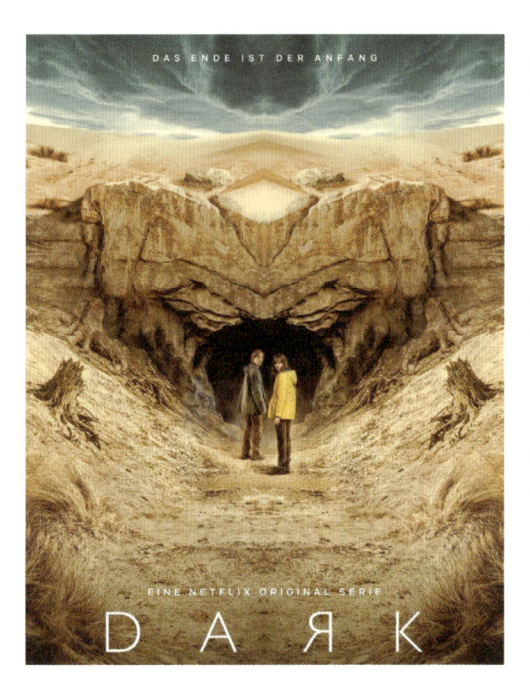

◁ Zuhair Murad, tarot dress displaying cards of the major arcana, Paris Fashion Week, 6 July 2022
A model walks the runway during Murad's Haute Couture Autumn/Winter 2022–23 show.

▷ Maria Grazia Chiuri, 'Tarot Card' coat, Paris Fashion Week, 3 July 2017
Influenced by the Visconti–Sforza deck, this design formed part of the Christian Dior Haute Couture Autumn/Winter 2017-18 collection.

connected with both Dee and Crowley, for summoning angels. A recent successful televisual adaptation of occult-themed historical-fantasy novels comes from American history professor and novelist Deborah Harkness (b. 1965), who has not only written the scholarly *John Dee's Conversations with Angels* (1999), but also the best-selling *All Souls Trilogy* (2011–14).

Sometimes, however, literature leads to other forms of occulture. The tarot novel *Il castello dei destini incrociati* ('*The Castle of Crossed Destinies*', 1973) of Italian writer Italo Calvino (1923–1985) and the dramatic imagery of tarot cards has been a source of inspiration for high fashion. Italian designer Maria Grazia Chiuri (b. 1964), creative director of Dior, commissioned an embroidered 'Tarot Card' coat for the Autumn–Winter 2017–18 collection, based on the 15th-century Visconti–Sforza deck. This was followed by a collection for the 2018 Dior Resort show, in collaboration with the shamanic healer Vicki Noble (b. 1947), who with artist Karen Vogel co-authored the 1981 feminist

Tarot-inspired sculptures in the Tarot Garden, Pescia Fiorentina, Italy
Created in the Tuscan village of Pescia Fiorentina by French-American artist Niki de Saint Phalle, the Tarot Garden officially opened on 15 May 1998 and features twenty-two sculptures, each inspired by a card in the major arcana.

Motherpeace tarot deck. Chiuri then went on to create a new Haute Couture collection for Spring–Summer 2021 inspired by Calvino's novel. For the 2021 science fiction epic *Dune*, based on the novels of Frank Herbert (1920–86) costume designer Jacqueline West used the High Priestess card (together with the Queen of Wands and Queen of Cups) as a source for her design for the black dresses of the secretive matriarchal sisterhood of the Bene Gesserit. The occult can also be found in more affordable couture: Brisbane-based Black Milk Clothing has released several limited edition items based on the colourful alchemical and kabbalistic engravings in the first edition of Heinrich Khunrath's *Amphitheatre of Eternal Wisdom* (1595): the *Eternal Wisdom Tee Dress* (2017), *Eternal Wisdom Kimono* (2018), and the amusingly named *Eternal Wisdom Long Sleeve Evil Mini Skater Dress* (2021).

From the catwalk to the comic book, occulture is versatile and most definitely present in the works of ceremonial magician and comic book writer Alan Moore (b. 1953), member of The Moon and Serpent

Grand Egyptian Theatre of Marvels, which performs occult 'workings' set to music, the first eponymous recording released in 1996. Moore's occult knowledge is especially prominent in the thirty-two issues of his *Promethea* comic book series (1999–2005). In Issue 12, for example, he explores the tarot, including images of an at times distinctly Crowley-influenced major arcana. In Issue 13, he turns to the Kabbalah and develops it over the next ten issues, introducing readers, for example, to the 10 spheres of the *sefirot* on the Tree of Life and their 22 interlinking paths, as well as their connections with specific tarot cards.

Last but by no means least, occult themes lie behind some popular video games. These include *The Council* (2018), set in the 18th century, which centres on the members of a fictional secret society called the Golden Order that seeks occult artefacts; *Goetia* (2018), a Victorian mystery in which the player becomes the ghost of a girl, Abigail Blackwood, with reference to ceremonial magic and Solomonic seals; and the tongue-in-cheek *Astrologaster* (2021), based on the life of English physician, astrologer and alchemist Simon Forman (1552–1611). Anyone interested in the Golden Dawn may be intrigued to know of the virtual reality initiation *Virtual Temple: Order of the Golden Dawn* (2017), described as a 'simulation game'.

Although some of these adoptions of occult material may seem trivial or at least light-hearted, they should not be automatically dismissed. Occult thought is resilient and nothing if not adaptable. It has survived over the centuries, adapting to cultural changes, finding new media in which to transmit its practices and beliefs. Sometimes mainstream, sometimes an undercurrent or part of counterculture, what may appear conservative and traditional today was often cutting-edge in its day, avant-garde, innovative, challenging and transgressive. Today the occult seems to be enjoying a renaissance, its syncretic, eclectic and polymorphous nature holding great appeal to many seeking other wellsprings of inspiration to nourish their imagination.

Barrington Coleby, *The Hermit*, c. 1971 — This haunting image appeared on the inside cover of the 1971 album Led Zeppelin IV and closely resembles the card of the same name from the Waite-Smith Tarot.

GLOSSARY

Adam Kadmon primordial man, divine light with a human form, in a state of pure potential.
Anima Mundi the soul of the world, with the cosmos considered to be a living being.
Anthroposophy 'human wisdom', a spiritual movement founded in the early 20th century by Rudolf Steiner, who advanced the belief in an objective, intellectually comprehensible spiritual world, accessible to human experience.
Archaeus (or **Archeus**) an invisible alchemical spirit that exists in living things; the artist, physician and occult power of nature.
Ascendant the astronomical or astrological point of the zodiac rising on the eastern horizon at any given moment, typically at the moment of an individual's birth. It is said to indicate the direction of one's path in life, how one interacts with one's surroundings and the persona one presents to the world.
Asiyah action and *Olam Asiyah*, the world of action, the lowest of the four spiritual worlds of the Kabbalah, representing purely material existence.
Astral Plane variously said to be the plane of existence crossed by the soul in its astral body between death and rebirth; the world of the celestial spheres, populated by angels and spirits; or more generally the spirit world where the souls of the dead exist.
Atzilut emanation, and *Olam Atzilut*, the world of emanation, the highest of the four kabbalistic worlds, the closest to God, the realm of pure divinity.
Automatic writing a psychic ability where the practitioner's pen is moved by spirits, enabling them to produce writing without consciously thinking.
Azoth from *al-zauq*, the Arabic term for quicksilver. Used by alchemists to refer to both primal and ultimate matter.
Bereshit the first Hebrew word of the book of Genesis, meaning 'In the beginning'; hence *Bereshit* denotes the work of creation in Kabbalah.
Beriah or **Beri'ah** creation, and *Olam Beriah*, the world of creation, the second of the four kabbalistic worlds, the abode of the archangels.
Bestiary a compendium of natural and mythical beasts with illustrations, descriptions and the natural and moral associations of the beasts.
Cartomancy fortune telling or divination with a deck of cards.
Chakra often translated as a wheel: focal points in the body according to Hindu and Buddhist philosophy. There are traditionally seven, rising from the base of the spine to the crown of the head.
Channelling acting as a conduit for an entity that is disembodied or on another plane of existence, often the channeller is in a seance or in a trance state.
Chiromancy palmistry, character analysis or fortune-telling by reading the aspects of a person's hands.
Chrysopoeia 'gold-making', a term used in ancient Greek transmutational alchemy.
Chymiatria chemical medicine, the use of minerals, metals and plants in the creation of medicine.

Cryptography the development of encoded writing to ensure secure, private communication.
Crystallomancy crystal gazing or divination with a crystal.
Ectoplasm a term used in spiritualism for a substance or spiritual energy manifested by mediums.
Ein Soph literally infinite or without end, a kabbalistic term to denote the ineffable God, prior to any self-manifestation or emanation.
Electrum a naturally occurring alloy of silver and gold; **Electrum magicum** is a magical alloy of the seven metals of medieval alchemy, made through a process of astral magic.
Elixir often considered to be a liquid that can convert base metals into noble metals (silver and gold) or cure human ailments; in Chinese alchemy it was said to grant immortal life.
Emet Hebrew for 'truth'. It is formed of the first, middle and last letter of the Hebrew alphabet, denoting the totality of the divine plan.
Empyrean heaven a classical term for the highest heaven, the abode of God and souls in salvation.
Extrasensory perception or **ESP** paranormal or psychic abilities including telepathy, clairvoyance, and precognition.
Freemasonry or **Masonry** medieval stonemason guilds that developed into fraternal organizations. Members join lodges, some more occult than others.
Gematria the kabbalistic practice of calculating the numerical value of a Hebrew name, word or phrase by using the alphanumeric nature of the Hebrew alphabet. Through *gematria*, concordances and significances can be divined between words or phrases with the same numerical value.
Goëtia sorcery, often considered malefic and involving demons and evil spirits, transmitted through grimoires.
Hermetism a religio-philosophical system based on the *Hermetica*, teachings of the mythical sage Hermes Trismegistus; **Hermeticism** is the broader range of teachings and practices of alchemy, astrology and magic said to be derived from Trismegistus.
Hyle primal matter before it has been given any shape or form.
Jindan the golden elixir of internal Chinese alchemy.
Jyotisha from the Sanskrit word for heavenly body, denoting Hindu or Vedic astrology.
Klifot a kabbalistic term for the evil or impure spiritual counterparts to the *sefirot*; representing the *Sitra Achra*, the other side or the side of impurity.
Lapidary a compendium of precious and semi-precious stones, popular in the Middle Ages, often associating stones with astrological and medical properties.
Macrocosm–Microcosm the analogical relations between the greater and lesser worlds, i.e. the universe and the human being.
Martinism a form of Christian mysticism first transmitted through a Masonic high-degree system established around 1740 in France by the theurgist and theosopher Martinez de Pasqually.
Merkavah literally Hebrew for chariot, a form of Jewish mysticism based around Ezekiel's vision of the chariot and angels in the Old Testament. *Merkavah* was focussed on ascent to the *hekhalot* or heavenly palaces and the throne of God.

Metoposcopy a form of character analysis or divination in which the expert reads the pattern of lines on the subject's forehead.

Necromancy the magical practice of communicating with the dead and summoning apparitions, which developed into a darker form of magic involving spirits, demons and angels.

Neidan a Chinese, Taoist form of internal physical and spiritual alchemy where the human body is thought of as a cauldron in which the three treasures of essence, breath and spirit are mixed. The goal was to promote long life and create an immortal spiritual body.

Neoplatonism a version of Platonic philosophy that emerged in the 3rd century CE and reinterpreted the ideas of Plato, famous representatives being Plotinus, Porphyry and Iamblichus.

Notarikon a kabbalistic term for deriving a sentence or idea from a word, using the letters of the word as the initial or final letters of words in a sentence, like an acronym. Also, a method of using the initial, middle or final letters of words in a sentence to form a word.

Ouroboros an ancient symbol depicting a serpent or dragon swallowing its own tail, symbolizing eternity or, in alchemy, repeated digestion of material.

Parapsychology the study of psychic phenomena including extrasensory perception, clairvoyance, telepathy, precognition, telekinesis and other paranormal subjects, such as ghosts.

Pentagrammaton the five-letter name for God, YHSVH, originating in 15th-century Christian Cabala.

Philosophers' Stone an alchemical substance, connected or identified with the elixir, capable of turning base metals such as mercury into gold or silver.

Physiognomy the practice of assessing a person's character from their appearance, particularly their face.

Quadrivium the four subjects considered the foundation for the study of philosophy and theology in medieval education of the liberal arts: arithmetic, geometry, music, and astronomy.

Rosicrucianism a spiritual and philosophical brotherhood that was Protestant in origin and arose in Europe in the early 17th century with the publication of two anonymous manifestos, the *Fama Fraternitatis* (1614) and *Confessio Fraternitatis* (1615), calling for a universal reformation of the arts and sciences.

Scrying a divinatory practice involving gazing into something reflective (e.g. a crystal, mirror or polished sword), to receive revelatory visions and messages.

Sefira/Sefirot emanations of the divine (usually described as ten in number) that appear on the kabbalistic Tree of Life.

Shem HaMephorash literally the explicit name, in Kabbalah it is most commonly the four-letter name for God, the Tetragrammaton, although 12, 22, 42, or 72 letter versions also exist.

Shemot 'names', i.e. the names of God. The Tetragrammaton is sometimes called simply *Hashem*, 'the name'.

Spagyria or **spagyrics** a term coined by Paracelsus, a medical approach in which substances, including poisons, were separated into the primordial elements, refined, purified and recombined to separate healthy properties from toxins and make more potent medicines.

Spiritism a reincarnationist and spiritualist doctrine founded on the existence, manifestations and teachings of spirits, established in France in the mid-19th century by writer and educator Allan Kardec.

Spiritualism a movement popular in the 19th and early 20th centuries, according to which an individual's awareness survives after death and can be contacted to provide insights for those still living.

Suffumigations the burning of incenses, generally of plant origin, to produce fumes as part of some magic rituals. The incense was burned so that the smoke rose upwards, for example through a table on which a magic seal was placed, so that it purified or charged the object and also provided a subtle medium in which a spirit could manifest.

Synchronicity a notion first introduced by the depth psychologist Carl Jung, concerning events that appear meaningfully related despite the absence of any causal connection, whether a significant 'coincidence' or divinatory practices like tarot and the *I Ching*.

Taoism or **Daoism** a Chinese religio-philosophical tradition with an emphasis on living in harmony with the Tao, the way, best known through the classic work, the *Tao Te Ching* and practices like tai chi and qigong.

Temurah substituting letters in words to discover new meanings, one of three methods used by Kabbalists to interpret texts.

Tetragrammaton the four letter divine name, YHVH (Yahweh).

Tetraktys a triangular figure of ten points arranged in four descending rows (one, two, three, and four points per row), of great significance to Pythagoreans.

Thelema literally ancient Greek for will or desire, an occult organization or new religious movement founded by Aleister Crowley.

Theosophy a religio-philosophical movement drawing inspiration from Eastern Hindu and Buddhist thought and Western occult philosophies, established in the United States in 1875, its best-known representative being Helena Blavatsky.

Theurgia or **theurgy** magic with a divine connection, religious purpose or magic performed with the intent for the practitioner to be unified with the gods.

Transmutation the alchemical notion of transforming one substance into another, best known in the idea of turning base metals, such as lead or copper, into the noble metals, silver and gold.

Tria prima or '**three principles**' an alchemical notion promoted by Paracelsus, who argued that all matter consisted of mercury, sulphur and salt, respectively the spirit, soul and body of things.

Trivium grammar, logic and rhetoric: the verbal counterpart to the quadrivium.

Waidan ancient Chinese external alchemy, the counterpart to *neidan* or internal alchemy, with a focus on creating elixirs of immortality by heating natural substances, such as minerals and metals, in a crucible.

Yetzirah formation, connected with **Olam Yetzirah**, the world of formation, the third of four kabbalistic worlds. Also connected to the famous proto-kabbalistic text, the *Sefer Yetzirah* or *Book of Formation*.

FURTHER READING

BACKGROUND & GENERAL READERS
Hanegraaff, Wouter J. (ed.), *Dictionary of Gnosis & Western Esotericism* (Leiden: Brill, 2006).
Luck, George, *Arcana Mundi: Magic and the Occult in the Greek and Roman Worlds, A Collection of Ancient Texts* (Baltimore, MD: The Johns Hopkins University Press, 1985).
Magee, Glenn Alexander (ed.), *The Cambridge Handbook of Western Mysticism and Esotericism* (Cambridge: Cambridge University Press, 2016).
Maxwell-Stuart, Peter G. (trans. & ed.), *The Occult in Early Modern Europe: A Documentary History* (New York: Palgrave Macmillan, 1999).
Monod, Paul Kléber, *Solomon's Secret Arts: The Occult in the Age of Enlightenment* (New Haven, CT: Yale University Press, 2013).
Partridge, Christopher (ed.), *The Occult World* (Abingdon: Routledge, 2015).
Wilson, Colin, *The Occult: A History* (New York: Random House, 1971).

HERMES TRISMEGISTUS
Copenhaver, Brian P., *Hermetica: The Greek 'Corpus Hermeticum' and the Latin 'Asclepius' in a new English Translation, with notes and introduction* (Cambridge: Cambridge University Press, 1992).
Faivre, Antoine, *The Eternal Hermes: From Greek God to Alchemical Magus*, trans. Joscelyn Godwin (Grand Rapids, MI: Phanes Press, 1995).
Fowden, Garth, *The Egyptian Hermes: A Historical Approach to the Late Pagan Mind* (Princeton, NJ: Princeton University Press, 1986).

ASTROLOGY
Campion, Nicholas, *A History of Western Astrology, Volume II: The Medieval and Modern Worlds* (London: Continuum, 2009).
Dooley, Brendan (ed.), *Companion to Astrology in the Renaissance* (Leiden: Brill, 2014).
Günther Oestmann, H. Darrel Rutkin and Kocku von Stuckrad (eds.), *Horoscopes and Public Spheres: Essays on the History of Astrology* (Berlin & New York: Walter de Gruyter, 2005).
Page, Sophie, *Astrology in Medieval Manuscripts* (Toronto: University of Toronto Press, 2002).
Tester, Jim, *A History of Western Astrology* (Woodbridge: The Boydell Press, 1996).

ALCHEMY
Atwood, Mary Anne, *A Suggestive Inquiry into the Hermetic Mystery* (Belfast: William Tait, 1918).
Cheak, Aaron (ed.), *Alchemical Traditions: From Antiquity to the Avant-Garde* (Melbourne: Numen Books, 2013).
Linden, Stanton J. (ed.), *The Alchemy Reader: From Hermes Trismegistus to Isaac Newton* (Cambridge: Cambridge University Press, 2003).
Morrisson, Mark S., *Modern Alchemy, Occultism and the Emergence of Atomic Theory* (Oxford: Oxford University Press, 2007).
Newman, William R. and Anthony Grafton (eds.), *Secrets of Nature: Astrology and Alchemy in Early Modern Europe* (Cambridge, MA: The MIT Press, 2001).
Newman, William R., *Promethean Ambitions: Alchemy and the Quest to Perfect Nature* (Chicago, IL: University of Chicago Press, 2005).
Nummedal, Tara and Donna Bilak (eds.), F*urnace and Fugue: A Digital Edition of Michael Maier's Atalanta fugiens (1618) with Scholarly Commentary* (Charlottesville, VA: University of Virginia Press, 2020).
Paracelsus, ed. and trans. Nicholas Goodrick-Clarke (Berkeley, CA: North Atlantic Books, 1999).
Principe, Lawrence M., *The Secrets of Alchemy* (Chicago, IL: University of Chicago Press, 2013).
Purš, Ivo and Vladimir Karpenko (eds), *Alchemy and Rudolf II: Exploring the Secrets of Nature in Central Europe in the 16th and 17th Centuries* (Prague: Artefactum, 2016).
Roob, Alexander, *The Hermetic Museum: Alchemy and Mysticism* (Cologne: Taschen, 1997).

ROSICRUCIANS & FREEMASONS
Akerman, Susanna, *Rose Cross over the Baltic: The Spread of Rosicrucianism in Northern Europe* (Leiden: Brill, 1998).
Bogdan, Henrik, *Western Esotericism and Rituals of Initiation* (Albany, NY: State University of New York Press, 2007).
McIntosh, Christopher, *The Rosicrucians: The History, Mythology, and Rituals of an Esoteric Order* (York Beach, ME: Samuel Weiser, 1997).
The Chemical Wedding of Christian Rosenkreutz, trans. Joscelyn Godwin (Grand Rapids, MI: Phanes Press, 1991).

KABBALAH
Dan, Joseph (ed.) and Ronald C. Kiener (trans.), *The Early Kabbalah* (New York: Paulist Press, 1986).
Dan, Joseph (ed.), *The Christian Kabbalah: Jewish Mystical Books & Their Christian Interpreters* (Cambridge, MA: Harvard College Library, 1997).
Halevi, Z'ev ben Shimon, *Kabbalah: Tradition of Hidden Knowledge* (New York: Thames & Hudson, 1980).
Idel, Moshe, *Studies in Ecstatic Kabbalah* (Albany, NY: State University of New York Press, 1988).
Pico della Mirandola, Giovanni, *On the Dignity of Man, On Being and the One, Heptaplus* (Indianapolis, IN: Hackett, 1998).
Reuchlin, Johann, *De Arte Cabalistica: On the Art of the Kabbalah*, trans. Martin and Sarah Goodman (New York: Abaris Books, 1983).
Scholem, Gershom, *On the Kabbalah and Its Symbolism*, trans. Ralph Manheim (New York: Schocken, 1969).

MAGIC
Agrippa, Henry Cornelius, *Three Books of Occult Philosophy*, trans. James Freake, ed. Donald Tyson (St. Paul, MN: Llewellyn Publications, 1993).
Attrell, Dan and David Porreca (trans.), *Picatrix: A Medieval Treatise on Astral Magic* (University Park, PA: Pennsylvania State University Press, 2019).
Betz, Hans Dieter (ed.), *Greek Magical Papyri in Translation* (Chicago, IL: University of Chicago Press, 1986).

Bremmer, Jan N. and Jan R. Veenstra (eds), *The Metamorphosis of Magic from Late Antiquity to the Early Modern Period* (Leuven: Peeters, 2002).

Bruno, Giordano, *Cause, Principle and Unity and Essays on Magic*, eds. Richard J. Blackwell and Robert de Lucca (Cambridge: Cambridge University Press, 1998).

Burnett, Charles, *Magic and Divination in the Middle Ages: Texts and Techniques in the Islamic and Christian Worlds* (Aldershot: Ashgate, 1996).

Clucas, Stephen (ed.), *John Dee: Interdisciplinary Studies in English Renaissance Thought* (Dordrecht: Springer, 2006).

Eamon, William, *Science and the Secrets of Nature: Books of Secrets in Medieval and Early Modern Culture* (Princeton, NJ: Princeton University Press, 1994).

Fanger, Claire (ed.), *Conjuring Spirits: Texts and Traditions of Medieval Ritual Magic* (Stroud: Sutton Publishing, 1998).

Fanger, Claire (ed.) *Invoking Angels: Theurgic Ideas and Practices, Thirteenth to Sixteenth Centuries* (University Park, PA: Pennsylvania State University Press, 2012).

Ficino, Marsilio, *Three Books on Life: A Critical Edition and Translation with Introduction and Notes*, ed. and trans. Carol V. Kaske and John R. Clark (Tempe, AZ: Medieval & Renaissance Texts & Studies, 1998).

Graf, Fritz, *Magic in the Ancient World*, trans. Franklin Philip (Cambridge, MA: Harvard University Press, 1997).

Kieckhefer, Richard, *Magic in the Middle Ages* (Cambridge: Cambridge University Press, 1989).

King, Francis (ed.), *The Secret Rituals of the O.T.O.* (New York: Samuel Weiser, 1973).

Lévi, Eliphas, *Transcendental Magic, its Doctrine and Ritual*, trans. A.E. Waite (London: George Redway, 1896).

Lévi, Eliphas, *The History of Magic*, trans. A.E. Waite (York Beach, ME: Samuel Weiser, 2000).

Page, Sophie and Catherine Rider (eds.), *The Routledge History of Medieval Magic* (Abingdon: Routledge, 2019).

Peterson, Joseph H. (ed.), *John Dee's Five Books of Mystery: Original Sourcebook of Enochian Magic* (Boston, MA/York Beak, ME: Weiser Books, 2003).

Savage-Smith, Emilie (ed.), *Magic and Divination in Early Islam* (Aldershot: Ashgate, 2004).

Yates, Frances A., *Giordano Bruno and the Hermetic Tradition* (London: Routledge & Kegan Paul, 1964).

Zambelli, Paola, *White Magic, Black Magic in the European Renaissance* (Leiden: Brill, 2007).

Zika, Charles, *Exorcising Our Demons: Magic, Witchcraft, and Visual Culture in Early Modern Europe* (Leiden: Brill, 2003).

OCCULTISM & SPIRITISM

Ahern, Geoffrey, *Sun at Midnight: The Rudolf Steiner Movement and the Western Esoteric Tradition* (Wellingborough: Aquarian Press, 1984).

Bogdan, Henrik and Martin P. Starr (eds.), *Aleister Crowley and Western Esotericism* (Oxford: Oxford University Press, 2012).

Bogdan, Henrik and Gordan Djurdjevic (eds.), *Occultism in a Global Perspective* (Abingdon: Routledge, 2014).

Butler, Alison, *Victorian Occultism and the Making of Modern Magic* (London: Palgrave Macmillan, 2011).

Crabtree, Adam, *From Mesmer to Freud* (New Haven, CT: Yale University Press, 1993).

Gauld, Alan, *A History of Hypnotism* (Cambridge: Cambridge University Press, 1992).

Gilbert, Robert A., *The Golden Dawn Companion* (Wellingborough: Aquarian Press, 1986).

Godwin, Joscelyn, *The Theosophical Englightenment* (New York: State University of New York Press, 1994).

Jonsson, Inge, *Visionary Scientist and The Drama of Creation* (West Chester, PA: Swedenborg Foundation, 1999).

Kemp, Daren and James R. Lewis (eds), *Handbook of New Age* (Leiden: Brill, 2007).

Owen, Alex, *The Place of Enchantment: British Occultism and the Culture of the Modern* (Chicago: University of Chicago Press, 2006).

Treitel, Corinna, *A Science for the Soul: Occultism and the Genesis of the German Modern* (Baltimore, MD: Johns Hopkins University Press, 2004).

Webb, James, *The Occult Underground* (La Salle, IL: Open Court, 1974).

Wilson, Leigh, *Modernism and Magic: Experiments with Spiritualism, Theosophy, and the Occult* (Edinburgh: Edinburgh University Press, 2013).

TAROT

Crowley, Aleister, *The Book of Thoth: A Short Essay on the Tarot of the Egyptians* (London: Chiswick Press, 1944).

Decker, Donald and Michael Dummett, *A History of the Occult Tarot: 1870-1970* (London: Duckworth, 2002).

Dummett, Michael, *The Visconti-Sforza Tarot Cards* (New York: George Braziller Inc., 1986).

Farley, Helen, *A Cultural History of Tarot: from Entertainment to Esotericism* (London: I.B. Tauris, 2009).

Kaplan, Stuart, *The Encyclopedia of Tarot*, 4 vols (Stamford, CT: US Games Systems, 1978-2003)

Ouspensky, P. D., *Symbolism of the Tarot* (London: Kegan Paul, 1938).

Waite, A. E., *The Pictorial Key to the Tarot* (London: Rider, 1911).

Wirth, Oswald, *Tarot of the Magicians: The Occult Symbols of the Major Arcana that Inspired Modern Tarot* (San Francisco, CA: RedWheel/Weiser, 2012).

NEW AGE & OCCULTURE

Asprem, Egil, *Arguing with Angels: Enochian Magic and Modern Occulture* (Albany, NY: State University of New York Press, 2012).

Hanegraaff, Wouter J., *New Age Religion and Western Culture: Esotericism in the Mirror of Secular Thought* (Leiden: E. J. Brill, 1996).

Jung, C. G., *Psychology and Alchemy*, trans. R. F. C. Hull (Princeton, NJ: Princeton University Press, 1968).

Jung, C. G., *Psychology and the Occult*, trans. R. F. C. Hull (London: Routledge, 1982).

Lewis, James R. and J. Gordon Melton (eds.), *Perspectives on the New Age* (Albany, NY: State University of New York Press, 1992).

Partridge, Christopher, *The Re-Enchantment of the West Volume I: Alternative Spiritualities, Sacralization, Popular Culture, and Occulture* (London and New York: T&T Clark International, 2004).

Sources of Illustrations

Every effort has been made to locate and credit copyright holders of the material reproduced in this book. The author and publisher apologize for any omissions or errors, which can be corrected in future editions.

a = above, b = below, c = centre, l = left, r = right

Front cover The John Rylands Research Institute and Library (German MS 3). The University of Manchester **Back cover** Wellcome Collection

1 Allard Pierson, University of Amsterdam (HS. PH317) **2** Wellcome Collection **4** Courtesy of Peter Diem. © DACS 2023 **6–7** The John Rylands Research Institute and Library German (MS 3). The University of Manchester **8** Charles Walker Collection / Alamy Stock Photo **11** Photo © Governatorato SCV – Directorate of Museums **12–13** Courtesy of Science History Institute, Philadelphia **14** U.S. National Library of Medicine **15** Smithsonian Libraries and Archives, Washington DC **16–17** The British Library archive / Bridgeman Images **18** Christine Webb / Alamy Stock Photo **19** The British Library archive / Bridgeman Images **20** Bibliothèque nationale de France (Français 135) **21al** Beinecke Rare Book and Manuscript Library, Yale University **21ac** The President and Fellows of St John's College, Oxford **21ar** Wellcome Collection **21bl** Frankfurt University Library **21bc** Harris Brisbane Dick Fund, 1932 / The Metropolitan Museum of Art (32.18(1-2)) **21br** Bibliothèque nationale de France (RES-R-1438) **22l** Samuel H. Kress Collection / National Gallery of Art, Washington (1957.14.1069) **22r** Samuel H. Kress Collection / National Gallery of Art, Washington (1957.14.862.a) **23** Biblioteca Medicea Laurenziana, Florence **24–25** Wellcome Collection **26** Rijksmuseum, Amsterdam (RP-P-BI-1459) **28** Wellcome Collection **29l** Historic Images / Alamy Stock Photo **29r** Bibliotheca Philosophica Hermetica, Amsterdam **30r** Charles Walker Collection / Alamy Stock Photo **31** The George Washington Masonic National Memorial **33** Christie's Images / Bridgeman Images **34** Bibliotheca Philosophica Hermetica Collection, Amsterdam **36** Bibliothèque de Genève **39a**, **39c** Sailingstone Travel / Alamy Stock Photo **39b** imageBROKER.com / Alamy Stock Photo **40–41** The University of Glasgow (MS Hunter 229 (U.3.2)) **42–43** Wellcome Collection **44l** Photo Juraj Lipták / LDA Saxony-Anhalt **44r** The Trustees of the British Museum (K.8538) **45l** Photo Josse / Bridgeman Images **45r** Novapix / Bridgeman Images **46–47** Wellcome Collection **48** Danvis Collection / Alamy Stock Photo **49** Bibliothèque nationale de France (Arabe 2583) **51** Bayerische Staatsbibliothek, Munich **52–53** Courtesy of the Ministry of Culture – Gallerie Estensi, Biblioteca Estense Universitaria, Modena **54** The British Library archive / Bridgeman Images **55** Azoor Photo / Alamy Stock Photo **56** Zentralbibliothek Zürich (SCH R 201) **57** Getty Research Institute **59** Used by permission of Leyla Rael Rudhyar **60** PBL Collection / Alamy Stock Photo **63** Beinecke Rare Book and Manuscript Library, Yale University **64l** The Egyptian Museum, Cairo **64c** Biblioteca Nazionale Marciana, Venice (Gr. Z. 299 (584)) **64r** Bibliothèque nationale de France (Grec 2327) **65a** Zentralbibliothek, Zurich **65bl** Biblioteca dell'Accademia Nazionale dei Lincei, Rome **65bc**, **65br** Getty Research Institute **66l** Millard H Sharp / Science Photo Library **66r** Charles D. Winters / Science Source / Science Photo Library **67** Photo Christie's Images / Bridgeman Images **68l** Bibliothèque nationale de France (RES-R-1438) **68br** Bayerische Staatsbibliothek, Munich **69al** Bibliothèque nationale de France (FM-ICONOGR-ATLAS (1)) **69ar** Deutsche Fotothek **69bl** The University of Glasgow Library **69br** Bibliothèque nationale de France (RES-R-1438) **70** Bibliothèque nationale de France (Ms-975 réserve) **72–73** Österreichische Nationalbibliothek, Vienna **74** The John Research Institute and Library (German MS 3), The University of Manchester **75** Topkapi Sarayi Ahmet III Library, Istanbul **76** Bayerische Staatsbibliothek, Munich **77al** Zentralbibliothek, Zürich **77ac** The British Library archive / Bridgeman Images **77ar** Bibliothèque nationale de France (RES-R-1438) **77bl** SLUB Dresden **77bc** Complutense University of Madrid **77br** Album / Alamy Stock Photo **78** Zürich, Zentralbibliothek **80** Science Museum Group Collection © The Board of Trustees of the Science Museum **81** Wellcome Collection **82–83** The Huntington Library **84** The Picture Art Library / Alamy Stock Photo **85** Francis A. Countway Library of Medicine **86–87** Bibliotheca Philosophica Hermetica Collection, Amsterdam **89** University of Wisconsin – Madison. Libraries. (Flat Shelving Duveen D 897) **90** Image courtesy of Estate of Leonora Carrington and Mixografía © Estate of Leonora Carrington / ARS, NY and DACS, London 2023 **93** Bibliothèque de Genève **94–95** Bodleian Libraries, University of Oxford **96** University and State Library of Saxony-Anhalt Martin-Luther-University Halle-Wittenberg **97** Wellcome Collection **99** Heritage Image Partnership Ltd / Alamy Stock Photo **100** Getty Research Institute **101** Photograph by Simon J. Downham, 2018 **102** By kind permission of Matthew Jaffe **103l** Cornell University Library **103r** Bibliothèque de Genève **104** Museum of Fine Arts, Boston (90.108) **106** The Picture Art Collection / Alamy Stock Photo **108 Photo** Saint Louis Art Museum. Funds given by Mr. and Mrs. George Schlapp, Mrs. Francis A. Mesker, the Henry L. and Natalie Edison Freund Charitable Trust, The Arthur and Helen Baer Charitable Foundation, Sam and Marilyn Fox, Mrs. Eleanor J. Moore, Mr. and Mrs. John Wooten Moore, Donna and William Nussbaum, Mr. and Mrs. James E. Schneithorst, Jain and Richard Shaikewitz, Mark Twain Bancshares, Inc., Mr. and Mrs. Gary Wolff, Mr. and Mrs. Lester P. Ackerman Jr., the Honorable and Mrs. Thomas F. Eagleton, Alison and John Ferring, Mrs. Gail K. Fischmann, Mr. and Mrs. Solon Gershman, Dr. and Mrs. Gary Hansen, Nancy and Kenneth Kranzberg, Mr. and Mrs. Gyo Obata, Jane and Warren Shapleigh, Lee and Barbara Wagman, Anabeth Calkins and John Weil, Museum Shop Fund, the Contemporary Art Society, and Museum Purchase; Dr. and Mrs. Harold J. Joseph, estate of Alice P. Francis, Fine Arts Associates, J. Lionberger Davis, Mr. and Mrs. Samuel B. Edison, Mr. and Mrs. Morton D. May, estate of Louise H. Franciscus, an anonymous donor, Miss Ella M. Boedeker, by exchange 1:1991. © Anselm Kiefer Courtesy Thaddaeus Ropac gallery, London · Paris · Salzburg · Seoul **109** Leonard Nimoy, courtesy R. Michelson Galleries **110–111** The Picture Art Collection / Alamy Stock Photo **113** Courtesy of the Library of the Jewish Theological Seminary, The National Library of Israel. '"Ktiv" Project, The National Library of Israel' **114** Wellcome Collection **116** The British Library archive / Bridgeman Images **119** Biblioteca Medicea Laurenziana, Florence **120** Museum August Kestner / Christian Tepper **121** Royal Library of the Monastery of San Lorenzo de El Escorial **122** Bibliothèque nationale de France (Français 1951) **123** The J. Paul Getty Museum, Los Angeles **124–125** Deutsche Fotothek **126l** The British Library archive / Bridgeman Images **126r** Bibliothèque nationale de France (Latin 9333) **127** The Metropolitan Museum of Art. Gift of Mr. and Mrs. Gordon S. Haight, 1980 (1980.228.1, .2a, b, .3) **128** Wellcome Collection **129** The U.S. National Library of Medicine **130** History & Art Collection / Alamy Stock Photo **132–133** Wellcome Collection **134l** Wellcome Collection **135** Wellcome Collection **137** Stephen Frost / Alamy Stock Photo **138** Bibliothèque nationale de France (Latin 7330) **141** Vatican Apostolic Library **142–143** Universitaetsbibliothek Leipzig **144** Cultural Collections, Library of the University of Newcastle, Australia **145** Picatrix Biblioteka Jagiellońska (BJ Rkp. 793 III) **146, 147** [Talisman] The Trustees of the British Museum (OA.1366) **147** [Manuscript illustrations] Cultural Collections, Library of the University of Newcastle, Australia **148** Magite Historic / Alamy Stock Photo **149** The Metropolitan Museum of Art. Purchase. Friends of Islamic Art Gifts, 1998 (1998.199) **150** Wellcome Collection **151** Bibliothèque nationale de France (Latin 7330) **152** KHM-Museumsverband / Kunsthistorisches Museum Wien, Kunstkammer **154–155** SLUB Dresden **157** The Metropolitan Museum of Art (43.106.1) **158** Birmingham Museums Trust. Presented by the Trustees of the Feeney Charitable Fund, 1925 **161** Courtesy of the University of Oslo Library Papyrus Collection **162** The National Library of Israel **163** National Central Library of Florence / Alamy Stock Photo **164** Wellcome Collection **165al** The British Library archive / Bridgeman Images **165ac** National Central Library of Florence / Alamy Stock Photo **165ar** Harold B. Lee Library **165bl** University Library, Leipzig **165br** The Trustees of the British Museum (1897,0813.10) **166** Bibliothèque nationale de France (Latin 9336) **168–169** Wellcome Collection **170** The British Library archive / Bridgeman Images **171l** Kassel University Library (4° Ms. astron. 3 110:51v) **171r** Kassel University Library (4° Ms. astron. 3 215:104r) **172** Wellcome Collection **173** The Trustees of the British Museum (1966,1001.1) **175** The Herzogin Anna Amalia Bibliothek, Klassik Stiftung Weimar (Q 455 (b)) **176** Courtesy the artist, Annely Juda Fine Art, London and P.P.O.W., New York **178** The Trustees of the British Museum (1859,0625.72) **181** Hulton Keystone / Getty Images **182** Wellcome Collection **183** Douglas Glass / Paul Popper / Popperfoto / Getty Images **184** History and Art Collection / Alamy Stock Photo **185** Moviepix / Getty Images **186, 187** Biblioteca Medicea Laurenziana, Florence **188** The Metropolitan Museum of Art. Gilman Collection, Gift of The Howard Gilman Foundation, 2005 (2005.100.384 (1–48)) **190** Photo La Gazette Drouot 2023 **191l** ARCHIVIO GBB / Alamy Stock Photo **192** Bibliothèque nationale de France (RESERVE FOL-DC-3684 (1)) **194** Charles Walker Collection / Alamy Stock Photo **195l** The Egyptian Museum, Cairo **195r** Underwood Archives Inc / Alamy Stock Photo **197** Museum of Witchcraft and Magic, Boscastle **198** Courtesy of Peter Forshaw **201al, 201ac** The Morgan Library & Museum, New York **201ar** Beinecke Rare Book & Manuscript Library, Yale University **201bl** The Morgan Library & Museum, New York **201bc** Beinecke Rare Book and Manuscript Library, Yale University **201br** The Morgan Library & Museum, New York **202** Wellcome Collection **203–204** Courtesy of Peter Forshaw **205** Wellcome Collection **206–210** Courtesy of Peter Forshaw **211** With kind permission from Johan Dreue **212** Courtesy The Magic Circle Collections / Darren Martin **213** Courtesy of Peter Forshaw **214** The Trustees of the British Museum (1973,0616.21.1-38) / With kind permission of use by the John Trinick Estate **215** *The Craftsman*, vol. XXIII, no. 1 (1 October 1912) **216–219** Rider-Waite Tarot deck images used with permission The Random House Group Limited. Rider-Waite is a registered trademark of U.S. Games Systems, Inc. All rights reserved. **222** Royal Museums of Fine Arts of Belgium, Brussels / Photo: J. Geleyns **225** The Solomon R. Guggenheim Foundation, Peggy Guggenheim Collection, Venice, 1976. © 2023 Artists Rights Society (ARS), New York / ADAGP, Paris and DACS, London 2023 **226** Photo: Belvedere, Vienna. Artothek of the Republic of Austria, permanent loan to Belvedere, Vienna. © DACS 2023 **227** Richard Morris **228** Jennifer Guidi, *Body Mind Spirit (The Seven Chakras)*, 2019. Graphite, coloured pencil and acrylic on paper, [image] 15.51 × 12.7 cm (6 ½ × 5 in.), [framed] 45.01 × 41.28 cm (17 ¾ × 16 ¼ in.). Photo by Brica Wilcox, courtesy of the artist **229** [Rock Crystal, Selenite, Amethyst, Lapis Lazuli, Turquoise, Peridot, Malachite, Rose Quartz, Carnelian, Tiger's Eye, Red Jasper, Ruby and Bloodstone] 123RF.com. [Diamond] Björn Wylezich / Alamy Stock Photo. [Purple Fluorite] Vladislav Gajic / Alamy Stock Photo. [Aquamarine] PjrRocks / Alamy Stock Photo. **230** Photo: AAG Auctioneers. © DACS 2023 **231** Rijksmuseum, Amsterdam (RP-T-1960-243) **232** ARTGEN / Alamy Stock Photo **233** Photo: Peter Harrington Rare Books. © ADAGP, Paris and DACS, London 2023 **234–235** © Estate of Leonora Carrington / ARS, NY and DACS, London 2023 **236** Getty Images **237** Photo by Michael Putland / Getty Images **238** Judith Collins / Alamy Stock Photo **240** Photo by Steve Schapiro / Corbis via Getty Images **242** Courtesy the artist, Annely Juda Fine Art, London and P.P.O.W., New York **243** Courtesy of Cinematerial.com **244l** Photo by Richard Bord / Getty Images **244r** Photo by Dominique Charriau / WireImage / Getty Images **245** Jean-Pierre Dalbéra **247** Barrington Colby Mom

INDEX

Illustrations are in **bold**.

Abiff, Hiram 28
Abū Ma'shar 49, **49**, 50, 54, **138**
Abulafia, Abraham 97, 242
Adam and Eve 22, **68**, 127
Adam Kadmon 96, **97**
Age of Aquarius 58, 236
Agrippa, Heinrich Cornelius 23–7, 117, 127–34, 140, **144**, 153, 156, 171, 184, 231
Al-Kindi 49–50, 148, 149, 174
Albarn, Damon 242
Albertus Magnus **77**, 121, 123
alchemy: basic overview 61, 66; China 66, **67**; early history 18, 62; etymology 62–6; Greece 71; India 66–7; Islamic 71–5; Kabbalah 105; laboratories **60**, 72–3, 81, **84**, 88; *magnum opus* (Great Work) **70**, 88; New Age 232; Renaissance 79; Scientific Revolution 28; symbols **14**, 79, **82–3**, **86–7**; tarot 220; theosophy 85; triad 68, **69**, **74**, 81; Zosimos of Panopolis 67–71. *See also* philosophers' stone
Alemanno, Yohanan 97
alembic **72–3**, **80**
Alfonso X of Castile and León 18–19, **121**, 121–2, **141**, 153, **163**, **165**
alphabet: Kabbalah 98–100, 105, **110–11**, 140, 153; occulture 243; ritual magic **168–9**; tarot 204, 205, 207, 209
amulets **113**, 150–1. *See also* talismans
angels **104**, **106–7**, **110–11**, 131, 160, 162, **166**, 167, **168–70**, 174, 196
Antonia of Württemberg, Princess **106–7**, 108
Apollonius of Tyana 189
Aquinas, Thomas 19, 61, 150–1
Arabic texts 18–19
archetypes **59**, 196, 200
Arcimboldo, Giuseppe **130**
Arroyo, Stephen 58
Assagioli, Roberto 58
astral travel 112, 189, 213
Astrological Psychology Institute 58
astrology: astral magic 139, 140, 148–9, 156; astrology **141**; basic overview 37; early history 15, 38–45; influences on substances 19–22; Islamic 49, 50; Kabbalah **36**; lapidaries 121–2; metoposcopy **132–3**; New Age 232, 224; political 184; Renaissance 50–4; split from astronomy 56; theosophy 57–8; types 45–9; Vedic 57. *See also* zodiac
astronomy 50, 56, 79, 140, 144
Atalanta fugiens (Maier) 21, **68**, **69**
athanor **16–17**, **34**, **72–3**
Atwood, Mary Anne 85
auras 226, 228

Bahir (*Sefer ha-Bahir*) 92
Bailey, Alice 224
Baphomet **186–7**, **190**, **192**
Barrett, Francis **150**, 184
Bartholomaeus Anglicus 20
Beatles 236, **236**
Bembo, Bonifacio 200, **201**
Bernardus Silvestris 50–4
bestiaries 122, **122**, **123**
bezoar stones **127**
Bhagavadgita 109
Bird of Hermes **77**, **82–3**, **85**
Black Sabbath 241
Blake, William **104**, **178**
Blavatsky, Helena Petrovna 30–1, 112, 190–1, **191**
Blue Öyster Cult 241
body: four humours 20; influence of the zodiac **46–7**
Boehme, Jacob 28, 85, 109
Bowie, David 237–41
Boyle, Robert 28
Brauner, Victor 232
Brazil 185
Breton, André 232, **233**
Brown, Dan 242
Bruno, Giordano 27, 140, 148
Buddhism 190, **230**
Bureus, Johannes 241
Byrhtferth of Ramsey 21

calendars **154–5**, 174, **192**
Calvin, John 55
Calvino, Italo 244–5
Campanella, Tommaso 55–6, 156
Capra, Fritjof 226
Cardano, Girolamo 237
Carey, Danny 242
Carrington, Leonora 233, **234–5**
cartomancy 32, 202, 204–5
Chaboseau, Augustin 32
Chaboseau, Jean 220
chakras **228–9**
chaos magick 196, 230
character. *See* personality
China, alchemy 18, 66, **67**
chiromancy 136, **238–9**
Chiuri, Maria Grazia 244–5
Christ: astrology 55–6; bestiary allegories 122; Christian Cabala 102, **106–7**, **110–11**; theurgy 167
Christian Cabala: divine names 102; early history 23, 92, 97–8; Kabbalistic Order of the Rose-Cross 32; key texts 103–8; Seal of God **110–11**. *See also* Kabbalah; Khunrath, Heinrich
Christianity: alchemy 80; astrology 48, 54–6; New Age **230**; spiritualism and spiritism 189
cinnabar 66, **66**, 67, 68
clairvoyance 189, 193
Clavicula Salomonis 160, **162**, **190**
Cleopatra the Alchemist 62, 64
clothing: occulture 244–5; talismanic **149**
Constant, Alphonse Louis 30, 180
Cosmographia (Bernardus) 50–4
cosmos: harmony 136; natural magic **124–5**, 131. *See also* astrology
Court de Gébelin, Antoine 202–3, 204
Crowley, Aleister 32, **181**, 187, 194–6, **197**, 213, 214–15, 224, 236, 241, 242
cryptography 27
crystallomancy 174
crystals **228–9**
cucurbit **72–3**, **80**

Dalí, Salvador 232–3
De occulta philosophia libri III (Agrippa) 23–7
Dee, John 145, **173**, 242, 243
Delaage, Henri 30
della Porta, Giovanni Battista 27, **128–9**, 134–6, 171
Delville, Jean **222**, 231

demons **19**, **78**, 148, 160, 172–3, 174, **175**, **194**
Dickinson, Bruce 241
divination: astrology 45, 48–9, 50, 55–6; mirrors 156; physiognomy 129; stones 118; tarot 189, 202, 203–5, 212, 213
divine man 163–6
divine names **16–17**, 97, 98, 100–2, 105, **110–11**, 171
Dogme et Rituel de la Haute Magie (Lévi) 14, 30
Dragon Rouge 241
dragons **34**, **63**, **67**, **76–7**, **82–3**, **230**. *See also* ouroboros
dreams 163, 167, 170
Dune (2021) 245
Dürer, Albrecht **157**

eagles **34**, **65**, **68**, 74, **78**, **86–7**
Egypt: alchemy 18, 62, **64**; astrology 38, **39**, 44; natural magic 131; occultism **195**; Sphinx **26**; tarot 202–3
electrum **152**, 156
elements, four 19, **20–1**, **68**, 74, **86–7**, **93**, 127–31, **130**
Emerald Tablet (Hermes) **9**, 10–14, **12–13**, 75, 243
Empedocles 20
Enlightenment 27, 56, 84, 180
Esalen Institute 226
Etteilla 204–5, **208**
exorcisms **113**, 148, 162, 172–3
Ezekiel 96, **104**, **106–7**, **230**

fashion 244–5
Faust, Johann **165**, **175**
Fendulus, Georgius **138**, **151**
Ficino, Marsilio 22, **22**, **23**, 126, 139, 148, 151–3
Findhorn Foundation 224–6
Firth, Violet Mary 112. *See also* Fortune, Dion
Flamel, Nicolas 88, 243
Flournoy, Théodore 183
Fludd, Robert **57**, **124–5**, 136, 197
Fludd's head **24–5**
Forman, Simon 246
Fortune, Dion 112, 179. *See also* Firth, Violet Mary
fountains 79, **82–3**, **86–7**
Fox, Catherine and Margaretta 184
Freemasons 28, **31**, 32, 57, 202, 230–1
Freher, Dionysius Andreas 29
Fulcanelli 88, 241

Galen 49, 84
Ganellus, Berengarius 171, **171**
Genesis 96
geometry 140
Germany 31, 85
Ghāyat al-Ḥakīm **145**, 153
Gikatilla, Joseph **99**
Gilly, Carlos 86
Glahn, Frank **203**, 220
gold. *See* transmutation
Golden Dawn 32, 85, 88, 109, 112, 180, 191, 193–4, 196, 211–14, 246
Golem 102, **102**
Grant, Steffi **197**
Greece 18, 38, 71
Greek Magical Papyri 160, **161**
Greene, Liz 58
grimoires 160–2, **168–70**, 174, **190**
Großschedel, Johann Baptist 174
Guaita, Stanislas de 30, 32, **193**, **206–7**, 209, 210–11, 231

Hagecius ab Hagek, Thaddaeus **132–3**
Hall, Manly Palmer **100**, 220

Hare Krishnas 236
Harkness, Deborah 244
Harris, Frieda 215
Hartmann, Franz 31
Helmont, Frans Mercurius van 103
herbals 123–6, 131–4, **135**
hermaphrodites. *See* Rebis
Hermes Trismegistus **4**, **9**, 10–14, **11–13**, 22, 44, 75, 118, **119**, 243
Hermetic Brotherhood of Luxor 191
hexagram 14, **65**, **100**
hieroglyphs 103, 203
Hinduism 57, 190, **230**
Hippocrates 20, 49, 84
Hitchcock, Ethan Allen 85
homeopathy 81
homunculus 74
horoscopes 38–44, **42–3**, 45–9, **57**, 156, **157**, 184
Horus 62
Huber, Bruno 58
Hudson, Frederick Augustus 188
humours, four 20
hypnotism 29, 183

I Ching 67
Iamblichus 22, 163
ilan **90**, 92, 108
immortality 66
India 18, 57, 66–7, 118, 236
Isis **11**, 62, 190

Jābir ibn Ḥayyān, Abū Mūsā 71, 74
John of Morigny 170
John of Rupescissa 80
Jung, Carl 58, 85, 183, **183**, 196, 224

Kabbala denudata (Knorr & Helmont) 103–8, 109, 189
Kabbalah: alchemy 105; alphabet 98–100, 105, **110–11**, 140; astrology **36**; basic overview 91; divine names 100–2; early history 22–3, 92; etymology 92; European spread 96–7; occulture 241–2, 246; tarot 112, 205, 210, 211; Zohar 92–6. *See also* Christian Cabala
Kabbalistic Order of the Rose-Cross 32, 193, **206**, 231
Kardec, Allan 185
Kepler, Johannes 55
kerotakis 62
Khunrath, Heinrich **12–13**, **16–17**, 102, **110–11**, 156, 187, 243, 245
Kircher, Athanasius **15**, 103, 136
klifot 96
Knapp, John Augustus 220
Knights Templar 28, **186–7**
Knorr von Rosenroth, Christian 103, 109, 189
knowledge, Fludd's head **24–5**
Kurtzahn, Ernst 220

lapidaries 120–2, **121**
Lasenic, Pierre de **198**, 220
Led Zeppelin 236–7, **247**
Leo, Alan 57
Leowitz, Cyprian 50
Leuchter, Jeremias Daniel 29
Lévi, Éliphas **8**, 14, 30, 37, 180, **186–7**, 189, **190**, 194, 199, 205–9, 210
Lilly, William 56
lions **34**, **68**, **82–3**, **86–7**
lodestones 19, 120
Luria, Isaac 105
Luther, Martin 54–5

Mackenzie, Kenneth 211
macrocosm 14, **15**, 50, **77**, **93**, 102, 196

254   INDEX

Madonna 241–2
magi 18, 55, 211
magic: astral, defined 139; development 18–19; etymology 118; natural, defined 117, 118–19, 135; ritual, defined 159. *See also* astrology; nature; rituals
magic circles **33**, 164–5, 172, 173, **232**
magic squares 141–3, 146–7, 153, **157**
magicians **114**, 126–7, 160–2
magnetism 19, 136, 150, 182
Maier, Michael **21**, **68**, **69**, 77
mandrake 126, **126**, **134**
Marbode of Rennes 120–1
Marlowe, Christopher 159, **165**
Martinist Order 32, 220, 231
Maslama al-Qurṭubī 153
mathematics: astral magic 140–4, 148–9; Kabbalah 100
Mathers, Samuel Liddell MacGregor 32, 109–12, 194, 211–3
Matta, Roberto 232, **233**
medicine: alchemy 81–4; astrology 46–7, **54**; four humours 20; sympathetic magnetism 136, **137**
Melanchthon, Philipp 55
Mellet, Comte de 203–4, 205
mercury **63**, 66–7, 68, 71, 74, 76, **78**, **86**–**7**
Merkavah (Chariot) 96
Mesmer, Franz Anton 29, 182
mesmerism 29, 182
Mesopotamia 18, 38
metempsychosis 105
metoposcopy **132**–**3**, 136
microcosm 14, **15**, 50, 77, 102, 196
mirrors 156, 172
moon: alchemy **63**, 68, **74**, 75, 76, 79, **82**–**3**, **86**–**7**; astrology 38, 45, 48, **53**; talismans **143**, **150**
The Moon and Serpent Grand Egyptian Theatre of Marvels, 245–6
Moore, Alan 245–6
Morgan-Le-Fay **158**
Morienus 79
Moses **11**, 22, 91, 92, 106–7, **226**
Moses ben Shem Tov de Léon 92–6
Mozart, Wolfgang Amadeus 230–1
Muḥammad Ibn Umail 74, **75**
Müller, Friedrich Max 109
Murad, Zuhair **244**
music 136, 140, 145–8, 230, 236–42
Mylius, Johann Daniel **14**, **21**

names, divine **16**–**17**, 97, 98, 100–2, 105, **110**–**11**, 171
nature: cosmos **124**–**5**, 131; herbals 123–6, 131–4, **135**; magic 117, 118–19, 131
Nebra sky disc **44**
necromancy 153, 172–3
New Age: alchemy 232; astrology **58**, 224; counterculture 224–6, 233–6; occulture 32, 227–30, 233, 243–6
Newton, Isaac 28, 75
Noël, Francois-Nicolas **68**
numbers: astral magic 140, 143–4; astrology 153; Kabbalah 98–100, 153

occult sciences: Blavatsky 190–1; first use of term 27; list of studies 140
occultism: Dion Fortune 112, 179; first use of term 29; Mesmer 182; spiritualism 184–5, 189–90; Swedenborg 180; tarot 32, 189, 209–15, 220; Thelema 195–6, 224. *See also* Golden Dawn; Theosophical Society
occulture 32, 227–30, 233, 243–6
Oedipus Aegyptiacus (Kircher) **26**, 103, 136
Oetinger, Friedrich Christoph 108–9
Olympiodorus 71
Ordo Templi Orientis (O.T.O.) 32, 187, 195
Orpheus 22, 118, **148**
Osthanes 18
ouroboros **8**, 14, 62, **64**–**5**, **93**

P-Orridge, Genesis Breyer 223, 230
Page, Jimmy 236–7
palmistry 136, **238**–**9**
Papus (Gérard Encausse) 30, 32, 193, 209–10, 231
Paracelsus 68, 81–**4**, **152**, 156, 231
parapsychology 32
Péladan, Joséphin 30, 32, 231
Pelagius 170
Pelecanos, Theodoros 64, **64**
pelicans **82**–**3**, 122
pentacles **190**
pentagrams 110–11, **163**, **171**, 173, **186**–**7**, **230**
personality: astrology 58; metoposcopy **132**–**3**, 136; physiognomy **128**–**9**, 135–6
Petrus Bonus **21**, 80
philosophers' book **16**–**17**
philosophers' stone **14**, **16**–**17**, **34**, **65**, 68, **68**, 74, 76, 78, 79
phoenix **14**, **110**–**11**, 118
physiognomy **128**–**9**, 135–6
Picatrix **145**, 153
Pico della Mirandola, Giovanni 22–3, **22**, 97–8, 101, 112, 126–7
Pippet, Wilfrid 214, **214**
planets: astrology **15**, 40–1, 45, **48**, 50, **52**–**3**, **55**, 121–2; herb associations 131–4, **134**; Kabbalah **93**; talismans 142–3, **146**–**7**, 149, 151–3
planispheres **44**
Plato 22
Platonic solids **21**
Pliny the Elder 118
Plotinus 22
Poisson, Albert 88
predictions. *See* prophecy
Preston, William **31**
Proclus 21, 22, 163
prophecy. *See* divination
Pseudo-Dionysius the Areopagite 163–7
psychiatry 58, 85
Ptolemy, Claudius 44–5, 50
Puységur, Marquis de 182–3
Pythagoras 22, 98, **100**, 140, 148, 185

Queen 241

Race, Victor 182–3
Radonvilliers, Jean-Baptiste Richard de 29
Ragon, Jean-Marie 30
Ranson, Paul 232, **232**
ravens **33**, **34**, 74–5
Rebis 68, **76**–**7**, **89**
Recanati, Menahem 97
Regardie, Israel 196
Reich, Wilhelm 196
Renaissance 18, 50
Reuchlin, Johannes 98, 101–2
Reuss, Theodor 32
Revelation **168**–**9**
Rhazes 74
Richet, Charles 31
Ripley Scroll **82**–**3**

rituals: *goëtia* (sorcery) 162, 171–4; grimoires 160–2, **168**–**70**, 174; theurgy 162–71
Rivail, Hippolyte Léon Denizard 185
Rosarium Philosophorum **69**, 77, 79
Rosicrucians 30, 32, 55, **56**, 57, 84, **86**–**7**, 194
Rowling, J. K. 242–3
Rudhyar, Dane 58, **59**

sacrifices 153
salamanders **123**, 131
salt 68, 81, **86**–**7**
Satanism 196
Schubert, Hans 220
Schweighardt, Theophilus 56
Scientific Revolution 27, 56
scripture interpretation 98–100
seals 142–3, **146**–**7**, 149, 171
séances **185**, 189
secret writing 27
Secretum Secretorum **19**, 123
sefirot 92, **94**–**5**, 96, 100, 106–7, **108**, 110–11, 209
senses, Fludd's head **24**–**5**
serpents **68**, 76. *See also* ouroboros
sex magic 32, 195
Shekhina **109**
Sheldrake, Rupert 227
Shelley, Mary 231
Shimon bar Yochai 92
Sibly, Ebenezer 183–4
Silberer, Herbert 85
skeletons **86**–**7**
skulls **86**–**7**, **114**
Smith, Pamela Colman 214, **215**, **216**–**19**
snakes **230**. *See also* serpents
Society, Anthroposophical 31
Society for Psychical Research 31
Solomon 127, 160, 167
somnambulism 180, 183
souls 68, 105, **106**–**7**, 131
Spare, Austin Osman **212**
sphinx **26**, 209
spirit photographs **188**
spiritism 185
spirits, evil **16**–**17**. *See also* demons
spiritualism 184–5, 189–90
St Cyprian **2**, **168**–**9**
St John's Wort **116**
St Paul 174
Star of David **93**
steganography 27
Steiner, Rudolf 31, **191**, 191–3
Stephanus of Alexandria 71
Stonehenge **227**
stones: bezoar stones **127**; divination and summonings 118; lapidaries 120–2; New age therapy 228–9
substances: occult qualities 19–22; sympathies and antipathies 120, 131; transmutation 62, 66, 71, 80, **86**–**7**; triad in alchemy 68, **69**, **74**, 81
sulphur **65**, **66**, 68, 71, 74, 76, **86**–**7**
summonings **114**, 118, 160–2
sun: alchemy **63**, 68, **74**, 75, 76, 79, **82**–**3**; animal associations 131; astrology 38, **52**; herb associations **134**; talismans **143**
Surrealism 231
Swedenborg, Emanuel 29, 180, 189
Symbolism 231
sympathies and antipathies 120, 131
synchronicity 58

Tabulae Theosophicae Cabalisticae **16**–**17**
talismans: Arabic 149; astral **142**–**3**, **146**–**7**, 149–50, 153; red jasper **120**
tarot: alchemy **220**; cards **198**, 200–2, **203**–**8**, **210**, **212**–**13**, 214–15, **216**–**19**, **242**; cartomancy 209; history 199, 200, 202–6, **221**; Kabbalah 112, **205**, 210, 211; New Age **225**, 232, 233, **234**–**5**; occultism 32, 189, 209–15, 220; occulture 237, 244–5, 246; Surrealism 232, 233
television, occulture 243–4
Temple of Solomon 28, **106**–**7**
Tetrabiblos (Ptolemy) 44–5, 50
Tetragrammaton 98, **101**, 101, **111**, 111
Tetraktys 98, **100**, **110**–**11**, **168**–**9**
Thābit Ibn Qurra 150
Theatrum Chemicum 84, **85**
Thee Temple ov Psychick Youth (TOPY) 230
Thelema 181, 195–6, 224
Thenaud, Jean 102, **103**
Theosophical Society 30–1, 57, 180, 190, 191
theosophy 30–1, 57–8, 85, 190–1
Therion 241
Thoth 10, 204
toads **33**, **82**–**3**
Toorop, Jan 231–2
Torah 92, 100
transmutation 62, 66, 71, 80, **86**–**7**
Tree of Life, Kabbalah **90**, 92, **94**–**5**, **97**, **99**, 103, 105, **108**, 112, 209, 240
triad in alchemy 68, **69**, 74, 81
Trinick, John Brahms **214**
Trithemius, Johannes 23, 27, 144, 173–4

Urban VIII, Pope 156
Utriusque Cosmi Historia (Fludd) **24**–**5**, **124**–**5**, 136, 197

Vachier, Philippe 209
Vedic astrology 57
Velvet Underground 233–6
video games 246
Vigenère, Blaise de 27
Virgil 18
Virgin Sophia **86**–**7**

Waite, Arthur Edward 88, 194, 211, 214, **215**, **216**–**19**
Westcott, William Wynn 32
Weyer, Johann 174
Wicca 196
William of Auvergne 118
Wilson, Colin 32
Wirth, Oswald **206**–**7**, 209–11
witches **172**, 232
Woodman, William Robert 32
Woodstock Festival 236

Yetzirah (*Sefer Yetzirah*) 91, 92, 100, 102, 112
yin and yang **67**, 211, **230**
yoga 112, 196, **228**–**9**

Zakariyā' al-Qazwīnī **48**
Zappa, Frank 241
zodiac: Egypt **39**; elements 20; Kabbalah **36**; lapidaries 121–2; New Age 224, 237; signs **15**, 40–1, **49**, 55, **151**. *See also* horoscopes
zodiac man 46–7, **54**
Zohar (*Sefer ha-Zohar*) (Moses ben Shem Tov) 92–6, 105
Zoroaster 18, **19**, 22, 54
Zosimos of Panopolis 67–71
Zukav, Gary 226

ACKNOWLEDGMENTS

I would like thank everyone at Thames & Hudson who put so much energy and expertise into bringing this volume to fruition, especially Jane Laing, Florence Allard, Rebecca Pearson, Lotte Roberts, Sadie Butler and Tristan de Lancey. It has been a pleasure to work with them. Gratitude to the archives that have granted permission to use their images. Last but not least, thanks to family, friends, students and colleagues who have encouraged and supported me in this project.

ABOUT THE AUTHOR

Peter Forshaw has a doctorate in Intellectual History and is Associate Professor of Western Esotericism in the Early Modern Period at the Centre for History of Hermetic Philosophy, University of Amsterdam. In addition to editing several volumes on occult and esoteric subjects, he is the author of *The Mage's Images: Heinrich Khunrath in his Oratory and Laboratory* and served as editor-in-chief of *Aries: Journal for the Study of Western Esotericism* for 10 years. He has contributed to TV and Radio programmes including BBC Radio 4's *In Our Time* series and Channel 5's *The Philosophers' Stone – The True Story*.

FRONT COVER
Illustration from Hermes, *Alchymia Naturalis Occultissima Vera*, 18th century.

BACK COVER
Two pages from *Clavis Inferni* or 'Key of Hell', attributed to Saint Cyprian, 18th century.

PAGE 1
Detail of God's all-seeing eye from the title page of a manuscript copy of Abraham von Franckenberg's *Raphael oder Artzt-Engel* (1676).

PAGE 2
'The Greatest Bond', from *Clavis Inferni* or 'Key of Hell', attributed to Saint Cyprian, 18th century.

PAGE 4
Kurt Regschek, *Hermes Trismegistos*, 1990. A modern image of the Egyptian sage standing inside a magic circle in the form of an ouroboric snake.

PAGES 6–7
Hermes, *Alchymia Naturalis Occultisima Vera*, 18th century: left, concentric circles of the four elements, from which grows a tree; right, a salamander, symbol of the philosophers' stone.

First published in the United Kingdom in 2024 by Thames & Hudson Ltd, 181A High Holborn, London WC1V 7QX

First published in the United States of America in 2024 by Thames & Hudson Inc., 500 Fifth Avenue, New York, New York, 10110

Occult © 2024 Thames & Hudson Ltd, London

Text © 2024 Peter Forshaw

For image copyright information, see pages 252–253

Interior designed by Anıl Aykan at Barnbrook

All Rights Reserved. No part of this publication may be reproduced or transmitted in any form or by any means, electronic or mechanical, including photocopy, recording or any other information storage and retrieval system, without prior permission in writing from the publisher.

British Library Cataloguing-in-Publication Data. A catalogue record for this book is available from the British Library.

Library of Congress Control Number 2024935259

ISBN 978-0-500-02713-4

Printed and bound in China by C&C Offset Printing Co. Ltd

MIX
Paper | Supporting responsible forestry
FSC® C008047

Be the first to know about our new releases, exclusive content and author events by visiting
thamesandhudson.com
thamesandhudsonusa.com
thamesandhudson.com.au